ARMS AND ARMOUR OF THE WESTERN WORLD

BRUNO THOMAS · ORTWIN GAMBER · HANS SCHEDELMANN

Arms and Armour of the Western World

McGRAW-HILL BOOK COMPANY

NEW YORK · TORONTO

Translated from the German by Ilse Bloom, FIL (Eng.)
and William Reid

CONTENTS

The Heroes' and Vassals' Armoury which the Archduke Ferdinand II of Austria (1529–95) began to assemble in 1547 and which he eventually arranged as a museum in the castle of Ambras, situated above the seat of his court at Innsbruck, is probably the most famous of its kind. Apart from his own parade and everyday arms he systematically collected the arms and armour of his ancestors and of practically every outstanding military leader of the renaissance, whether friend or foe. As royal property the collection was removed to Vienna when the French and Bavarians invaded the country, and on the occasion of the Congress of Vienna in 1814/15 it was set up in the baroque assembly rooms of the imperial Belvedere Castle, the single-storey summer palace of Austria's greatest war hero, Prince Eugene of Savoy. Before this museum was dissolved about 1889 by decree of the Emperor Franz-Joseph I and amalgamated with the imperial armoury – to form the largest Western collection of arms and armour, then housed in the Kunsthistorische Museum – Carl Goebel, the fashionable Viennese artist, was commissioned to paint a picture of the Belvedere exhibition as a permanent record. Goebel's colourful interiors make a natural backcloth for his lively studies of visitors in contemporary costume.

In 1936 the *Waffensammlung* was moved from the Kunsthistorische Museum across the Ringstrasse to the Neue Hofburg.

Vienna, Gemäldegalerie, 3631

CARL GOEBEL, VIENNA, 1875
*The second armour gallery
of the Royal Ambras Collection
at the Untere Belvedere in
Vienna*

INTRODUCTION

In this age of push-button warfare, arms are losing their aura of splendour and the magic of regimental panoply is vanishing; but this volume is as little concerned with the weapons of the industrial age, the era of mass production, which falls into a category of its own, as it is with the executioner's sword and axe. It avoids the false romanticism of chivalry as it does the tiresome technicalities of modern times and the hair-raising sensationalism of all other periods of history. But how can the instinctive, deep-rooted respect for weapons and the way they are treasured be explained? Why have men of every age equipped themselves with arms of the most superb artistic design? Whence comes the ever present inclination to preserve arms, to place them in graves for a later life, to collect them and to surround oneself with them while alive? The reasons are many, one of the most important being certainly their value as mementoes. Man feels gratitude towards a weapon which has saved his life, which accompanies and protects him in a critical situation, which, by its mere presence has staved off attacks on him. The sight of his arms awakens memories of the terrors of mortal peril, of the improbability of rescue. But they speak also of comradeship, of the selflessness of a friend in danger, of risking one's own life for the protection of dependants and one's country's possessions and culture, for a good cause or for an ideal. Thus regarded, the weapon is not a symbol of survival or of the prevention of total annihilation but of the commitment of man to the greatest good. ✒— The carefully preserved weapons of all cultures focus special attention on this aspect — sacrifice. He who is unable — both inwardly and outwardly — to defend himself against that which he recognises to be evil or believes he ought to recognise as evil, against impending dissolution, against the threat to all that makes life worthwhile, surrenders himself and not himself alone. Even if opinions differ on the concept of pledge and sacrifice, if people, parties and nations are divided by it, pure sacrifice weapon in hand for one's fellow, for one's neighbour, was and is something real. It is not just the senseless, criminal, tragic sacrificing of the individual or the masses in the turmoil of war. ✒— Nothing expresses quite so clearly the involvement of life with death as does the weapon which has accompanied mankind from his very beginnings. Since his first intellectual awakening, man has sought to improve his means of self-protection by using an increasingly more sophisticated tool than his bare hands. With this weapon he secured his vital food. The tool that preserved his life accompanied him in death, to the extent that our entire knowledge of the most ancient arms is primarily based on grave-finds. The reason for the perennial fascination which arms exercise is to be found in the perpetual contribution they have made to the preservation of the human race. Here we have one of the roots of their artistic development through the millennia. ✒— On the other hand, apart from the purposes of defence and self-preservation, one of the foremost characteristics of arms was the demonstration of strength (even if it was borrowed), of manhood, of superiority, of pride in victory, of the will to freedom and independence. Human nature is ever inclined towards abuses, and weapons have proved no exception. Status-seeking, the lust for power and the desire to dominate play a large part in the urge to carry arms. ✒— In the disciplinary scheme of the medieval doctrine of virtue, man was presented, at least in theory, with an ideal toward which he should strive. As one of the four cardinal virtues strength ranks next to wisdom. But it is tempered by moderation which should prevent any excesses and should teach man self-restraint. Above all these virtues towers justice whose task it is to intervene, by force of arms if necessary, with the sword of justice,

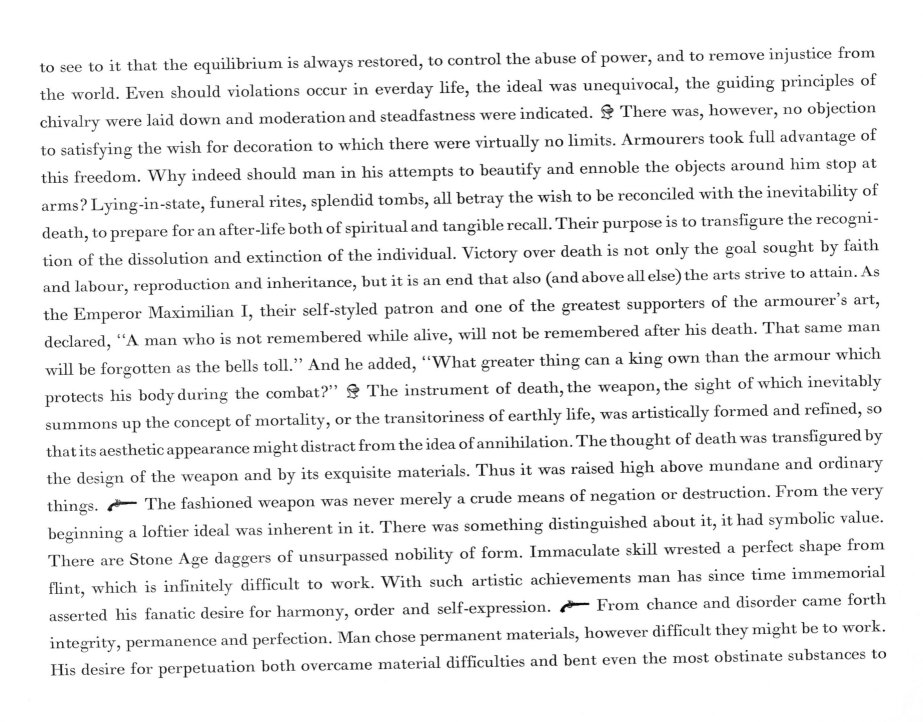

to see to it that the equilibrium is always restored, to control the abuse of power, and to remove injustice from the world. Even should violations occur in everday life, the ideal was unequivocal, the guiding principles of chivalry were laid down and moderation and steadfastness were indicated. There was, however, no objection to satisfying the wish for decoration to which there were virtually no limits. Armourers took full advantage of this freedom. Why indeed should man in his attempts to beautify and ennoble the objects around him stop at arms? Lying-in-state, funeral rites, splendid tombs, all betray the wish to be reconciled with the inevitability of death, to prepare for an after-life both of spiritual and tangible recall. Their purpose is to transfigure the recognition of the dissolution and extinction of the individual. Victory over death is not only the goal sought by faith and labour, reproduction and inheritance, but it is an end that also (and above all else) the arts strive to attain. As the Emperor Maximilian I, their self-styled patron and one of the greatest supporters of the armourer's art, declared, "A man who is not remembered while alive, will not be remembered after his death. That same man will be forgotten as the bells toll." And he added, "What greater thing can a king own than the armour which protects his body during the combat?" The instrument of death, the weapon, the sight of which inevitably summons up the concept of mortality, or the transitoriness of earthly life, was artistically formed and refined, so that its aesthetic appearance might distract from the idea of annihilation. The thought of death was transfigured by the design of the weapon and by its exquisite materials. Thus it was raised high above mundane and ordinary things. The fashioned weapon was never merely a crude means of negation or destruction. From the very beginning a loftier ideal was inherent in it. There was something distinguished about it, it had symbolic value. There are Stone Age daggers of unsurpassed nobility of form. Immaculate skill wrested a perfect shape from flint, which is infinitely difficult to work. With such artistic achievements man has since time immemorial asserted his fanatic desire for harmony, order and self-expression. From chance and disorder came forth integrity, permanence and perfection. Man chose permanent materials, however difficult they might be to work. His desire for perpetuation both overcame material difficulties and bent even the most obstinate substances to his will. Out of the hardest stones and every metal, he wrought the form which he envisaged. Evidence of this is provided by the arms of such primitive peoples as the nomadic and peasant civilisations. How much more true is it of weapons which were produced by the highly developed cultures of the East and West! ⚘ Until well into the 16th century the medieval knightly custom prevailed by which a great ruler would go into battle in the greatest panoply. His life-risking challenge was a festival that frequently turned out to be the feast of death. The armours that Charles V took on all his campaigns—and in respect of nearly every one of them we know the reason for its creation and how the order was placed on the occasion of a particular action—are masterpieces of the plastic arts in steel and priceless examples of decoration in gold and silver. It goes without saying that no less care was devoted to the arms used for sporting combat that took place in front of the ladies, as for example the joust, shooting contests, hunting, or indeed on any such solemn occasion. ⚘ The function of the weapon had to be matched by such technical perfection as the gravity of the affair demanded. If an armour failed in fencing, jousting or hunting, it could cause loss of life. A weapon was not only for looking at, although its effect on the eye was certainly taken into consideration by client and maker. As in architecture, its importance lay in its efficaciousness, since in both disciplines production is backed by engineering skill and technical knowledge. A building must not collapse and an armour or a gun must not show any sign of strain even after the severest use. This is the maker's very first duty to his client. In spite of the many theatrical characteristics of parade arms, it is this that prevents their deviating into pure fantasy, one might even say artificiality, into which so many fields of the arts and crafts have strayed. Excesses in the decoration of arms are possible. They are however, well protected against the ill-conceived principle of "art for art's sake". The treacherous falsification of the 19th century is unmasked precisely when its confused romanticism is examined from the standpoint of utility. ⚘ On the other hand, court arms, as we have said, must never be mere tools and instruments, never merely sober and functional. Reduced to a simple formula, the defensive armour is always costume, reinforced apparel, and the weapon of attack an appurtenance of dress or a fashionable accessory. Both great categories of

arms were elements of dress, predominantly masculine attire, closely tied to the textile clothing with which they were carried. Arms and costumes were linked and interrelated, sharing identical features of fashion and style. In every age, frequently on every occasion and in every detail, it remains to be ascertained which part was the determining factor, lending itself to further development, forming taste and deciding style—civilian attire or the knight's war apparel that evolved into the uniform, the correct equipment for which is specified in detail along military lines. There is good reason for calling our representative journal *Waffen- und Kostüm-kunde* (The Study of Arms and Costume, published in five languages). But there are still more reasons for producing magnificent arms than man's inclination to impress and cut a dash with the opposite sex, a wish that may explain some aspects of plain and parade arms, although by no means all. The completed weapon is never merely a thing of beauty, nor just a tool. Behind it inevitably lies a profounder thought. Arms always contain and express symbolic values. In German it amounts to an identification of hero and weapon in the word "rapier" or "broadsword". Either one is entitled to bear arms, a certain kind of weapon, or one is not. One may be in duty bound to bear arms, or one may be strictly debarred from so doing. In other words, arms are and were, probably in all periods of human society, also a mark of the invidual's social position, a clearly discernible, easily recognisable badge of his rank. By the mere process of production they acquire a deeper significance. They have to be seen against this background. From the outset they possessed some qualities which went beyond the mere purpose of protection; they have no words and yet they speak. Successive epochs under-stood the language of symbols and forms that is spoken by the feudal sword, the sceptre and the dagger of honour. This language may in the course of time have become incomprehensible, and fallen into oblivion; that which lay beneath the surface is lost to memory. From the spiritual point of view arms lose their value when this happens. All we are left with then is the empty husk. The mystery and unspoken ideas which surround all arms have thus become a secret. For example, arms found in prehistoric graves present us with such riddles. The most accurate technical tests and analyses of materials are of no use in such circumstances and a purely

comparative examination of forms is bound to be superficial. But the weapon only derives its real significance from its more profound associations. There are peasants' arms, citizens' arms, those of the nobility, of great rulers and purely symbolic weapons. Until well into our own times the type of weapon has indicated the military rank, a tradition which is carefully protected by prohibitions and regulations. The servant received the weapon which his lord considered suitable. The rising middle class attempted to gain prerogatives, insisting in the 18th century on its right to courtesy and students' daggers. Infantry and cavalry were not only separated by law and rank and by varying needs with regard to equipment, but also by the individual type and form of arms of attack and defence that were either permitted or inadmissible. At the very beginning of the 16th century the Emperor Maximilian I had his triumphal procession painted on parchment to depict the social order as it existed in his imagination, the various strata of society being strictly distinguished by their equipment in a picture that expresses an idea which probably never corresponded to reality. Only with the militarism of the 18th century and the ensuing period was this wishful thinking realised in the sphere of military uniforms. Every type of arm arose from bare necessity and basic causes, in turn assuming its due symbolic significance. It was a perpetual cycle of being in the ascendant, falling back and sinking into oblivion, a process in which we, on the threshold of a classless society, in the age of the masses, are still engaged. The simplest of weapons is the original and most ancient one. And the oldest has come to be regarded as the most distinguished article in subsequent periods, especially latterly. The simplest and the most sensible styles of costume and of armour had one basic attribute in common—they lasted. But it is just through their lasting quality, through their antiquity, that they gain distinction. A man of distinction comports himself with dignity, moves with quiet assurance. If a garment is richly patterned and embroidered, if an armour is embossed and damascened, then its artistic excellence is dependent on the way in which the detail is harmonised, how the whole is put together and to what extent it can be taken in at a glance. But elegance is in constant danger of being mocked when its time is past. It is but a short step from the divine to the ridiculous. This happens when the knight in armour becomes the subject of cheap music-hall jokes, when the official's sword is ridiculed because it is carried by an incorrigible civilian. ❧ To trace the origin of various types and forms of arms would involve staging a play in reverse; to uncover unknown and lost links; to determine unexpected connections that cut across space and time. ❧ The knotty stick, the cudgel carried by the peasant or journeyman, became the club, the mace, the *Kürissbengel* of the knight, the badge of rank of the cavalry officer, the baton – particularly in the East – the *Regiment,* a simple unadorned staff like the officer's cane still in use in some Western armies, the elaborate marshal's baton and eventually the sceptre in the hand of the sovereign. The victor's simple wreath of leaves became the diadem on the helmet of king and emperor. There was a close relationship between the *Spangenhelm* and the arched crown. The accolade was given only with the double-edged cross-shaped sword. The smaller version, the dagger, possessed the same high social status. The single-edged asymmetrical knife in all its variations, such as the hunting sword and the sabre, were for long considered inferior. In this group of arms only the dagger was elevated and honoured by the aristocracy. ❧ It took two hundred years for the Swiss peasants' weapon, the murderous halberd, to become the esteemed weapon of the bodyguards of the Hapsburgs, whose expulsion from Switzerland it had brought about. The knife-shaped glaive, however, used by the aristocratic bodyguards, always retained more dignity. In the military sphere the various types of hafted weapons indicated the precise rank of corporal, ensign and officer. As late as the 13th century the crossbow was proscribed by Papal Bull as a treacherously quiet and unfair weapon. Around 1500 it was the favourite equipment of the Archmaster of the Hounds of the Holy Roman Empire, as the Emperor Maximilian I called himself. As far as he was concerned, he categorically rejected firearms. This was no doubt also due to the fact that the black arts were the ignoble invention of aspiring commoners and that the weak, with the aid of chemistry, derived from them undeserved advantages. His grandson, the Emperor Charles V, however, left a superb collection of his own pistols. Among the nobility this gave to this type of arm a tremendous impetus that lasted right into the 19th century, culminating in the cases of precious duelling pistols. The list of arms which rose or fell in the weapon hierarchy

14

and whose evaluation underwent characteristic changes, could be continued *ad liberandum*. That specific arms were affixed above the tombs of the dead was testimony of veneration and high esteem. The selection was made according to a strictly determined combination of helmet, shield and flag. All three – together with the far more perishable material of the knight's costume and horse trappings – carried heraldic symbols, the owner's personal coat of arms. It was not by chance that the knight's spurs were also hung above the tomb. This was the one piece of equipment which was by custom presented by his mother to the young squire or page. Long-established rules, which may be traced back to the earliest times, laid down the weapon's role in the sphere of festivities. Not only did the sword dance of the North, the "fantasia" of the Levant, demonstrate skill in the handling of arms, but dance and play, particularly tournaments, led into regions ruled by magic. Processions of all kinds were the forerunners of the theatre. Theatre and opera themselves represent the well planned and executed transformation of a real person into a fictitious one, a disguise in which one individual acted the part of another. This whole sphere cannot be imagined without arms. The renaissance or baroque prince, in the role of Roman emperor, simulating an ancient or a biblical hero, or even dressed as an Indian potentate, was the leading and central figure in the play which he presented to a public that crowded the amphitheatre or stood by the roadside. Their aim and ambition was a creditable comparison, a historic and spiritual relation and the enhancement of their own worth. Thus the fashionable field armour became the muscled cuirass *all'antica* and the helmet the Roman *cassis*. The visor took the form of a lion's mask, the helmet crest that of a dragon and the shield boss was designed as Medusa. In this way the wearer indentified himself with Hercules and Perseus, with Caesar and Augustus. This equation, in which arms and armour play the greatest part, was not formulated for fun, but always for reasons of propaganda and usually with political intent. (After all, the heir to the throne did not receive his name in baptism by chance. After due consideration he was linked with an illustrious model, a famous predecessor whom he was to emulate, with whom he was to identify himself, just as he himself was identified with the hero that he, weapon in hand,

personified in pompous pageantry.) ❧ Above all, the tournament with its millennia-old roots vested claims and dreams in a highly complicated system of arms and equipment to be used for this purpose according to rules rigidly laid down and, one might almost say, sanctified. Heralds, heraldic experts, learned festival organisers and court historians took charge of the performance and saw to it that the prescribed forms were adhered to in accordance with their masters' wishes. As a first step, evidence of worthy, that is to say, aristocratic, ancestors had to be provided. (In monarchies this system of preferential treatment of the privileged classes has continued even in present-day constitutions and politics.) This explains why the most ancient forms of the tournament were, as a matter of course, the preserve of the very highest circles, why the equipment took such a costly form that only the most powerful were able to afford it. ❧ Thus the obsolescent type of helmet for the ancient contest with clubs, the helmet with an open barred visor, became the helmet crowning the coat of arms of the aristocrat. By contrast, the helmet for the tilt, which after all was also used in the "journeymen's jousts" of the bourgeois sons of Nuremberg patricians, and which is historically more recent, crowned the citizen's coat of arms. In this connection one need only recall the coat of arms surmounted by a jousting helm which Dürer designed for himself. Ancient history endured everywhere underneath the outward appearance and surface of arms. Against a spiritual background was spread a close network of symbolic concepts, rank and dignity, achievement and merit. Glory and the apotheosis of the hero were expressed in the weapon, but one has to know how to perceive and read them. The expression "read" must be taken literally here: parade arms with their decoratively placed representations, reaching back into the Old Testament and to classic mythology, contain a great many literary allusions. ❧ Second in order of importance after their use in the field in actual battle, was the use of arms in war exercises, in the preparatory school for serious battles, in the formal duel, the joust, or in field conditions simulating group combat, the knights' massed tournament which was a kind of manoeuvre, military exercise or skirmish on horseback and on foot. By various progressions, the whole gained the added attraction of refinement. Around 1500, the Emperor Maximilian I laid down and had illustrated the rules for the most diverse kinds of tournament in greater detail than anyone else. Just because he preserved these ancient customs, he earned the title of "The Last Knight" at the end of the Middle Ages and the beginning of a new era. ✐— Not only were arms and armour specially ordered for impending campaigns, for which sovereigns and commanders as well as the great mass of the infantry wanted to be equipped in the latest and most modern manner; tremendous orders for arms were placed too for tournaments which were announced and prepared well in advance, and for which the competitors frequently travelled long distances, and on which detailed reports were published. Those who devote themselves to scientific research into ancient arms must always bear this in mind. One must find out when and why, for what purpose arms that have been handed down to us were accumulated. They were made not only for wars, but also for great meetings and festivities at which arms never before displayed – unusual, sensational, amazing arms – were to be shown; at which unheard-of splendour was to be manifested to enhance the reputation and fame of the participants. Tournaments and *concours d'élégance* for horse and rider, equipment and sporting achievement were an indispensable part of weddings which themselves were often associated with the conclusion of peace treaties and alliances. No historical study of arms is possible without knowledge of the relevant dates. The same applies to the proclaimed competitions in archery and shooting with crossbow and target gun and to the hunts organised by the courts, all of which afford definite dates. Not only had the noble mourners to appear in their finest equipment at princes' funerals and exequies, but the deceased's favourite arms and favourite horse had to parade in the funeral procession. ✐ Moreover, parade arms were the most popular presents made to courtiers, dignitaries and generals in recognition of successful political, diplomatic and military services rendered. Individual arms, which were originally used by the ruler himself, often must be sought in the collections of his descendants. On the other hand, courtiers frequently left their own memorable and outstanding arms to the princely armoury in order to ensure that they and their families were not forgotten by their lord, and to gain access to a Valhalla of immortality. As a young man the esquire first came in contact with ceremonial weapons at the symbolic ceremony of recep-

tion into the order of knighthood, of the accolade. Even beyond his allotted life-span the weapon bore testimony to the prince's servant, to the historic importance of his position and not least to his artistic sense. After all, an element of the latter must always be at hand–noblesse oblige! ♟ The acquisition of armour was a costly affair, so that it should be possible to discover a concrete and convincing reason for its production. There is evidence of parade arms having been widely popular as Christmas presents, ordered, say, by the princess for her prince. The demand for beautiful arms on the occasion of awarding distinctions, at diets and fealty ceremonies, but above all for coronations, is of even greater significance. ♟ Sword and sceptre then lay before the prince as symbolic arms. The former was attached to his belt and he took the latter in his hand. He used yet another sword for the accolade and a third was carried upright before him in procession. That at any rate was the procedure at coronations of an emperor. A case in point is the so-called sabre of Charlemagne; or the Ceremonial and the Mauritius swords were used. On the occasion of these ceremonies the seven Electors of the Holy Roman Empire surrounded their newly-crowned lord and bore the arms and equipment to which their rank and function entitled them. One or two grades further down, the process was repeated with some changes in the case of kings and dukes. They too selected their dignitaries and their court. In this instance also the court marshal carried the sword, the standard-bearer the banner, the master of ceremonies the baton, the umpire the shield, the master of hounds and master falconer the finest equipment for their respective types of hunting, and so on. These highly significant insignia may to-day be found in the royal and national treasure-houses of the West and in the armouries which acquired them for their intrinsic worth. In Europe they cover a span from the 9th to the 19th century. Every single example of the earliest specimens is an unsurpassed and unique major work of the armourer's and goldsmith's crafts. Their constitutional character and their political distinction preserved them from constant wear and tear and from being melted down, and it is significant that these are the earliest historical arms that have survived in museums. With them the weapon became the highest symbol complying with the imperial motto ''justitia regnorum fundamentum''. They not only stood for power, but represented justice at the highest level. A step down the scale the silver sword of the municipal judge occupied the same position, followed by the Synod sword publicly displayed on market days, to proclaim law and order. Such arms are not bloody; on the contrary, their existence and physical presence serve to prevent bloodshed. ⚬— In this connection we need only recall the guards' arms, especially their hafted weapons. These troops, of divers number and social rank, protected the sovereign, represented him, and proclaimed his arrival with his escutcheon and emblems borne on their spears and halberds, which usually are dated with the year of their production. Thus they provide the most certain evidence that weapons were not made or ordered fortuitously. The dates always correspond to the beginning of a reign, an oath of fealty ceremony, or a coronation. History, which can be reconstructed, is therefore reflected in them; it stands behind every weapon. It has to be traced back and revived in every instance if we aspire to a true comprehension of the weapon as a document of the mind and of civilization, of technology and art. ⚘ Almost every type of weapon is matched by its own craft or crafts. As more than one was usually required to create it, close and devoted cooperation was needed. There is hardly any raw material that is unknown to arms. Forged iron, steel, and cast bronze come to mind in the first place and, quite apart from the decorative and refining artistic processes using precious metals and any other valuable material which one can imagine, no arms can be produced without wood, leather and textiles. Every historical armoury is simultaneously a manual of art and craft techniques and a comprehensive museum of these arts and crafts. ⚘ Shirts of mail, collars and trousers of mail were laboriously interlinked and rivetted by wire-workers. The armour occupied not only the armourer but also the polisher and the finisher, who was responsible for the strappings and linings, the padding and the leather gloves. Saddler and heraldic painter, making the horse's equipment and shields, were above all timber and leather experts, the latter also painting the heraldic devices. Spur-makers cut the spurs, stirrups and snaffles. The cutler forged the short blades. Sword and dagger employed quite a number of trades: swordsmith, hilt-maker, scabbard-maker, belt-maker and lastly the sword cutler who assembled the various parts and undertook the sale. Hafted weapons needed both bladesmiths and haft-makers. With the invention of firearms the mechanical and technical side advanced on all fronts. The precision toolmaker, even the watchmaker, the inventor and engineer appeared on the scene and became of ever greater importance in the field of the gunsmith's craft. The crossbow-maker joined the steel bow to the wooden shaft, the so-called stock. A toolsmith made the cranequin, the spanning device, for him. Barrelsmith, locksmith and stockmaker worked jointly on firearms. The gunsmiths' guilds, for example the Vienna Guild, laid down that every part of the masterpiece had to be made by the master himself, and that it had to be delivered within a specified period. Frequently, however, the gunsmith assembled the whole from parts of varying provenance, each bearing its own signature and sometimes a different date and place of manufacture, and controlled the weapons' distribution. On behalf of their highly-placed clients the inventors dealt unceasingly with the problems of breechloading, self-spanning, multi-shot and repeating guns, while the large-scale development of numerous types of ignition mechanisms progressed from the matchlock to the wheel-lock, the snaphance lock and finally to the flintlock. All these trades and crafts, quite capable on their own of producing pure works of art, evolving beautiful and functional forms, advancing both technically and aesthetically towards admirable achievements of manual work perfectly suited to their purpose, were joined by the decorative artists. Blueing and burnishing steel gave not only a protective layer to the delicate polished metal, but offered at the same time an opportunity for colourful decoration to be artistically applied. Painters covered the surfaces of arms and shields with decorative patterns. Etchers applied their etching (scenes and ornament) to all types of arms, engraved masterpieces being created particularly on the surface of armour sculptured on a monumental plane. It may be flat etching, for which the pattern was etched out of the blued surface; or it may be sunk and finely gilded or blackened. *Goldschmelz* is a German process which gives arms a look of great luxury: very shallow patterns etched on the polished surface are filled with gold to give a result that shows up particularly well against a dark blue ground. Engraving as a mechanical principle is, in contrast to the chemical process of etching with acid, the most ancient type of decoration practised from the Middle Ages

Mail-maker   *Armourer*

to our time. Iron chiselled in relief was the supreme decoration on swords, daggers, and firearms. Coiners and medallists sometimes entered the field, leaving arms that are major works of art. Defensive arms in particular became gala pieces as a result of the embossing of their iron surfaces, damascening and the refinement produced by final engraving with the burin completing the effect. ❦ In this way the weapon closely approached the goldsmith's art. The gilding of surfaces was either applied by firing, burnishing or as painter's gilding. The first process is based on an amalgam cover; to this heat is applied in order to evaporate the mercury, which is "fumed off". Gilding with leaf gold is carried out in the same way as is the production of the gold background on medieval altarpieces, by applying very finely beaten gold leaf. When using the inexpensive painter's gilding, gold dust *(or moulu:* ground gold) is dissolved in varnish and brushed over the surface. Gold and silver damascening consist of fretted silhouette-like patterns that are hammered on to the surface. When applied to a roughened surface, it is flat, struck damascening; when sunk into grooves or standing proud like a relief, it is encrusted damascening. Bronze, silver and gold mounts which may also be enamelled translucently or opaquely with melted glass or even set with precious and semi-precious stones, occur on parade arms in the "fall of the Middle Ages", the refined late gothic period, and later when the exaggerated renaissance style was approaching its end, and during the extravagant baroque. Oriental splendour may have had a stimulating effect on all this. In their superior planning the masters frequently combined every artistic possibility in a single valuable object. ❦ Every trend in textile design was utilised to produce highly impressive effects by using gold and silver thread, painting with the needle in flat, raised and appliqué embroidery on velvet, silk, satin, damask and gold brocade, on armour bases, the lining of shields, helmet covers, saddle blankets, horse trappings, hunting bags and sword belts. Leather, too, was embroidered, painted and lacquered. The stocks of small arms and their accessories, above all the powder flask, presented the stockmaker, who was a kind of specialised cabinet-maker, with every opportunity to show his skill. The art of wood-carving was combined with inlaid work in ivory, bone, stag-horn, tortoise-shell and mother-of-pearl. These inlays were either flat and engraved, or chiselled

Bladesmith   *Crossbow-maker*   *Gunsmith*   *Stockmaker*

in relief. Some stocks are made of solid ivory; others, again, are set in gold with the entire surface veneered with tortoise-shell. Masters and artists signed with their marks or names, frequently several of them on one piece which they had mutually wrought into a finished work of art in miniature. As previously mentioned, armour was not only a technically ingenious body-protection but in its developed forms became the constantly changing and newly designed festive costume of the nobility, a stylised entity of beaten steel in the shape of a flexible cover for the body. Swords, hafted weapons and firearms in their refined distinction were the knight's indispensable accessories, and he was the representative of an older aristocratic world. All types of arms followed every trend of the great art of each period. There is evidence that the great masters of the creative arts had their own personal attitude towards arms. Thus Dürer and Holbein, Aldegrever and Flötner, Delaune and Bérain, made their own designs for arms. At the very least, however, the beautiful weapon fascinated them all, time and again, as a model. They reproduced arms perfectly in study designs, portraits and paintings of battles, on tombs and figures of the saints and thus handed down pictures of them to posterity. Jan van Eyck and Konrad Witz, Uccello and Castagno, Michael Pacher and Bernt Notke, Verrocchio and Leone Leoni, van Dyck and Rembrandt are but a few names that come to mind in this connection. If we want to understand the contents of their works to the full, we have to know the arms which they inserted with such devotion into their compositions. The artistic development of the individual Western weapon, as far as it has survived in museums, stretches—with a few exceptions—like an arch from the romanesque, which dominated the whole of Europe, to the neo-classical on the eve of the machine age; from about 1200 to about 1800. All this is inconceivable without the preliminary stages, moulded on three continents by the advanced civilisation of classical antiquity and the peoples of the steppes wandering across Eurasia. We could never understand the form-language spoken by the European armourers in their works without taking into consideration the preliminary and earlier eras of our continent and the constant fertilisation from the Orient through centuries. Here we have confined ourselves to European thought and feeling, lest the presentation dissipate itself in the immeasurably wider spheres of foreign cultures, and in order to set a limit to the boundless subject of "beautiful arms". Contemporary historical research by archaeologists has succeeded in unearthing some original arms from tombs and homes of the pre-romanesque age, in most cases fragments that need to be augmented and reconstructed by scientists. It is only between about 1200 and 1400 that the Church supplies us with intact funeral arms and crown jewels, including weapon insignia from the romanesque and gothic periods. The first conscious attempts to preserve and protect were therefore made for religious and constitutional reasons. The new men of the renaissance and baroque developed a modern feeling for the historical, a completely new concept of time, and with it a critical historical sense. They were the first to know of the collecting, preserving and handing-down of past and contemporary products of human skill, of tools, arms among them; and they were motivated by purely secular considerations. The earliest carefully assembled armouries containing the personal armour of the great date back to the beginning of the renaissance. A little later the more or less standard equipment of troops began to be preserved. Thanks to a conscious historical attitude, arms and armour have since been collected within the framework of museums as nostalgic monuments to saved life or tragic death, to culture and art, for contemporary display as well as for the information of posterity. ❧ It was a rewarding venture to select the most beautiful and best preserved from the superabundance of objects produced in the course of six centuries and now to be found in the collections of the Western Hemisphere in Europe and North America. To some the result may come as a surprise. As our selection was made solely from the standpoint of skill and artistic perfection, it leads to remarkable knowledge of the personalities of all the most prominent clients and the greatest masters, their national origin and place of work. ❧ There were only a very few high-ranking rulers, emperors and kings, electors and dukes who really gave a powerful and decisive impetus to the artistic design and development of arms by their patronage and as substantial clients. Some of them completely exhausted their financial resources in the process. They were emulated by their courtiers and subsequently by a larger, but less successful circle. ❧ In the field of the armourer's craft, too, it was to the great civilised nations of Europe that the signif-

icant achievements were due. In the forefront stood the Italians and Germans, followed by the French and the Spaniards, the Dutch and the English. 🜚 As far as the armourer's art is concerned there were basically only a few really important centres of production during the four centuries from 1400 to 1700. The following are the most famous of these, from which numerous works are known. First and foremost is Milan; in the German region, the free imperial cities of Augsburg and Nuremberg, the princely residences of Innsbruck, Landshut and Dresden; and also Greenwich in England. It has not yet been possible to locate any significant production in France and Lower Germany, regions that have left us no masters' names. It may be possible eventually to find evidence of centres in Paris, Cologne and perhaps Brunswick. In the Netherlands, Brussels, Antwerp and The Hague; and in Italy, Brescia must be taken into consideration. At the fringes of Europe there are the armour production centres of Calatayud in Aragon, Eugui in Navarre and Arboga in Sweden. At first sight this seems an odd list of names that does not to fit into the history of art. This is because armourers are to an unusual degree dependent on external conditions, on the available iron, assured supplies of charcoal, running water and not least upon the princely support of the workshops. 🜚 The armourer's art has produced a number of great masters who have to be evaluated as creative artists of the highest class. Credit for technical advances and original invention is similarly due to them. Their genius gave tremendous impetus to further developments. They combined perfect skill with perfect artistic achievement. In many cases whole families were at work and the knowledge and experience gathered by succeeding generations passed from father to son, both of whom may have served one prince. 🜚 Several great names have to be kept in mind: from Milan the Missaglias (real surname Negroni), Negrolis (really Barini), Serabaglio, Piccinino, della Cesa; from Augsburg the Helmschmids, Sigman, Frauenpreiss, Peffenhauser, Hieronymus Ringler; from Nuremberg Hans Ringler, von Worms, Siebenbürger, Lochner; from Innsbruck the Treytz, Seusenhofers, Witz, Topf; from Landshut Deutsch and the Grossschedels; from Dresden and Berlin the von Speyers; Greenwich had Kirkner and Halder; Antwerp Libaerts. Many of these have only recently been recognised as personalities and artists of stature. It is to be hoped that the mystery of the origin of the many anonymous works of this noble craft will one day be solved. We would then at last possess an allround conception of the masters and their *œuvres*, the evolutionary trends and the interchange of relationships and influences. In this context much research remains to be done on the 16th and 17th centuries. ♟ The production of defensive arms and plate armour was concentrated in a limited number of fertile workshops. As far as offensive arms and accessories are concerned, the position is rather different. A decentralised production was desirable simply because most types were in daily use. It was necessary to establish workshops everywhere because of the many demands made on the smaller items of equipment, their repair and maintenance. And yet it will be found that as regards swords, daggers and hafted weapons the decisive achievements and the outstanding works emerged at a few specific places, that large-scale centres of production were responsible for the mass delivery of quality articles and that individual orders from the courts were linked with traditional places or with residences. Only a few places are really famous for blades: Solingen, Passau and ultimately Munich; Toledo and Milan (so far no identified works exist for Brescia). Research is confronted with an immensely wide field when it tries to find the origin of the many types and forms of *armes blanches* and hafted weapons. ⚒ The position of firearms is quite different, as they are far more frequently marked, signed and dated. Here there are great differences from nation to nation and various schools may be distinguished. Workshops of amazing efficiency emerged in towns, market places and even in tiny villages. Masters left their marks on barrels, locks and stocks. ⚒ During the Middle Ages the work is mostly anonymous but the renaissance saw the emergence of the craftsman's individuality. The power of the guilds increasingly found expression in the quality mark system with the result that not only architects, artists and sculptors but the crafts too shed their anonymity. This is the measure of the divergence between the 16th and 15th centuries. In the baroque of the 17th and 18th centuries, even the least significant collaborator was frequently mentioned, especially on firearms, complete with his initials and signature; the engraver appears on the lock-plate; the carver on the stock; the maker of the decorative inlays, the brass founder or the silversmith on the mounts; the iron-chiseller, damascener,

artist, and gilder on the barrel, which was often imported from far afield. Since the baroque was in fact the golden age of firearms, the highly developed self-assurance of the workers and the personal ambition of the masters, who may be traced right back in to their villages, only serve to benefit research. The significance of the great centres such as Nuremberg, Paris and Brescia has long been recognised. In the last two and a half decades our knowledge of historical firearms has broadened out and deepened to an unprecedented extent. Many hundreds of names of masters in all branches have come to light, to be recorded in thick volumes whose lists come from collections from all over the Western world, the remoter districts of which reveal their peculiar characteristics. ✸ Among the German courts, Dresden was regarded as one of the most significant centres. Munich followed, its iron-chiselling school of Wetter, Sadeler and Spät, whose works covered the entire field of weapons of attack and their accessories, taking the lead at the end of the 16th century. Now, however, it has become clear that, next to this and after the imperial residence of Prague, Vienna must be considered as being peripheral to the armourers' craft. Augsburg, Salzburg, Ferlach and Teschen are yet to be written-up but the material has already been prepared. London's achievements are being surveyed. With Madrid and Ripoll the Spanish gunsmiths' craft has been summarily treated as have those of Stockholm and Denmark. Italy and North America have been the subjects of extensive studies. Holland's importance becomes ever clearer, and here not only Maastricht is noteworthy. Above all, the German regions as far as the easternmost border territories of German cultural influence provide a broad field of study for future research. It will not only have to be concentrated on the artistic activity of the courts and the princes' patronage of the craft, but also on the townships that independently fulfilled demands of all kinds. ✸ When tracing the original background to this joint Western activity, paying attention to the beginnings, seeking the great impetus, the turning point and the inspired novelty, we shall encounter not only the fundamental masters who prepared the ground and at the same time left behind perfect masterpieces, but also a small number of clients of high standing whose role it is impossible to exaggerate. They brought together the forces and selected those best suited to their purposes.

The armoury at Augsburg (peep-show picture)

They engendered the opportunities and provided the means. They supplied exquisite personal taste which was thrown into the balance. Their enthusiasm and demands often appear to have been boundless; they inspired the masters of their choice to achievements which, without them, would never have been realised. Thus they actually participated in the development, placing their orders with a particular purpose in mind. But the great reformers and inventors also turned to them because they sensed their understanding, their grasp of essentials, their instinct for progress, their magnanimity and their genius. ✒ A selection of the most beautiful and significant, of the earliest and most magnificent arms and armour places these clients in the foremost ranks of patronage. With a sure eye for what was effective, they stimulated the great masters to design for them according to the latest standards of elegance and fashion and to do so convincingly. In their wake coursed an ever-widening stream of amateurs and followers whose independence decreased as their numbers grew. The study of arms must not be pursued from a purely comparative point of view alone, without reference to the bearer of the arms. Without taking note of the client, one cannot do justice to the object and comprehend it as an entity. Outstanding masters produced their highest achievements for outstanding rulers. How could it be otherwise? ✜ It is not quite so easy to discover and name the influential patrons of the 15th century. Too few objects have been preserved. That arsenal of Europe, the gigantic weapon manufactory of Milan produced not for a single patron but for the whole world. The Burgundian dukes presumably played a vital part in the field of precious arms, imposing their style on and influencing it both by their orders and as collectors. The Emperor Frederick III (1415–93), for one, left behind a number of arms from which we may deduce his expertise as well as the unusually high demands he made on his armourers. ✜ His son Maximilian I (1459–1519) at the early age of twenty revealed himself to be one of the greatest patrons and reformers in the entire field of arms and armour, possibly the greatest ever to live in the West. The objects he left behind, mainly in Vienna, also stamp him as a unique personality in this sphere. Among them are gothic and early renaissance armours and tournament equipment as well as armour pattern books, swords, crossbows and falconry equipment, even parts of the

frontier fortifications which defended his country, together with explanatory illustrated manuscripts. This legacy, which fills entire museum galleries, contains South German and Tyrolean, Italian, Dutch and Burgundian works. Henry VIII (1491–1547) was inspired to emulate him, and this subsequently bore rich fruit in the British Isles. Maximilian I also set the high standards which his grandson the Emperor Charles V (1500–58) felt bound to maintain. This ruler possessed an exceptionally keen critical faculty in art matters. The fame of the venerable Real Armería in Madrid is based on the arms treasures handed down by Charles V and which, in terms of their importance, rival those of the "Last Knight". Every aspect of the advanced renaissance finds expression in them. The French kings were not only Charles V's opponents in the field of politics, but also as connoisseurs and patrons of the armourer's art. It is becoming manifest that the son of Francis I (1494–1547), Henry II (1519–59), must be counted among the few great initiators. His parade arms are pure manifestations of the mannerist trends of his time. His artistic aspirations in the field of parade arms and their actual continuation and fulfilment after his early death found a champion of consequence in Eric XIV of Sweden (on the throne from 1560 to 1568). This had not a little influence on succeeding Swedish kings. Meanwhile, from around 1545, two Hapsburgs of the Austrian line assume the utmost importance in ordering fine arms. In Vienna it was the Emperor Maximilian II (1527–76) whose magnificent inheritance is opening up unexpected new fields for current research. At the same time, his younger brother the Archduke Ferdinand II (1529–95) collected the arms and armour of friend and foe, of the past and the present, his own and those of members of his family, at his residence in Prague and later at Innsbruck for his own unique Hall of Fame, the Heroes' Armoury that found a home at Ambras Castle in the vicinity. Maximilian II's contemporary in Madrid was his cousin, King Philip II of Spain (1527–98), who had similarly refined tastes. For his generation the Emperor Rudolph II (1552–1612), residing at the Hradchin castle in Prague, set the highest standard for the courtly late renaissance style. His lands bordered on the territories of the dukes and electors of Saxony and Bavaria, where large armouries had been established in Dresden and Munich.

They brought together arms that had been in the magnificent collections of the princes in the 16th century and found their culmination under the Electors Christian II of Saxony (1583–1611) and Maximilian I of Bavaria (1573–1651), precisely in the period and the spirit of Rudolph II. ⌐— Meanwhile, the French King Louis XIII (1601–43) had developed a fanatical taste for beautiful arms. Louis' traditional attitude towards armour – his own was uniquely valuable – and his revival of the armourer's art would justify our calling him "The Last of the Knights". It was in his reign that the flintlock began its triumphant progress across the world. His son, the Sun-King, Louis XIV (1638–1715), brought about and lived to see the complete supremacy of French firearms. The standards which he demanded for his arms were adopted in the whole of Europe. He was a great moving spirit, whether by initiating Versailles and the Hôtel des Invalides in Paris, as the father of a style of interior decoration, or as the personal patron of particularly extravagant arms. In his day and long after his death the successors and imitators building castles based on his original ideas were legion. From emperors and kings, princes and barons of the Holy Roman Empire down to petty princes, all were fascinated by him. In exactly the same way, in the armourer's craft, the Europe of the late baroque, of the rococo, of the neo-classical, of the Empire style – that is, until Napoleon I (1769–1821), – lived on, stimulated by stylistic trends emanating from France since Louis XIV's time. ⌐— Thus we have the extremely attractive spectacle of a tremendous variety of beautiful arms whose ramifications reached out to tiny and remote places. Admittedly, during the 17th and 18th centuries arms which were the equal of the French were also produced in Brescia, Maastricht, London, Madrid, Vienna, Munich, Berlin, Heidersbach in Thuringia, and Schwäbisch-Gmünd, and one could clearly feel a breath of the national and local peculiarities to which they owed their freshness and vigorous attraction. But the unique personality is missing, the man who, with great determination, turned the wheel of progress, and as instigator, client and user opened closed doors and explored new worlds. In the 18th century we no longer find a Maximilian I or a Charles V. ☙ One may say this, however, also of the late period of individual arms – the finest and best documented examples are to be found in the old armouries of

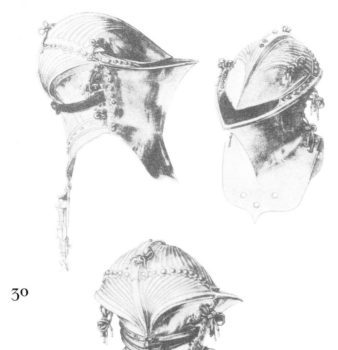

30

Europe. It is not by chance that the selection we present here falls back almost exclusively on dynastic collections which to-day are still in the South Tyrolean Churburg, in Vienna and Madrid, Munich and Dresden, Berlin, Paris and London, Stockholm and Copenhagen, and Turin and Florence. Similar objects are responsible for the fame of the largest modern collections of historical arms – in New York and Leningrad. The importance of any contemporary private collection depends on its possession of beautiful arms that can be traced to the ancient armouries. ✎ The prominent patron at an artistically appointed residence; the outstanding master to whom he turned and who was usually technician and artist in one, working at a place that had long been famous; the particular political grounds for its production, that is to say, its historic background – these together constitute the prerequisite and the guarantee that an old weapon shall become a precious document of pragmatic history, of cultural history and of the history of technology and art.

Bruno Thomas

King Ferdinand I – later to become Emperor–(left) and Frederick II, Elector and Pfalzgraf bei Rhein. Detail of the painting "Staghunt of the Elector John Frederick of Saxony near Torgau" by Lucas Cranach the Younger (1544). Vienna, Kunsthistorisches Museum.

Philip
daubigny
1665. fre,

A Paris chez van Merlen, rue St Iacques a la ville d'Anuers, Auec Priuil. du R.

1

THE PLATES

1 SICILY (PALERMO), BEFORE 1220

The Ceremonial Sword of the imperial regalia, originally the property of the Emperor Frederick II of Hohenstaufen of the medieval Swabian dynasty (1194–1250; Emperor, 1220)

Frederick II, King of Sicily from 1197 and of Germany from 1212, carried this state sword when being crowned Emperor by Pope Gregory IX in Rome. Its cross-shape follows the dignified style of the Middle Ages. The long double-edged blade bears the mark of the crooked cross. Around 1335 the Emperor Charles IV replaced the original brazil-nut pommel by the then fashionable disc pommel engraved with the Imperial Eagle and the Lion of Bohemia. The magnificent decoration of the hilt and scabbard, with their strongly coloured enamel and filigree on gold further enriched with pearls and rubies, derives from Byzantine-oriental culture. One of the ornamental plates on the scabbard shows an early example of the single-headed Imperial Eagle, the ancient symbol of Jupiter Capitolinus, proof of the deliberate continuation of the ancient Roman *Imperium* with its supra-national philosophy. The precious decoration of this unique weapon stems from the court art that was established by the Norman kings of Sicily, and which was carried out largely by Saracen craftsmen. This insignia formed part of the imperial regalia from the time of Frederick II.

Vienna, Weltliche Schatzkammer, XIII/16

2 SWITZERLAND, END OF THE 12th CENTURY, ALTERED DURING THE SECOND QUARTER OF THE 13th CENTURY

The equestrian shield of Seedorf, thought to have belonged to the Knight Arnold of Brienz

This war shield was originally rounded at the top and pointed at the base, a shape that we are familiar with from the famous Norman Bayeux tapestry (c. 1066). The function of this type of shield was to cover the heavily armed rider's left side from the face to below the knee, acting as a protective barrier. Remnants of the internal straps which formed part of its fastening have been preserved. The highly stylised figure of a lion is of silvered gesso set on a blue dyed leather cover. The lion is the heraldic device of the bearer, probably Arnold of Brienz, who founded the small Lazarite convent in 1197 at Seedorf on Lake Uri in the Canton of Uri whence the shield originates. It is the oldest Swiss heraldic relic.

From ancient times on, the lion was deemed a royal animal because of his courage, strength and beauty. In the Orient it was the privilege of kings to hunt him. Paintings show rulers and mythical heroes engaged in combat with the lion rearing up on its hind legs. From these oriental models the rampant figure of the lion was adopted for medieval coats of arms. The Seedorf shield appears to have been modernised between 1230 and 1250 by the removal of the upper curve, then no longer in fashion. This supports the view that this precious defensive arm was not originally intended as a funeral shield but was actually in everyday use for more than a generation.

Zurich, Schweizerisches Landesmuseum, LM. 3405

3 MILANESE MASTERS, c.1380–90

Half-armour from the armoury of the Governors of Matsch

In the castle of Churburg a unique treasure has been preserved in the ancient armoury owned and assembled by the two noble families of Matsch and Trapp. Its incomparable contents, the incunabula of the art of the armourer like this half-armour, date back to the late 14th century. The construction of the breastplate gives evidence of its antiquity, assembled as it is from steel lames in the oriental fashion. The helmet, a "houndskull bascinet" with pointed visor, is of similarly ancient appearance. Engraved brass strips bordering the plates form a decorative element carrying, both on the helmet and on the breastplate, a New Testament quotation blessing the armour. The scalloped vambrace and the gauntlets with their plaited pattern are actually the remnants of two other armours which date back to the same period – there were always many brothers in the Matsch family. The helmet bears their coat of arms as a mark of ownership. To complete the picture of this armour one has to imagine the missing leg-harness with its pointed shoes, a short-sleeved tight-fitting leather jacket over the mail shirt and a brocade cover for the originally lined mail collar. At this time shoulder defences of plate had not yet been developed. The master's mark proudly engraved on every part (*e.g.* on the breast, the "p" ascribed to Petrajolo Negroni da Ello, called Missaglia) proves that the fragments are masterpieces of Milanese craftsmanship.

It was there that the armourer's art was born and plate armour of steel was first evolved – even before the 14th century. Vambrace and leg-harness, helmet with articulated visor – all were brought to technical perfection at a surprisingly early date. Breast and shoulder defences emerged only later in the 14th century and one learns of their step by step development from Italian illustrations. The Milan tomb of Duke Bernabò Visconti, created around 1370, fits the period of the Churburg half-armour. The low-slung hip belt of leather was made around 1400. Being coloured and decorated but not metal-mounted, it was presumably worn with civilian clothes rather than with armour. *Churburg, near Sluderno, Gräfliche Rüstkammer, 13 and 364*

4 GERMAN, c.1400–10

Bascinet with hinged visor

The snout-like form of the visor and the pointed helmet-bowl gave this type of bascinet the name "houndskull". The articulated face defence emerged as a novelty during the early 14th century, in the second half of which the visored helmet became an accepted part of the military dress of the aristocracy. Artificial peculiarities were the artistic ideal of the time and so the armourers combined fantastic round visors (in Western Europe) or pointed visors (in Italy and Germany) with the pointed bascinet. From 1400 a new artistic epoch had a different ideal, to which the close configuration, the beautifully smooth shape, the harmonious gracefully changing contours of the Coburg bascinet bear witness. The German armourer who created them knew how to please his customers. The aesthetic attraction of its modelling and finish and the even blue of the surface remains unchanged to this day. From the constructional point of view the German master's habit of suspending the visor in the middle of the forehead is more ancient than the contemporary Milanese armourers' method of fixing it at the sides so that the visor pivoted on its axis. It is interesting to note that the German knight concealed the accompanying mail that protected his body to a far greater extent than did the Italian *uomo d'arme*. It was usually hidden underneath a pleated coat, reaching to the knee and with voluminous sleeves. Worn over it, the shining breastplate had to act as gleaming decoration against the colourful mass of fabric, giving eloquent expression to the common European "International Style" that so loved richness and colour.   *Coburg, Kunstsammlungen der Veste, A.I.1*

5 HUNGARY, 1419–25

Electoral Sword of Frederick I,
Elector of Saxony (1370–1428; Elector, 1423)

The crystal pommel of this magnificent sword from the Dresden Armoury is decorated with tiny labels bearing the coats of arms of Hungary and Bohemia as well as the Imperial Eagle of Germany, the heraldry of Sigmund I of the House of Luxemburg (1368–1437). He was King of Hungary from 1387, becoming King of Bohemia in 1419; King of Germany in 1410, and Emperor in 1433. All this gives credence to the story that Sigmund presented the sword to Duke Frederick I of Saxony when he officially invested him with the Electorate of Saxony at Ofen in 1425.

Not only the heraldry and the historic circumstances point to Sigmund I as the original owner but also the extremely rich and choice goldsmith's work. The parrying guard in imitation of twisted gnarled boughs conforms to the late gothic style of Central Europe that transformed abstract shapes into plants. One talks of a German "Bough Gothic" style. The scabbard is covered with crimson velvet around which a band of gilded silver with laterally attached gothic foliage is wound in a spiral in imitation of the hangings that are always slung around the scabbards of ceremonial swords. On the bands themselves, framed by silver-gilt wires, there is delicate enameling in the Hungarian colours of red, white and green. Filigree enamel was first seen in Venetian Italy during the 14th century. Hungarian goldsmiths adopted it and brought it to perfection. Presumably, therefore, it was a goldsmith at Sigmund's Hungarian court who created this splendid sword after 1419, but before the ceremony in 1425. It is the richest example to be preserved of any medieval reign.   *Dresden, Historisches Museum, A 34*

6 MILAN, MISSAGLIA AND CORIO WORKSHOPS RESPECTIVELY, AROUND 1450–55

Armours of Frederick I, Elector Palatine (1425–76; Ruler from 1451) and of a Governor of Matsch from Churburg

By around 1420 the Milanese armourers had evolved the armour cap-à-pie with all its parts and the next fifty years saw the development of an ever-growing ability to produce an elegant perfection of form with a few additional technical improvements. Among these were the tassets, shield-shaped plates attached to the fauld. In consideration of the different tasks carried out by the right arm, that wielded the sword, and the left, the bridle arm, the flexibility and weight of the armour varies. The Milanese masters endeavoured to achieve a smooth steel body cover that gave a sculptured effect. About 1450 they reached the peak of their fame. Little hindered by the guild restrictions, united in syndicates through opportunity or by necessity, they developed a productive capacity which practically secured them a monopoly in the West. This is why the majority of armour and armour parts of the 15th century to survive were made in Italy and why these works bear so many masters' marks in so many different arrangements.

The strong and dignified appearance of the armour from the Churburg Armoury, now in the Glasgow Art Gallery and Museum (right), is reminiscent of figures on frescoes by the masters Piero della Francesca and Andrea del Castagno. Only the tassets are missing. Its sole decoration consists of *pointillée* ornaments and the motto "AVANT". The work gives the impression of having been cast in one piece although in fact five masters were involved in its creation: the brothers Giovanni, Ambrogio and Bellino Corio, Dionisio Corio and Giovanni da Garavalle.

The example from the Vienna Armoury (left) shows that the Milanese knew how to adapt themselves to foreign tastes. The valiant and experienced warrior Palsgrave Frederick probably ordered it when he began his reign in 1451. As Count Palatine and a neighbour of the glorious and powerful Duchy of Burgundy, he obviously preferred Western European military dress, the excessively long and pointed shoes, large helmets with rounded visors, and shoulder pieces with discs such as were then worn in France and England. The most famous Milanese workshop, which was required to supply him with armour in this style, was owned by Tomaso Negroni da Ello, called Missaglia. Tomaso's son Antonio, Master Antonio Seroni, and Pier Innocenzo da Faerno – the creator of a magnificent horse-armour in the Historisches Museum, Vienna – cooperated and stamped it with their masters' marks.

Vienna, Waffensammlung, A 2 –
formerly Churburg Armoury 20; now Glasgow, Art Gallery and Museum

7 BURGUNDIAN, 1467–77

The sword of Charles the Bold, Duke of Burgundy (1433–77; Duke, 1467)

BURGUNDIAN, c. 1490

The ivory sword of Maximilian I (1459–1519; King, 1486; Emperor, 1508)

The rise of the Duchy of Burgundy, situated between Germany and France, as a new economic and political factor which was the result both of its craftsmen's diligence and of its sea trade, began at the end of the 14th century. Its dukes of the House of Valois were the equal of kings in prestige, wealth and splendour. Charles the Bold, the most ambitious of them, was not satisfied by mere equality but wanted to become a king himself. An excellently equipped army was to realise his far-reaching plans of conquest, the targets of his attacks being the Holy Roman Empire, Lorraine and the Swiss Confederation.

The Duke's own sword in the Vienna Schatzkammer conveys an idea of the unimaginable pomp and splendour at the court of Burgundy. The narrow thrusting blade is carefully polished. The gold mounts on hilt and sheath are decorated with the emblems of the exclusive Burgundian Order of the Golden Fleece which was founded by Charles' father, Philip IV, in romantic allusion to the saga of the Argonauts. Pearls, a ruby, and two charming little enamel plaques with the Crucifixion and the Madonna decorate the pommel. The pommel, hilt and sheath are carved out of narwhal horn, the most precious relic of the Middle Ages, symbolising purity and the Virgin Mary. To possess a whale's tooth was to provide protection against ill-fortune, disease and death. It was of no avail to the Duke. In 1476 he lost his conquests and treasures in battles against the Swiss at Grandson and Murten and, in 1477 before the gates of Nancy, his dominions and life itself.

In the same year the Emperor's young son Maximilian married the heiress to the Duchy of Burgundy. Thus the foundation-stone was laid for the international importance of the Hapsburg dynasty. The joint use of gold and ivory on the hunting knives that had belonged to Maximilian reveal the tastes prevailing at the court of Burgundy. Maximilian seems to have bought back the sword of his fallen father-in-law from the Swiss booty. Philip, the son of Maximilian and Maria, married the Spanish princess Johanna. The eldest son of this union was Charles V, on whose empire the sun never set, thus fulfilling the dreams of his great grandfather, in an even more splendid if completely unexpected manner.

Vienna, Weltliche Schatzkammer, XIV/9 – Vienna, Waffensammlung, D 259

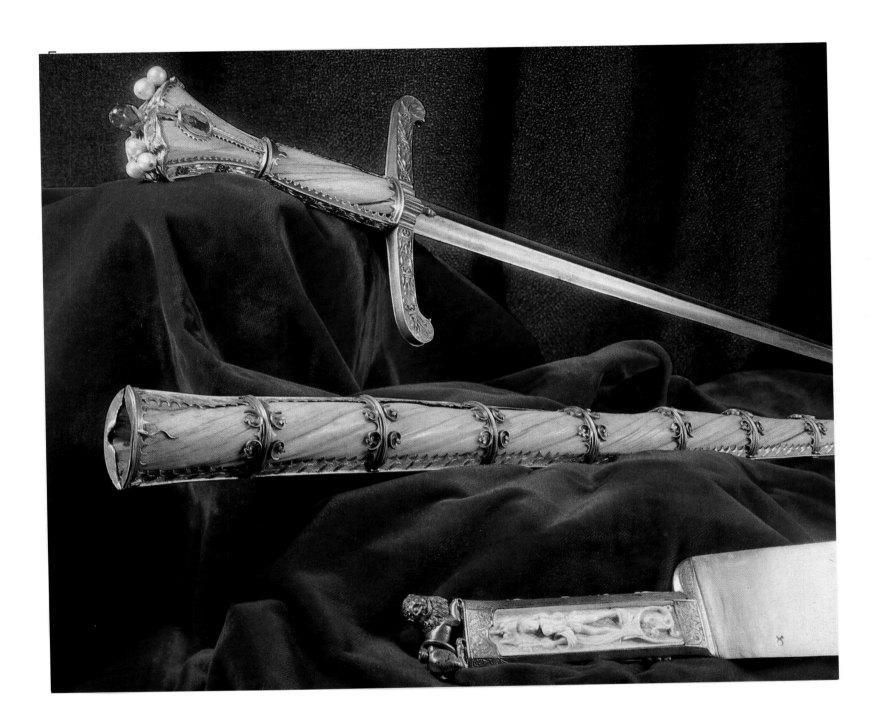

Two gothic maces of the Emperors Frederick III (1415–93; King, 1439; Emperor, 1452) and Maximilian I (1459–1519)

The two maces consist of base, plinth, buttresses and tracery windows that recall the domed gothic towers in Dutch paintings of the 15th century. The tracery of gilded brass shows vestiges of paint that prove that it was indeed meant to give the impression of a gothic building with its stained glass windows. The mace must be regarded as a sign of rank, a function that it was found to have in the old Egyptian empire and in most of the ancient civilisations of Mesopotamia some millennia before Christ's birth.

The two Vienna maces are part of the original stock of the Imperial Armoury. Whoever could have used them around 1475, and when was there any demand for such specimens? They must have been made for the battle of Neuss in 1474/75. In order to prevent the power-hungry Charles the Bold, Duke of Burgundy, from taking the besieged city of Neuss north of Cologne an army moved into the Rhineland led by the Emperor Frederick III and his son, the Archduke Maximilian, then just sixteen, who was later to become emperor. By the introduction of a variety of amusements the two noblemen succeeded in leading a very pleasant camp life. The front-paper of this book illustrates this well. Collapsible boards for chess and backgammon fit into the maces' hollow grips. The lost pieces must have been kept in the hollow shaft. The artist thought up something special for the Emperor, who was extremely interested in astronomy and astrology, in the sun-dial secreted below the detachable cap of the grip. The serious purpose of weapon and badge of rank mingles here with the light-hearted character of a fashionable little work of art.   *Vienna, Waffensammlung, A 153 and A 162*

9   WESTERN EUROPE, c.1470

Pole-axe, traditionally said to have belonged to Edward IV, King of England (1442–83; King, 1461)

The aristocrat would settle his disputes of honour or sporting duels in an arena, surrounded by referees and seconds and before spectators' tribunes. The weapon he preferred was the long hafted pole-axe, as shown here. The iron thrusting spike, hammer and hatchet appear to issue from the throats of lions and wolves at the socket of gilded bronze, itself decorated with engraved foliage and a knot of flowers. The hand-guard takes the shape of a heraldic rose above which floats a fiery cluster of clouds. Due to the symbols of the rose and flame this weapon has been ascribed to King Edward IV of England. Symbols and ornaments of this type were, however, widely used at the time so that this assumption is not necessarily valid. In view of the care and splendour with which this weapon was made and its particular style, it probably originated in the armoury of an aristocrat holding a high position in either France, the Netherlands or England.   *Paris, Musée de l'Armée, K 84*

Foot-combat helmet of Maximilian I (1459–1519: King, 1486; Emperor, 1508)

Particularly in Western Europe, the knights' duel on foot was regarded as a sport. As the husband of Maria (heiress of Burgundy 1457–82; married, 1477), Maximilian presumably first developed his marked preference for foot-combat at her pleasure-loving court. Two types of equipment were suitable: either the *Kempfküriss* with a flared skirt of iron, or the one which enveloped the body like close-fitting tights.

Lorenz Helmschmid, the outstanding royal armourer of Maximilian's father, Frederick III, created foot-combat equipment for Maximilian around 1485 – possibly for the festivities on the coronation of the young prince as Roman King in 1486. We can see what it looked like in a book left to us by the Helmschmid workshop, which contains sketches and illustrations recording the armour produced there. It came into imperial possession and from there, through a chief equerry to the Imperial Household named Thun, into the library of the Princes Thun at Tetschen in northern Bohemia.

Only the original helmet has been preserved, a masterpiece of forging. For a long time it was the prize possession in the armoury of Count Breuner, later Prince Ratibor, at his neo-gothic castle of Grafenegg near Krems in Lower Austria. Its bright rounded surface must once have given the impression of a polished steel ball, the firm smooth shape thus displaying its full charm. A comparison of the accurate sketch with the original is sufficient proof that this was the personal property of the sporting monarch.

Collection Carl Otto von Kienbusch, New York, 56

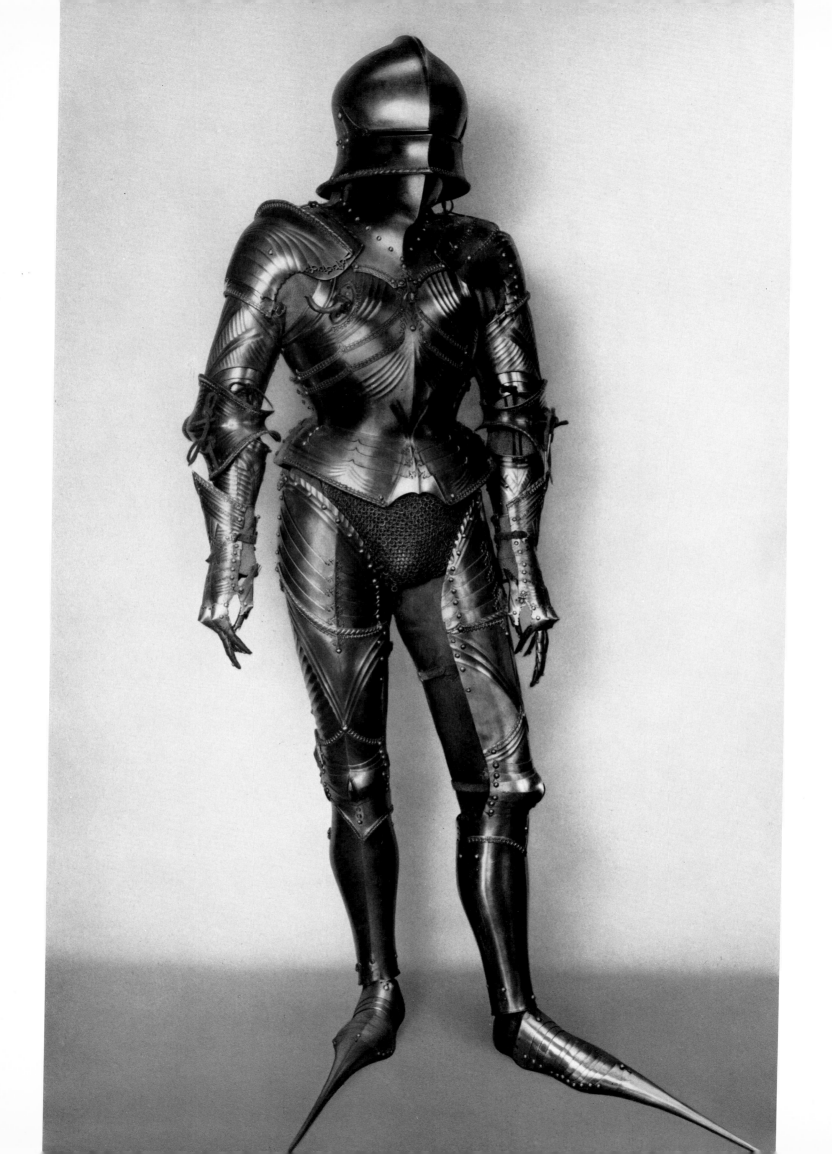

11 LORENZ HELMSCHMID, AUGSBURG, c. 1480

Late gothic armour of the Archduke Sigmund (1427–96; Lord of the Tyrol, 1439–90)

The first field and tournament armours made outside Italy had their origin in southern Germany around 1480. A single incomplete example in the Historisches Museum, Vienna, unfortunately lacking its helmet and vambraces, dates from the decade beginning 1450. Otherwise only individual parts, particularly helmets, from complete knightly armours have been handed down from the beginning of the German late gothic period in the late 15th century. The most excellently preserved early German *Küriss*, as the complete armour was called, is undoubtedly that of the Archduke Sigmund. Maximilian I (1459–1519) probably used it himself when a young prince and presumably presented it to his uncle Sigmund, who succeeded him in 1490 as Lord of the Tyrol, part of the Hapsburg Empire.

There is no earlier or later example of the armourer's art to match this one in its elegant perfection. Its maker's mark is to be found on the point of the neck-guard of the helmet, a typical German sallet. It is the mark of Lorenz Helmschmid, and stamped next to it is the Augsburg coat of arms. Lorenz was one of the most brilliant armourers of all time, a craftsman and artist of outstanding distinction who created around 1480 the "armour garniture" to be used for all purposes. He was a true creative master who served not only the Emperor Frederick III, but was even more active for his son Maximilian I, the self-styled "Last of the Knights".

The fashion ideal of the late Middle Ages is embodied in its purest form in this armour of Sigmund's. It is characterised by extreme slimness, pointed shapes, rippled effects that enliven its surfaces, and it possesses marked flexibility. The bright surfaces are edged with gilded ornamental bands patterned with lilies. This work of princely beauty reveals the German's special talent for line and the graphic, whilst the Italian armourer prefers large and simple sculptured forms.

The armour did not unduly burden the prince, who was small-boned and, moreover, wore corsets: it weighed only the usual forty pounds or so, which were fairly evenly distributed over the whole body. The rider's handling of the long equestrian lance was facilitated by a hinged lance rest. The bizarre pointed shoes had their origin in a peculiar whim of fashion of the period. As they were meant only to be worn on horseback, the points could be removed when the rider wished to go on foot. *Vienna, Waffensammlung, A 62*

The hand-pavise of Matthias Corvinus, King of Hungary (1443–90; King, 1458)

Numerous large, trapezoid pavises and small, rectangular hand-shields have been preserved from the 15th century; all were made with a wide, pronounced medial rib. Examples of this shape go back to western Slavonic sculpture and their traces are lost in the prehistoric darkness of Asia's steppes. In the early 15th century Czech Hussites were equipped with pavises, with which they carried heavy broadswords. The terror spread by the Hussites and their obvious military superiority led to the recruitment of Bohemian warriors for Central European armies and to the adoption of their arms.

A battle for power between the Emperor Frederick III and Matthias Corvinus, the son of the Hungarian regent Johannes Hunyadi, had long been raging in Hungary and devastated Lower Austria. In 1485 even Vienna, the imperial residence, fell to the victorious Hungarian king who reigned there in defiance of the Emperor until his death in 1490. During the war the Bohemian kings Georg Podjebrad and Wladislaw Jagiello had in turn been allied with both parties and Bohemian-Moravian foot-soldiers had fought in both armies. The attractive gilt gesso hand-pavise was modelled on the arms of this select troop and was probably made for King Matthias during his stay in Vienna by a Viennese artist. Around the combined coat of arms of New Hungary, Bohemia, Dalmatia and Ancient Hungary are grouped the king's further coats of arms and the inscription "Alma genitrix Maria interpella pro rege Mathia". From the charge on the Hunyadi shield, which impales the central coat of arms, Matthias adopted the surname Corvinus ("The Raven"). After the death of the King, who was not only a doughty warrior but an equally great lover of the arts – the works in his "Corvina" library are world-famous – the young Hapsburg Maximilian fought a quick and victorious campaign to recover the lands lost by his father. It must have been on that occasion that the Hungarian king's pavise came into his possession, as it was in the imperial armoury for three centuries before 1805, when one of Napoleon's generals took it to Paris. A long, heavy broadsword with gilded hilt in Vienna (A 123) may once have belonged to it.

Warriors with this type of Bohemian equipment that occur in the woodcuts in Maximilian's "Triumphal Procession" reminded the aging emperor of the happy victories of his youth.
Paris, Musée de l'Armée, I. 7

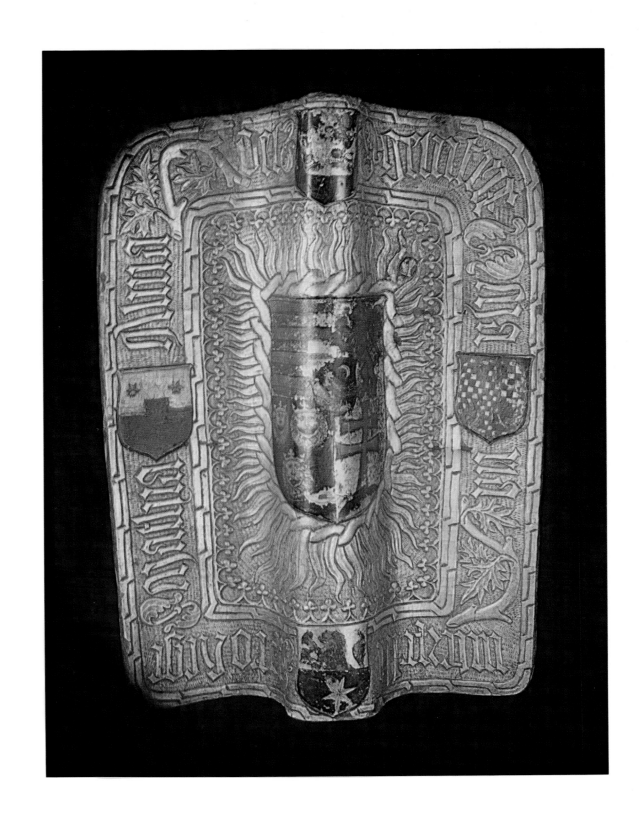

The "Feudal Sword", hunting sword and knife of the Emperor Maximilian I (1459–1519; King, 1486; Emperor, 1508)

When the Archduke Sigmund, Maximilian's uncle and predecessor as Lord of the Tyrol, died in 1496, the "Last Knight" ordered a unique garniture from his royal cutler at Solbad Hall. It consisted of a set of *armes blanches* (a generic term covering all swords and daggers) all in the same style and similarly decorated. Today it is dispersed in four places.

The giant bastard sword bears remnants of the maker's signature ... NS VON H ... and the date 1496 as well as a series of coats of arms and the initials of Maximilian I. The sword was part of his personal regalia and derives its name from its use during the oath of fealty by vassals to their lord and the distribution of feudal tenures that formed part of the ceremony.

(The sidearm which belongs to the same garniture was presumably a gift from the Emperor Charles V to his brother-in-law Christian II, King of Denmark, on his appointment to the Order of the Golden Fleece. Today it is in the National Museum in Copenhagen.)

A hunting sword contained the additional knives and had an elaborately ornamented leather scabbard.

Part of this garniture is a complete set of cutlery for the hunt in a similarly decorated leather case, comprising four different knives and one small fork. Its inscriptions and pictures would remind the nephew of his recently deceased uncle. Many materials in a great diversity of colours have been used and finished in a most artistic manner; steel that has been etched, decorated with *goldschmelz*, ground, chiselled, blued and gilded; cast silver, engraved bronze; inlaid wood and ivory, carved mother-of-pearl, cut and embossed leather. The rich sweep of the gothic style – scrolls, small figures, coats of arms, and saints – is developed in all its exuberance, yet forms an artistic entity of truly regal character.

Vienna, Weltliche Schatzkammer, XIV/4 – Vienna, Waffensammlung, D 11 – Kremsmünster, (Armoury of the Benedictine Abbey) 4.

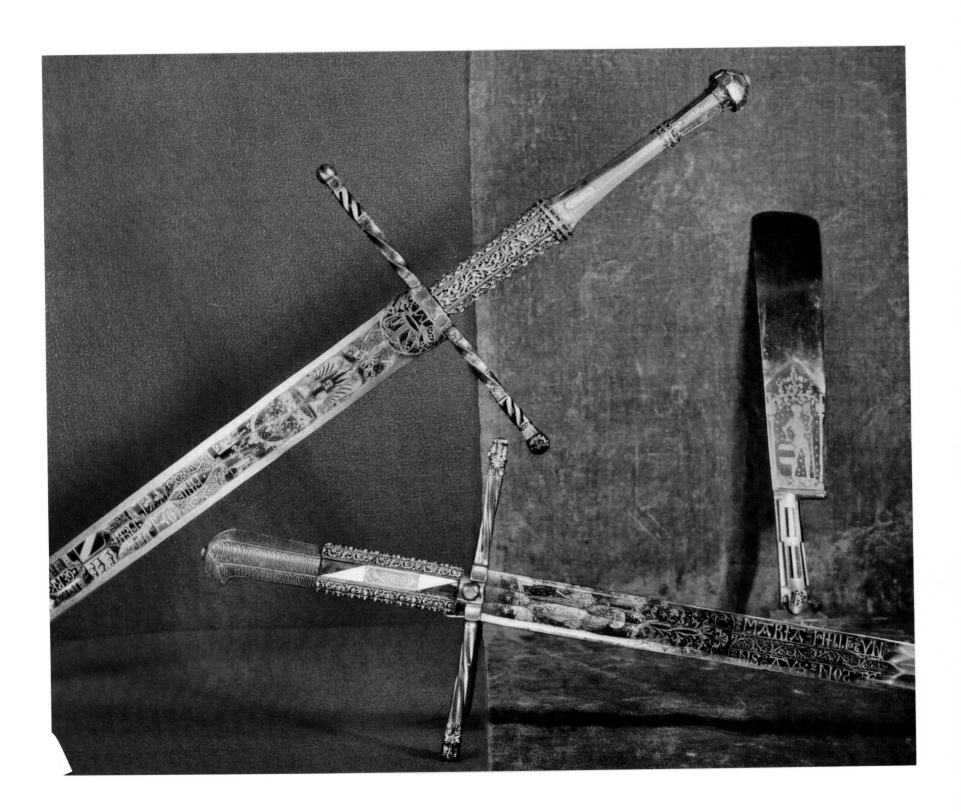

The parade sword of Maximilian I (1459–1519; King, 1486; Emperor, 1508)

ERCOLE DE'FIDELI, FERRARA-ROME, 1490–1500

Parade sword

In 1494 Maximilian I, then Roman King, married the Milanese Princess Bianca Maria Sforza for political reasons rather than for love. At the time a violent struggle was raging between the Holy Roman Empire and France over supremacy in Milan, and the Hapsburg considered it urgent to secure his claims by marriage.

Presumably, this parade sword with its pictorial allusions to love and marriage was one of the wedding presents (right). Putti and the god Cupid himself, and a vessel with a growing plant, the popular ancient symbol for being blessed with children, appear on the gilded etching of the blade. The inscription "IN DIO AMOR" (God is love) on a gold band around the hilt is probably a reminder of the holy sacrament of marriage. The compact, slender hilt with flat oblong pommel is reminiscent of the form of late gothic sword hilts, whilst the wedge-shaped blade, tapering towards its point, with a strong median rib, follows the Italian style. On this weapon German and Italian forms have been united to form an artistic entity, as in the case of Milan cathedral. The inlaid wood and mother-of-pearl of the hilt matches the inlaid choir stalls of Upper Italy, where the art then flourished.

On account of his skill, the Jewish goldsmith Salomone da Sesso was called to the court of Ferrara where he was converted to Roman Catholicism and took the Christian name of his godfather, the art-loving Duke Ercole d'Este. As a result of the planned marriage of Alfonso I, Duke d'Este, to Lucretia Borgia, Ercole "dei Fideli" (i.e. Ercole the Believer) moved to the notorious court of Prince Cesare Borgia. When the latter was overthrown in 1503, he transferred his services to Cardinal della Rovere, who later became the great renaissance Pope Julius II (1503–13). The goldsmith Ercole, who died in Rome in 1518, specialised in the production of precious swords and daggers with richly etched blades and gilded cast hilts. As the Vienna exhibit (left) is from the Hapsburg armoury, it must have been the property of Maximilian I or of his son Philip I, King of Spain, who had personal ties with Cesare Borgia. It is as beautiful as, but in a better state of preservation than, the so-called "reine des épées", a sword that Ercole created for the Borgia and which is in the collection of Prince Gaetani in Rome.   *Vienna, Waffensammlung, A 170 and A 455*

15 AN ITALIAN MASTER, c. 1480–90

Barbuta with lion's-mask cover

Early in the 14th century Italian scholars discovered, as a result of their industrious research, the magic world of antiquity. They sought the renaissance – the *rinascimento* – of a new and free man and its discovery was proclaimed with exultation. The arts were caught up in the spell of the new movement in which Greco-Roman antiquity had become the great ideal. In every expression of cultural life one endeavoured to behave *all 'antica*, a trend that inevitably affected arms too.

Although the late medieval helmet provided excellent protection for the face, it obscured the sight and made breathing difficult. Therefore a "barbuta", an open helmet with sight, had already appeared in the 14th century, particularly in Italy. It can hardly have been coincidence that in the course of the 15th century the shape of this barbuta became strikingly similar to the helmet worn by the heavily armoured foot-soldiers of ancient Greece. Italian warriors stationed on the Aegean Islands for the protection of Venetian and Genoese merchants' colonies may well have come across this Grecian type of helmet.

The New York helmet is given an even more antique appearance by being covered with an embossed and gilded lion's mask. The artist has been extremely successful in his portrayal of the royal beast's expression of savagery and strength. Its skilful maker was probably inspired by Roman representations of Hercules wearing the lion's skin, or he may somewhere have discovered pictures of the Etruscan god of Hades crowned with a lion's head. Presumably he worked in southern Italy, at Naples, where an unusually large number of classical remains were preserved. A warrior on the relief of the gate at Castel Nuovo, Naples, which was created around 1460, wears a barbuta decorated in this way. But the helmet in New York was made somewhat later, as hidden under the lion's mane is an articulated neck-guard, a technical innovation that was not introduced until between 1480 and 1490. This is a beautiful example of the Italian armourers' art from the period when the early renaissance was merging into its mature stage, and is the first original work of a series of preciously embossed armours *alla romana*.

New York, Metropolitan Museum of Art, 23. 141

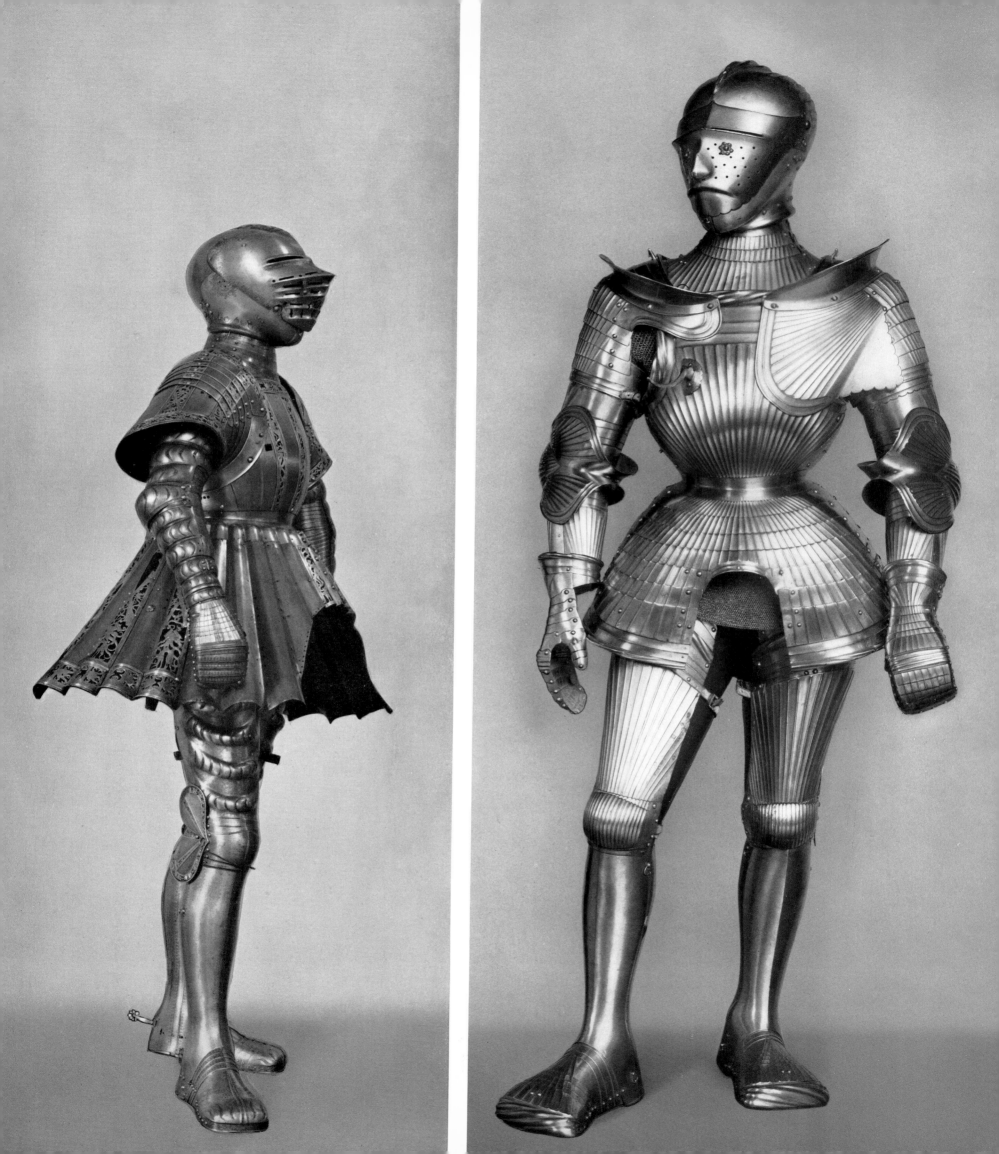

Armour with bases of the boy Archduke, later the Emperor Charles V (1500–58; King of Spain, 1516; King and Emperor, 1519)

In 1504 Maximilian I founded his own centre of armour production at the Innsbruck court. This was obviously modelled on the workshops of his Milanese relations by marriage. The highly talented Konrad Seusenhofer was put in charge and a number of masters and journeymen were engaged to carry out innumerable imperial orders. In 1512 Maximilian ordered parade armours for his young grandchild, Charles, and for his ally, King Henry VIII of England. They were to be equipped with wrought metal work and with iron bases or skirts derived from the costumes of the Dutch aristocracy. Only the helmet of Henry's armour is still in the Tower of London (IV. 22), but the charming and complete boy's armour made for Charles can be seen in Vienna. Like the so-called landsknechts' costume it is puffed and slashed and shows etched, gilded and blackened patterns. The most striking ornament, however, is the pierced bands of gilded silver with the emblems of the Order of the Golden Fleece against violet velvet. The hammered, brightly polished armour was actually sent to Augsburg for this unusual decoration to be fitted.

WILHELM VON WORMS THE ELDER, NUREMBERG, c. 1530–35

Fluted armour of Christopher, Duke of Württemberg (1515–68; ruler from 1550)

Nuremberg is the classic seat of fluted armour. Its parallel embossed flutes are purely a fashionable decoration that commands comparison with the contemporary costume of pleated textile. As early as 1500 the restlessly rippling gothic grooves clearly change into parallel flutes and emphasise the well-rounded, sharply defined surface curves of the armour. Some armour of this type comes from Innsbruck, from Augsburg, and some even from Milan, but the vast majority has its origin in Nuremberg, the centre of a tremendous armour production. The fashion lasted until about 1530–35. A single late specimen of this sort was created for the Emperor Maximilian II about 1557. The fashion with its beautiful lines experienced late revival in a whole series of armour made for the coronation of the Emperor Matthias in 1612. It was then that the romantic preference for all things "primitive" began under the influence of the Emperor Rudolf II, the great Dürer collector, whose interest resulted in the production of deceptive imitations of Dürer's art.   *Vienna, Waffensammlung, A 109 and A 237*

17 NORTH ITALIAN, 1494–1508

Lure, falcon and hawk's hoods of Maximilian I and his wife Bianca Maria Sforza (1472–1510 married, 1494)

The noble sport of falconry came to Europe during the early Middle Ages from the brilliant court of the Persian Sassanids in Ctesiphon and from the Arabian Abbasides in Baghdad. It was one of the privileges of aristocracy to own hunting falcons, carefully reared birds that were frequently worth their weight in gold. Therefore it is not surprising that participants in the hunt were keen to display the choicest falconry equipment.

In northern Italy, probably in her home town of Milan, the splendour-loving Queen Bianca Maria Sforza had truly regal falconry outfits made for herself and her husband Maximilian I, who was later to become emperor (1508). Her own coat of arms and her husband's royal arms appear on the small gilded and painted hoods of tooled leather. The smaller size was intended for falcons, the larger for hawks. Wearing it and deprived of sight, the bird remained quietly on the falconer's leather-gloved fist. As soon as the hood was removed, the bird spread its wings and pounced on its prey, usually heron or small game. A heron hunt being enjoyed by a lady and her escort is depicted on the charming embroidery of the silken lure. Two other lures of embroidered gold brocade have been preserved from the set. Only the matching hunting-bag, from which the falcons were fed after a successful hunt, is missing.

Though expensive and strenuous, this extremely thrilling sport is now enjoying a revival and has attracted many devotees. *Vienna, Waffensammlung, D 6, D 24 ff.*

Crossbow with windlass of Louis XII, King of France (1462–1515; King, 1498)

Connecting a shaft to a bow to make a crossbow is a technical achievement of great antiquity. As long ago as the first centuries A.D., the Chinese successfully used it to defend themselves against the invading Huns. Although the Church prohibited its use on several occasions in the Middle Ages because of its murderous impact, the crossbow nevertheless won acceptance. It has maintained its position as a hunting and sporting weapon well into modern times, even to the present day.

In the Middle Ages the cord was drawn with the aid of a belt-hook but human force proved insufficient when heavy steel bows replaced the composite wood and horn bow in the 15th century. A windlass of the block-and-pulley type was then used in Western Europe for this purpose, as illustrated here.

This most beautiful medieval crossbow is kept in Vienna. Its steel bow is etched and gilt, the gilded iron parts skilfully chiselled to show royal crowns among other motifs. The slender stock, varnished to a reddish brown, is delicately inlaid with bone; below it, the *porc épic*, the porcupine badge of Louis XII of France, and the coat of arms of Anne, Duchess of Brittany (1476–1514). Maximilian I had wanted to secure her rich inheritance for himself by marrying her in 1491, but the French King Charles VIII succeeded in literally taking his bride from him and marrying her himself. After his death in 1498 his royal successor, Louis XII, wedded the widow in 1499, a union commemorated by the coat of arms and symbol.

As the etching of the steel bow is similar to that found on Spanish blades, this hunting weapon was probably made in Spain where the crossbow makers were famed for their beautiful work. Philip I of Spain (1478–1506) may have ordered it as a diplomatic present but not sent it, owing to recurring diplomatic tension with France. This very choice weapon quite probably came into the possession of the great huntsman Maximilian I as heir to the estate of his son Philip who died 13 years before the father. *Vienna, Waffensammlung, D 1*

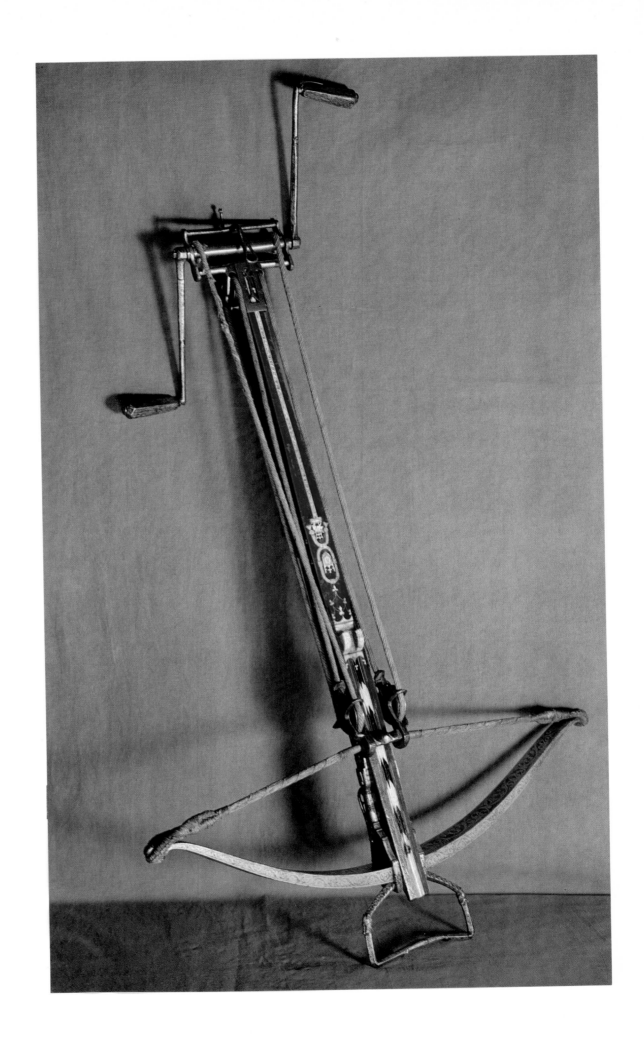

19 KOLMAN HELMSCHMID, AUGSBURG, c. 1505–10

Cap-à-pie armour for the field tournament and the "Freiturnier" of Andreas, Duke of Sonnenburg, Truchsess von Waldburg (assassinated in 1511)

The tournament, or *Freiturnier*, had all the characteristics of a military manœuvre. It created the impression of a small-scale cavalry battle in all its stages. Originally it had been intended as a practical exercise in armed combat but gentlemen considered it a choice opportunity to display their courage and skill before the ladies seated in the spectators' stands. There was great rivalry in the display of glamorous equipment. At the height of the Middle Ages tournaments were already being performed in a romantic setting, in the manner of a romance of chivalry or an allegory. Warlike theatrical performances became one of the foundations of European opera.

Despite its violence, the tournament was to remain a game whose participants were not to be injured in the combat. Therefore cap-à-pie armour was usually worn, strongly reinforced by double-pieces at neck, chest, the abdominal region and the left side. Apparently even heavier equipment with an added steel shield screwed against the neck and left side of the body became the rule at the court of Maximilian I during the fourteen-eighties. This triple-thickness cap-à-pie armour was later worn internationally for the tilt.

The most beautiful and best preserved example of such an armour was created by Kolman Helmschmid in Augsburg between 1505 and 1510. There are many signs to suggest that the work was originally intended for Maximilian I himself, who then presented it to his counsellor Sonnenburg as an expression of royal regard. Eventually Sonnenburg had to pay dearly for his Emperor's favour. Felix von Werdenberg was so jealous that he assassinated his unsuspecting rival in 1511.

Kolman Helmschmid, representing a younger generation, while equalling the genius of his father Lorenz, had fully comprehended the essence of the Italian renaissance. He turned away from the opulence and delicacy of his father's creations in the late gothic style and constructed an abstract steel cover of simple plastic forms and lines. The armour's only ornament is firegilt patterns against a blue ground, the decorative technique of *goldschmelz* that had been in use since the end of the 15th century. In its classic severity it is the counterpart of the works of a Hans Daucher or Hans Holbein the Younger, who convey the impression of having been raised on southern sunshine rather than under a German sky.

Vienna, Waffensammlung, A 310

20 F. DE GRAMPIS AND J. A. DE LITTIS OF MILAN (ARMOURERS) AND PAUL VAN VRELANT OF BRUSSELS (ENGRAVER-GOLDSMITH), LONDON, 1514–15

Armour with bases of Henry VIII, King of England (1491–1547; King, 1509)

The gift which the Emperor Maximilian I had for political reasons made to Henry VIII arrived in London at the end of May 1514. It was the Innsbruck armour with bases made by Konrad Seusenhofer. Its immediate effect was the creation of a very similar work, the king's armour with bases which is on the whole well preserved and still adorns the Tower of London. To imitate textile dress in this way did not serve any practical purpose whatsoever, but was merely a whim of fashion.

In a recent work, the English historian Claude Blair cleared up the story of its creation. In 1511 the two Milanese armourers Filippus de Grampis and Johannes Angelus de Littis obtained contracts from Henry VIII under which they were to work at his court armoury, where either one or both of them made this imposing armour. Payment for the rich engraving that covers its entire surface, and for the complete silvering was made to Paul van Vrelant of Brussels. By that time he was presumably resident in London, where he died in 1551. The armour was used for the great tournament at the royal palace at Greenwich in 1516.

The bases are bordered by a band with the initials HK for Henry of England and Katherine of Aragon, the first of the King's six wives, carried out in goldsmith's work. Curved openings enable the wearer to sit his saddle. The surfaces are covered with the King's Tudor roses and his Spanish spouse's pomegranates. These surrounded scenes from the legends of St Barbara and St George, England's patron saint. Stimulated by a Tyrolean armour, a major work of the English renaissance was thus created in the island kingdom by Italian and Flemish artists.

London, Tower Armouries, II-5

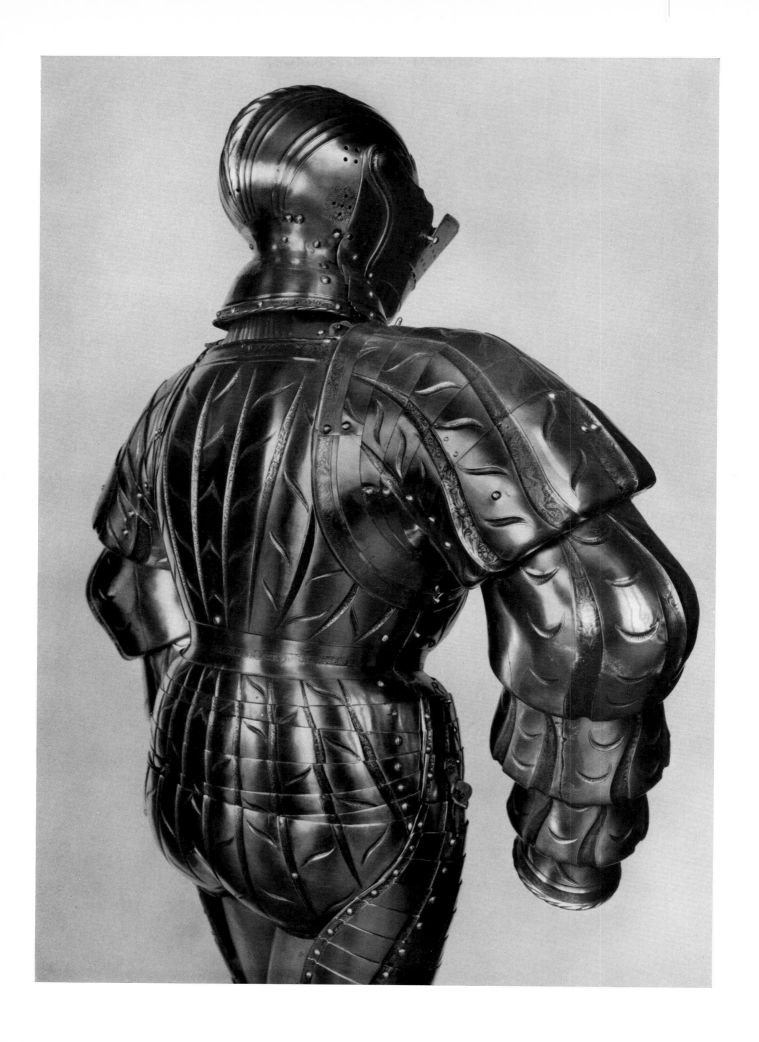

21 KOLMAN HELMSCHMID, AUGSBURG, c.1520

Costume armour of Wilhelm von Rogendorf (1481—1541)

The idea of translating gothic and renaissance textile dress into steel did not give Kolman Helmschmid much peace of mind either. The greatest armourer of his generation, son of Lorenz, one of his major creations was the armour garniture with voluminous puffed sleeves which is in Vienna. There is ample evidence that the owner was indeed the Lower Austrian aristocrat named there, who is known to have carried out the most delicate military and diplomatic missions, with which he was entrusted above all by Emperor Charles V. Near Pögg-stall he built the castle of Rogendorf which was based on Spanish models. Pieces bearing the closest likeness in form and decoration to the Rogendorf armour are kept to this day in Charles V's Real Armería in Madrid. These apparently include some parts which belong to the armour shown here, so it is not far-fetched to assume that the Emperor presented his merito-rious commander-in-chief, who had been so successful in Spain, the Captain of his Guards, and a Knight of Calatrava, with his own armour in the assembly in which it had last been used, for the sporting foot-combat.

The skilful and highly characteristic embossed work of the imperial court armourer is coupled with delicate and spirited etching by the artist, probably an important master like Daniel Hopfer the Elder of Augsburg. He was one of the so-called "minor artists" of the German renaissance who in truth were worthy assistants of those ingenious sculptors in steel, the armourers. *Vienna, Waffensammlung, A 374*

22 AUGSBURG, c. 1520–25

Three battle-axes from princely military equipment

As signs of command and authority, the battle-axe and war hammer are as old as the mace. Their use extends into the sphere of sacred things. In this context one should remember the cult axes of ancient Crete, the skilfully cast axes of the Luristan civilisation, the hatchet of Baal of Doliche, and the hammer of the Germanic god Thor.

Battle-axe and war hammer – frequently together – hung from the saddle of cavalry officers as a weapon of command during the late Middle Ages. They were still used for this purpose in the renaissance. The three examples shown here form a group that goes back to the early 16th century. The owner of only one, that with the uniformly blackened decoration, is known. It belonged to Otto Heinrich, Count Palatine of the Rhine (1502–59), Elector Palatine (from 1556), the founder of the Otto-Heinrich wing at Heidelberg Castle.

One axe is delicately decorated with *goldschmelz* on a blue ground. The other two show the blackened etched patterns which, though practised by Italian craftsmen in the 15th century, were only brought to their utmost perfection for the decoration of weapons by German artists in Dürer's time. The rounded armour surfaces were etched with acid and the patterns thus formed resulted, so to speak, in unprinted etchings, and these are called works in the "Hopfer-style" after Daniel Hopfer the Elder of Augsburg. Incidentally, he appears to have been among the first to utilise the technique of etching iron plates for the reproduction of his designs. His plates, smeared with printers' ink and then rolled off on to paper, gave us – apart from the famous ones by Albrecht Dürer – the first iron etchings. The classic engraving on copper plates was only developed later.

Vienna, Waffensammlung, A 299, A 298, A 387

23 THE STYLE OF GIOVANNI ANGELO MISSAGLIA, MILAN, c. 1525

Infantry officer's armour embossed with a diamond pattern

In keeping with their social structure, the medieval trading cities of the north and the city states of the Italian south had long possessed a militarily well-trained infantry. However, only as a result of the pioneering successes of the Swiss Confederates, the German landsknechts, and the Spanish infantry did they become the dominating arm of the service. A special type of armour was gradually developed in the course of the 15th century for those who fought in the front ranks of battle.

The foot-soldier could do without a number of parts of the rider's armour, such as the bolted-on lance rest and the double protection for the left arm. Thigh defences did not matter so much to him as they did to the horseman, and in fact they would have impeded his movements all too severely. A burgonet provided better vision than the horseman's visored helmet. Based on these considerations, the type that finally evolved at the beginning of the 16th century was variously named *Harnasch, Trabharnisch,* or *armatura da piede.*

The sons of peasants and burghers served in these new foot regiments alongside the offspring of knights. The *Trabharnisch* did not therefore—unlike the knights' cap-à-pie armour—imply any class distinction. Only the quality of its finish indicated whether the wearer was a common soldier, an officer or a very prominent person. The *armatura da piede* in the Bargello was at the very least the property of an officer of fairly high rank. The armour owes its brilliant highlights to the neatly embossed pyramids. The parts left plain are etched, by which means their ornaments and scalloped scrolls create the impression of bands of brocade. The restless exuberance of the piece not only matches the *lanzichenecchi*'s love for pompous and bizarre decoration, but is a sign of the period which was beginning to turn away from the classic style of a Raphael and Sansovino and about to cultivate an almost baroque taste like that of Michelangelo.

Florence, Museo Nazionale (Bargello), 756

Burgonet embossed with a diamond pattern of the Emperor Charles V (1500–58; King of Spain, 1516; Emperor, 1519)

Charles V, the Emperor Maximilian I's grandchild, came to the throne in 1516 and was elected Roman King and Emperor in 1519 in spite of all the endeavours of his rival, King Francis I of France (1515–47). At that time Charles was still an unknown quantity in international politics. The enterprising and martial Francis I, embittered by his electoral defeat and continually striving to break Spain's stranglehold on his country, remained his intransigent opponent. He revived France's old claim to Milan and expected few difficulties from the young man by whose abilities no great store was set. In the decisive battle of Pavia in 1525, Charles' German-Spanish army brought to a halt the victorious French advances in north Italy. The French defeat was complete and Francis himself was taken prisoner. With one stroke the young Emperor had become master of Europe, and all eyes were on him.

Kolman Helmschmid's work for the Emperor, the armour garniture embossed with a diamond pattern, was probably made during this period of triumph. After his grandfather's death Charles had taken over the Augsburg master as his royal armourer. With this garniture, Helmschmid followed the almost baroque taste of the period, which is manifested for instance in the Bargello armour. The embossed diamond pattern on the borders provides the highlight, and the work is further beautified by the finest gilded etching by an Augsburg artist. The puzzling letters "KD" which appear on the left shoulder can probably be interpreted as meaning "Karolus Divus", because "divus", the Divine, is part of the ancient imperial title. Apart from the traditional *Küriss*, the garniture consisted of double pieces for the tournament and of a new type of armour, the *Feldküriss*, of which the close burgonet shown here is a part. It is derived from the combination of a burgonet with the bevor found on West European armour of the late gothic period. Charles' father, Philip I, had something similar in his armoury. Now his son was using it in its most refined and highly developed form.   *Madrid, Real Armería, A 27*

25 DESIDERIUS HELMSCHMID, AUGSBURG, 1538

The field armour "de fajas espesas" of the Emperor Charles V (1500–58; Emperor, 1519)

The indefatigable Emperor conquered Tunis in the fortunate and victorious campaign of 1535, so putting an end to the excesses of the Muslim pirates. Then, with the peace of Nice concluded in 1538, he achieved a provisional compromise with King Francis I of France. In the same year an uprising called him to the Netherlands where the Protestant princes emerged as the result of the Reformation as new opponents of the Emperor of the Holy Roman Empire. The "Schmalkaldic League" was turning into a menacingly belligerent force. The order for a new field armour in 1538 probably arose from this situation. Desiderius Helmschmid, the son of the court armourer Kolman, who died in 1538, accepted it and put his skill at the Emperor's disposal on many future occasions. Charles V developed a tremendously extravagant taste in his armour that was hardly ever surpassed by any ruler before or after him. His armour garnitures with numerous extra pieces for all kinds of use in the field, for the tilt and tournament, became the leading fashion prevailing at every court in Europe. This armour is named *de fajas espesas* after its closely etched pattern of bands similar to the braided trimming then worn on Spanish court dress. A similar pattern often recurs on the Emperor's armours, all of which resemble each other and bear the stamp of a uniformly stylish and superb taste. We are again dealing with a so-called field armour with long articulated tassets and relatively light greaves and sabatons, which frequently were not worn at all.   *Madrid, Real Armería, A 129*

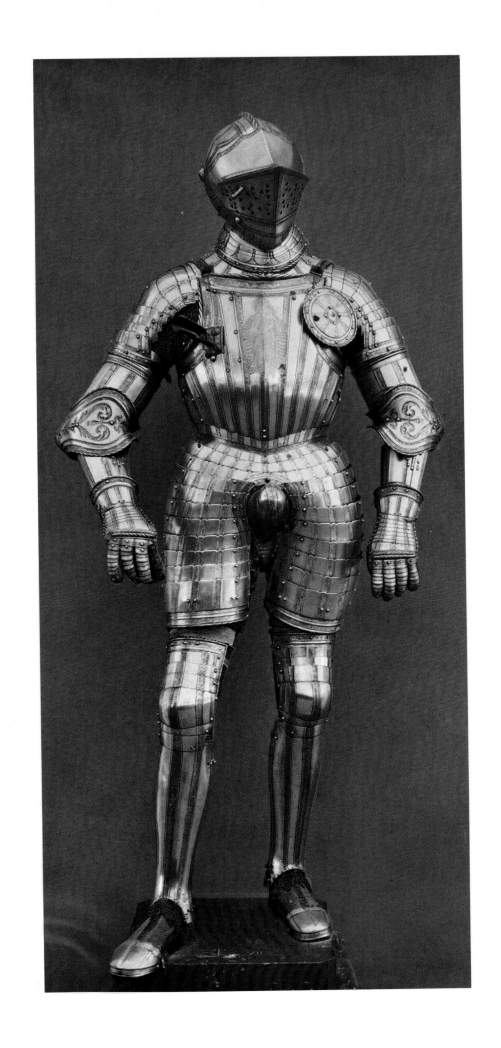

Damascened sword hilt

At the beginning of the 16th century Macchiavelli reported that the Spanish foot-soldiers armed with shield and sword were the only dangerous opponents of the Swiss and German landsknechts. Influenced by the Moors, the Spaniards during the final stages of the *reconquista*, the reconquest of Iberia from the Moors, had trained a light cavalry known to be efficient, as well as excellent infantry. The foot-soldier required a different type of sword from that of the horseman as, in his densely packed formation, he had less room for action and therefore a thrusting weapon was preferable to a cutting sword. The rapier, with a narrow thrusting blade and the typical hilt that protects the fist with a system of defensive bars, was thus created in Spain in the course of the 15th century – and Italy, then partly under Spanish rule, followed suit. However, it took the entire first half of the 16th century for the full development of this weapon and a systematic school of fencing. The rapier, once part of the ordinary warrior's equipment, then became respectable, at least when worn as a sidearm with civil dress, and was skilfully decorated.

The example shown here comes from a time when the construction of the hilt had almost been perfected. The hand itself is protected by quillons and knuckle bow; the index finger, which is laid on the blunt base of the blade when fencing, is protected by several curved arms. Although the whole gives an impression of profusion and complexity, its individual forms are, in accordance with Spanish taste, simple, austere, almost angular. The dark steel is decorated with delicate, unostentatious arabesques in gold damascening, a decorative technique that required precious metal wire to be beaten into the roughened steel ground. It had its origin in the East and became one of the decorative methods preferred by the metal-working craftsmen of the renaissance from about 1520–1530. Spain, the world power which had then taken the lead in military and political matters developed it and passed it on. In Toledo she possessed a production centre for the slender, flexible rapier blades which had long been famous and whose signatures were often imitated and even forged in Brescia and Solingen.

Paris, Musée de l'Armée, J. 70

27 LOMBARDO-FRENCH (THE CIRCLE OF THE BROTHERS NEGROLI OF MILAN), 1537–47

The black and silver parade armour of Henry II of France when Dauphin (1519–59; King, 1547)

On the sudden death of his elder brother Francis in 1536, Henry II unexpectedly found himself in the position of successor to the throne. From 1537 he was almost constantly in command during the numerous wars waged by his royal father, Francis I. In the same year the fascinating Diane de Poitiers, though twenty years his senior, entered his life. She was always to be closer to him than his wedded wife Catherine de' Medici whom he had married in 1534, so the monograms, repeated countlessly on this armour, have an intentional double meaning. They could equally well be interpreted as standing for Henri-Diane as for Henri-Catherine. His motto "donec totum compleat orbem" refers to claims to dominion – "No rest untils deeds cover the globe". The symbol of the waxing crescent moon has a similar meaning, symbolising in turn the activities of the goddess Diana who is surrounded here by quiver, bow and arrow, the black of night and the silver of moonlight. All these conventional symbols and colours can be seen on the extremely elegant armour of the young Henry II which finally found its way from the Royal Armoury in the Bibliothèque Nationale to the Musée de l'Armée. All royal emblems are absent except for the gilded laurel wreath of the triumphant victor that is wound across the forehead. The royal father had, it would seem, allowed the prince to bear this mark of honour. The entire black steel surface is covered with silver damascened bands decorated with the scrolls and symbols described. Contemporary and related parade armour made by Filippo Negroli of Milan and by his brother Francesco as well as by the Milanese Caremolo Modrone in Mantua for the Emperor Charles V most closely approach this design. Several of the numerous members of the Negroli family of artists worked for France. From the 15th century there was a constant flow of armourers from Milan to that country. Both the modelling and the decoration achieve such a high standard that one is tempted to ascribe them to those two most famous members of the Negroli family. There is, moreover, evidence that Filippo also worked for King Francis I of France.   *Paris, Musée de l'Armée, G 118*

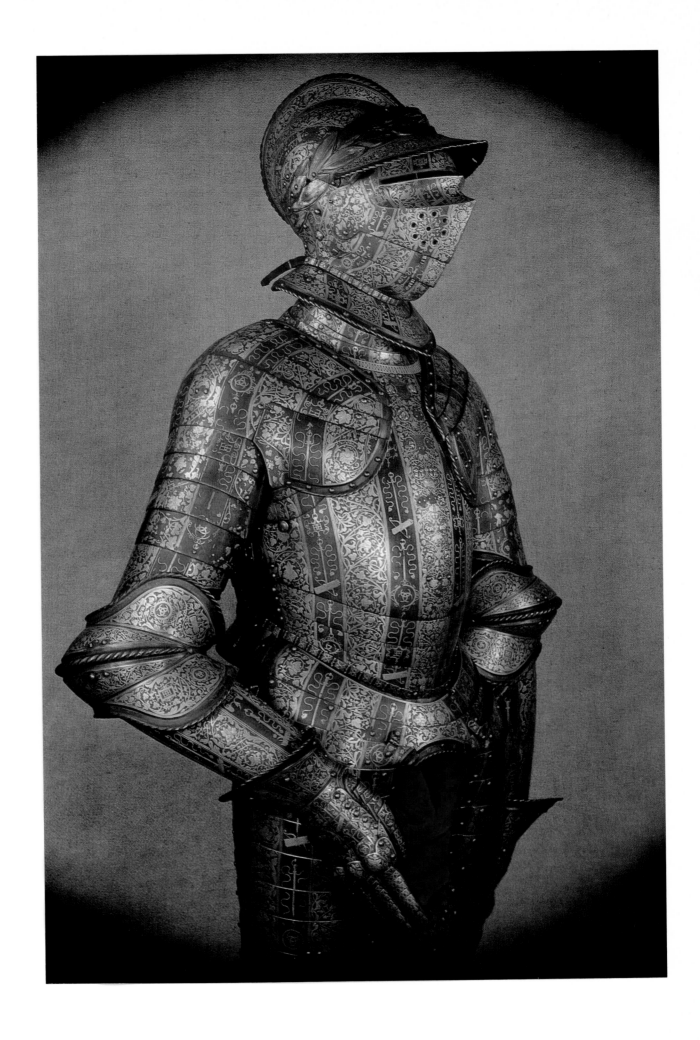

28 FILIPPO AND FRANCESCO NEGROLI, MILAN, 1541

The lion helmet and Medusa shield of the Emperor Charles V (1500–58; Emperor, 1519)

In 1535 Charles V crossed the seas to fight the pirates at Tunis. His equally bold campaign against Chaireddin Barbarossa in 1541 took him to Algiers to liberate the Christian slaves and weaken France's infidel allies. Though neither of these extremely hazardous undertakings was crowned with lasting success, they were celebrated for centuries. In the interval between the Roman emperors and Napoleon, Charles V was the only European ruler to set foot on African soil. As a memento of Algiers his particularly devoted brother Ferdinand I (1503–64; Emperor, 1558), who succeeded to the imperial throne, presented him with a gift in the form of the usual combination of burgonet and round shield carried in battle by Spanish infantry. It is inscribed with the donor's tribute to the hero and both items of armour are themselves covered with grandiose allusions. The open helmet in the style of ancient Rome, the "cassis", has been transformed into a gala piece and it and the shield are embossed with ornamental figures on a brown ground richly damascened in gold. The pivoted visor takes the shape of the Nemean lion's mask, which Charles V pulled over his head as did his Greek model Hercules to whom he felt himself allegorically associated through his motto PLUS ULTRA. The severed head of Medusa of the petrifying glance, entwined with its serpents, was raised by the Emperor in the face of his foes, as Perseus did to his enemies. It is an admirable example of Italian renaissance sculpture. To symbolise the Emperor's sea crossing, the entire circular surface is wreathed with a frieze of the gods of the seas and legendary figures, as well as with four medallions representing the heroes of Roman Africa: Scipio, Caesar, Augustus and Claudius, the legitimate predecessors of Charles V's Western empire. The amazed beholder is confronted with drama-filled visions, executed with an unprecedented profusion of forms and materials, a work of art in the mature style of the mannerist period, loaded with illustrations and symbols that have to be carefully analysed and read line by line.

The master was (Giacomo) Filippo Negroli, whose real surname was Barini and who was already highly praised by Giorgio Vasari in the history of art that he published in 1550. Although Lomazzo, writing in 1584, called him the inventor of the technique of embossing iron, of making embossed parade arms, this is in fact untrue. There is evidence that the Helmschmids of Augsburg had already practised this craft in 1477. But Negroli's figures are tremendously expressive, approaching the best Italian bronzes of the period, and led to a wave of similar creations throughout Europe. His brother Francesco, a goldsmith and damascening artist who acted as his assistant, is mentioned as Charles V's "dorador" and "deaurator" in Milan. Filippo produced a series of masterpieces for Charles V which can be seen in Madrid to-day, each differing from the one before, but he also worked for Charles V's royal adversary Francis I of France. All parties availed themselves of the services of a great artist who really knew how best to express and advance the desired political programme through the medium of parade arms.
Vienna, Waffensammlung, A 693

29 PETER PECH, MUNICH, 1542–50

Double wheel-lock pistol of the Emperor Charles V (1500–58; Emperor, 1519)

The revolutionary invention of gunpowder resulted in the development of the first primitive guns and small arms in the 14th century. Simple pistol-like weapons that were not easy to handle were known in the 15th century. They had to be fired manually, which was cumbersome. Only the invention of the mechanical tinder-box, which can probably be traced back to Leonardo da Vinci, created the technical prerequisite that equipped a gun with a lock mechanism to ignite the charge. Even the Emperor Maximilian I still hated this murderous weapon that could so easily be concealed and was so effective at long range. However, shortly after his death we already find the wheel-lock pistol in princely hands. The first specimens appear to have been made in Munich, then the seat of the Wittelsbachs, in the fifteen-twenties.

There the Emperor Charles V obtained his early and precious pistols, the majority of which are still preserved in his Real Armería in Madrid. At an early stage he appears to have recognised the pistol's merits as a weapon for light cavalry to which he, as a Spanish monarch, was particularly attached.

The weapon illustrated here combines technical ingenuity with the skill of a craftsman and artistic design. The Munich watchmaker, locksmith and master gunmaker, Peter Pech, stamped his initials PP on the barrel which is covered with etched and gilded scrolls. The entire lock is also gilded and decorated over-all with etching. One wheel-cover is adorned with the imperial double-headed eagle, the other shows Charles V's motto PLUS ULTRA and the Pillars of Hercules. The etcher was one of the circle of Munich artists, probably Ambrosius Gemlich. The stock of cherry wood, with a spirally carved butt and semicircular pommel cap, is inlaid with engraved and plain bone, an indication that this pistol may also have been used for hunting. A particularly interesting aspect of this early and beautiful piece is its ingenious construction with double locks to allow two shots to be fired from the two superposed barrels.

New York, Metropolitan Museum of Art, 14.25.1425 (W.H. Riggs bequest)

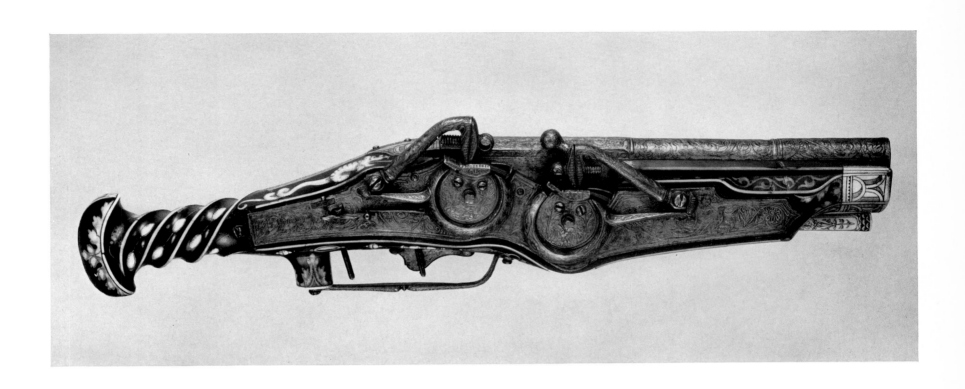

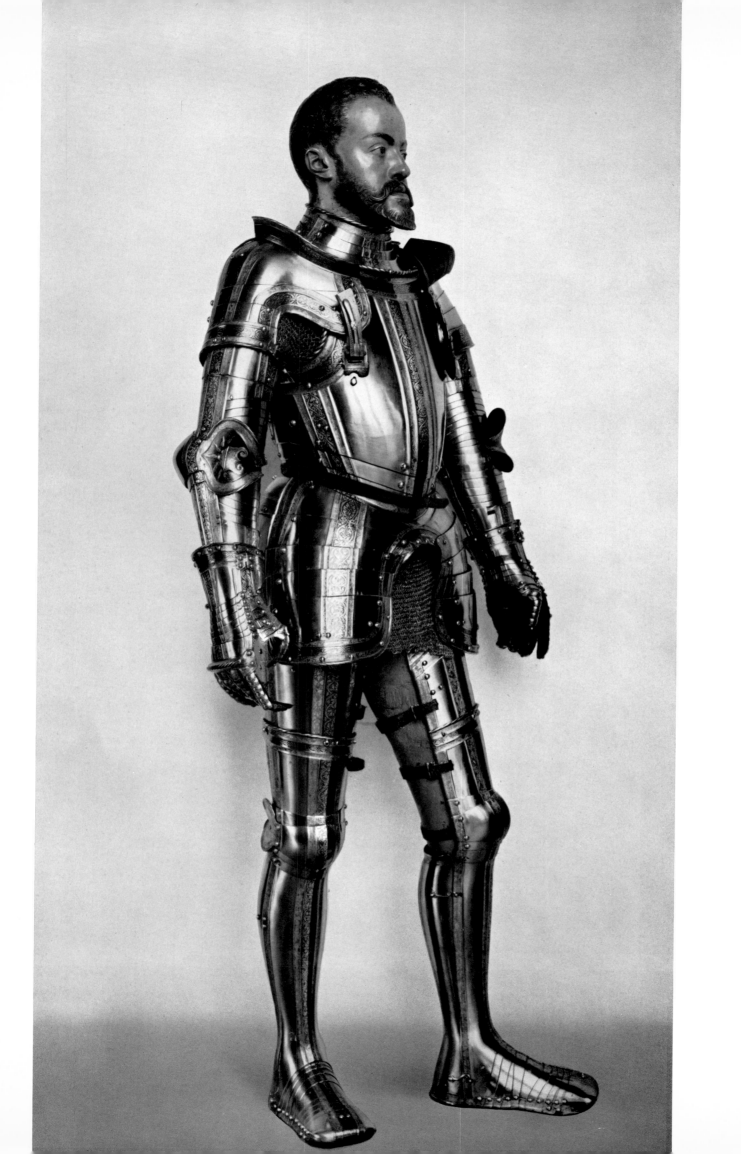

30 DESIDERIUS COLMAN HELMSCHMID (ARMOURER) AND
ULRICH HOLZMANN (ETCHER), AUGSBURG, 1546

Field armour of Philip II of Spain (1527—98; King of Spain, 1556; of Portugal, 1580)

The Austrian cousins Maximilian II and Ferdinand II were not the only ones to be well equipped with armour at the time of the decisive battle of Mühlberg against the Protestant forces in 1547. At the age of nineteen Philip II, Crown Prince of the Hapsburg Spanish line, took the field wearing a valuable armour that his father had just obtained for him from his favourite royal armourer in Augsburg. In 1572, as a memento of his father, Philip sent this historic armour to the Archduke Ferdinand for his Heroes' Armoury, a kind of Valhalla, at the castle of Ambras. The remainder of the very large garniture, bearing the date 1546, is to-day in Madrid. (It is said that parts of it were marked 1549, proving that work on one and the same garniture had continued for several years. After an interval of three years a Hapsburg prince must surely have received something else, something new! Those parts do not, in fact, belong to the armour of 1546.)

At that time nobody dressed so extravagantly as the members of the Hapsburg family. In spite of all their ambitious endeavours, even the king and princes of France never quite achieved the same profusion of armours in all their diversity. The classic plastic form is matched by the elegant, noble, reserved, yet radiant, richness of the decoration. Broad bands of perfectly etched patterns, gilded and blackened, represent ornament in its purest form. A small cartouche shows the VH mark of Ulrich Holzmann, one of a family of artists and craftsmen and the outstanding etcher of his day.

The figure is completed with a portrait head of Philip II in silver extremely realistically painted in oils. It was produced around 1556 by Pompeo Leoni of Milan, royal sculptor in Madrid, entirely in accordance with Spanish taste and must have come from a lost parade armour belonging to Philip from the Imperial Treasury, Vienna. From the artistic point of view it is a rare and superb specimen of the portrait heads which were known to have been used in the armouries of the sixteenth century.

Vienna, Waffensammlung, A 547. Vienna, Sammlung für Plastik und Kunstgewerbe, 3412

31 BARTOLOMEO CAMPI, PESARO, 1546

Parade harness "alla romana" of the Emperor Charles V (1500–58; Emperor, 1519)

By far the favourite armour workshop of Charles V was in Augsburg and belonged to Kolman Helmschmid and his son Desiderius. Since his victory at Pavia in 1525 the Emperor had obviously suppressed the arms production of Milan which had served the French King Francis I, taken prisoner on that occasion. It appears that in 1533 the Milanese genius Filippo Negroli was allowed to deliver a splendid example of his craftsmanship to the Emperor. From then on, northern Italy could again be counted among the suppliers to the imperial armoury, but it was not merely a question of fulfilling orders. The minor Italian princes, Gonzaga of Mantua and Montefeltro of Urbino, knew how to curry the Emperor's favour by presenting him with gifts. Guidobaldo II, Duke of Urbino, sent him an unsurpassed masterpiece bearing his initials, the mark of his goldsmith and armourer Bartolomeo Campi, the date 1546, the place of origin, Pesaro – the small Upper Italian capital on the Adriatic – and an inscription to the effect that at the urgent instigation of the Duke the work had been completed within two months, a task that would normally have taken at least a full year. Here is an unequivocal answer to the frequently asked question – how long was needed to produce such an opulent parade armour when the work was done by an eminent master with outstanding skill in every branch of his craft?

Charles V appeared in this armour as the triumphant Augustus. (After all, he did consider himself the legitimate successor of the Roman emperors.) The precise reproduction of antique costume accorded perfectly with the essence of the Italian renaissance and cannot be explained away simply as a theatrical masquerade. In this instance external appearances correspond to a profound human aspiration towards an ideal. Dressed in this way, the traditions of ancient Roman pageantry were continued by the Italian princes in their *trionfi* and by the northerners in their *entrées solennelles* or *joyeuses*. No less a person than Michelangelo clad the figures in his Medici chapel in Florence in armour of this kind. It is based on the ancient Grecian "muscled" cuirass of bronze, a material which is still being used here to a certain extent. The boots with their embossed toes translate into steel the plaited leather of the Roman military boot. The decoration of mounted masks and scales is antique. The combination of mail and lions' masks on the pauldrons and the shape of the burgonet with its wreath of oak leaves constitute the modern elements as does the damascening in gold and silver.   *Madrid, Real Armeria, A188*

32 SWITZERLAND, c.1550

A "Holbein dagger"

The dagger is one of the oldest arms known to mankind. The form illustrated here—its hilt in the shape of the Roman figure I with a broad double-edged blade—was already known in the Near East in the third millennium B. C. It reached the European Middle Ages from the art of Asia's steppes and at the turn of the 13th century it made its appearance as part of a knight's equipment and as a weapon of the burghers, particularly in the German region. In the renaissance it was most preciously decorated when great artists, among them Hans Holbein the Younger, created designs for such parade daggers. As Holbein worked in Basle for a considerable period, it is not surprising that this type of dagger, which had long been at home in German-speaking Switzerland, was brought to near perfection in that country. Based on his designs many different sumptuous specimens of the "Holbein dagger" were produced up to the end of the 16th century. Both aristocrats and landsknechts carried them at the right of their belts. Originally, the illustrations on the pierced and gilt scabbards were allegorical and instructive, but gradually patriotic motives were adopted, among them the legend of William Tell as it emerged in the 16th century. One of the most beautiful of the numerous Zurich models reproduces the well-known scene of the splitting of the apple.

The dagger's scabbard also contains a small knife and a steel for sharpening knives, tools for everyday use. This combination of short *armes blanches* with knives in a combined scabbard follows the tradition of the early Middle Ages.　　*Zurich, Schweizerisches Landesmuseum, IN 6971*

Foot-combat armour of the Archduke Ferdinand II (1529–95; Governor of Bohemia, 1547; Lord of the Tyrol, 1564)

MATTHÄUS FRAUENPREISS THE YOUNGER, AUGSBURG, 1549/50

Foot-combat armour of the Archduke Maximilian II (1527–76; Emperor, 1564)

By 1546/47 the conflict between the Emperor and the Protestant princes' Schmalkaldic League had become open war. At the battle of Mühlberg, Charles V achieved a glorious victory over his enemies whose commander-in-chief, Johann Friedrich, Elector of Saxony, fell into his hands together with the Landgrave Philip of Hesse. The Emperor had reached the zenith of his power and success. A few years later however, Moritz, Elector of Saxony, who had formed an alliance with King Henry II of France, deprived him of the fruits of victory by means of a sudden attack. The embittered Charles V abdicated in 1556.

But at the beginning of 1548, after the Battle of Mühlberg, the Emperor and his brother King Ferdinand I could, with absolute confidence, still command the princes to attend the Imperial Diet in Augsburg. The garniture which Ferdinand I had made by his Innsbruck royal armourer, Jörg Seusenhofer, for his younger son was completed for this occasion. The influence of Charles V's Augsburg armour can be seen in the finely banded pattern of this piece. The eagles of ancient Austria–now Lower Austria–are distributed on the plain interstices. Hans Perkhamer of Innsbruck created the original etched ornaments. The 87 parts of the "Eagle Garniture" can be assembled like the pieces of a puzzle into twelve different armours for use on horseback and on foot, in the field, for tournament, tilt and foot combat. The foot-combat armour, the *Kempfküriss* with its flared bases and puffed and slashed cuisses, is particularly attractive.

One of the consequences of the Mühlberg victory was the subjugation of the national and Protestant opposition in Bohemia, allowing the King of the Romans, Ferdinand I (1503–64; King, 1529; Emperor, 1558), to secure the Bohemian crown for his eldest son Maximilian II without difficulty. On that occasion the latter received exactly the same type of "Large Garniture" as his younger brother, this time made by the famous Augsburg armourer Matthäus Frauenpreiss the Younger. The leading Augsburg etcher of the time was Jörg Sorg the Younger, who only completed the magnificent decoration of broad gilded bands patterned with scrolls in 1550. This date appears on the base of the *Kempfküriss* whilst the engraver's notebook, preserved in Stuttgart, gives the year 1549 below sketches of the garniture.

These are two superb examples of a type of garniture with ingenious extra pieces that fits so well into this period–the beginning of the post-renaissance period of the mannerists with their love of the fanciful.

Vienna, Waffensammlung, A 638a and B 73

34 DESIDERIUS COLMAN HELMSCHMID (ARMOURER) AND JORG SIGMAN (GOLDSMITH), AUGSBURG, 1550

Splinted parade armour of Philip II of Spain (1527–98; King of Spain, 1556; of Portugal, 1580)

The history of the great armourers' art is one of princely patronage. Only a few leading connoisseurs and customers were ever able to induce the outstanding masters to give of their best, and Philip II belonged to this select group. He himself carried arms of superb elegance and when placing orders for them expected the highest of standards. His blued and gold damascened laminated parade garniture with decoration in relief, in the Madrid Real Armería, is undisputedly one of the most brilliant achievements of the armourer's art. Philip II wore it in 1551 when attending the Augsburg Diet where the succession to the imperial throne was negotiated.

The burgonet bears the full signature "Desiderius Colman" as well as the initials YS of the goldsmith and damascening artist Jörg Sigman and two dates, 1549 and 1550. Desiderius only struck his helmet mark on the saddle with the Augsburg coat of arms. (The opulent round shield, which is part of the garniture, was signed by Desiderius alone in 1552.) The work is designed in Charles V's preferred style and he must have ordered it for his eldest son in his favourite city of Augsburg. It became the earliest piece of German embossed work to be decorated with dense small-figured compositions entirely surrounded by tendrils and scrolls in such abundance that it is almost impossible to take in every detail. Filippo Negroli stimulated the whole of Europe with his versatile, diffuse and allegorical style that flourished at the Emperor's Madrid court around 1550. Augsburg was the first centre north of the Alps to follow this trend. Paris and Antwerp were to take it up later. With the exception of individual works by emigrant artists, there do not seem to have been any other European cities that produced these precious embossed armours.

But it was the armourers of Landshut who appealed to Philip II's personal taste and consequently he turned to them in subsequent years for armour garnitures, both for himself and for his unfortunate son Don Carlos (1545–68), made by Wolfgang Grossschedel (deceased 1562/63). They express a classic and perfect simplicity that is cool and reserved with a complete avoidance of anything obtrusive or exaggerated while plastic art and noble line remain conservative, and adhere to the high standards always demanded by Charles V.   *Madrid, Real Armería, A 239*

The blue and gold parade armour of Maximilian II (1527–76; King of Bohemia, 1549; Roman King, 1562; King of Hungary, 1563; Emperor, 1564)

This dark blue ceremonial costume of steel, with ornamental bands cast in bronze and heavily gilded, stood in the Emperor's armoury in the Renngasse, close to one of Vienna's tiltyards, with its owner's name given as the Emperor Charles V. Right from the start all the world's armouries ascribed such sumptuous specimens to this monarch, with Benvenuto Cellini usually being named as the maker—and with equally little reason. Heraldry once again proves its tremendous importance in the study of arms. As well as a second breast- and backplate the half-chanfron of this garniture was in the Hermitage in Leningrad, formerly the Tsar's armoury. Pieces which were part of Napoleon's booty from Vienna were sold at Dresden around 1930. The chanfron had the coat of arms of Maximilian II of Austria, Charles V's nephew and son-in-law. Its composition shows that he had been crowned King of Bohemia but not yet Roman King nor King of Hungary, so the armour may be assumed to have been produced between 1549 and 1562. In fact, the helmet shows the engraved date of 1557 at the centre point of the brow.

The armourer must have hailed from Augsburg but it is impossible to state either his name or that of the goldsmith. Maximilian had come from Spain where he had married the Spanish Princess Maria in 1548. That is why he wanted, instead of the usual burgonet, a pointed Spanish iron hat with turned-down brim, the so-called *capacete*, and a round shield as used by Spanish infantry, to accompany this garniture. At that time the prince's armour was certainly still being paid for by his father Ferdinand I, emperor since 1558, who left an armour garniture in Vienna, dated 1537, the work of the Innsbruck royal armourer Jörg Seusenhofer. It cestifies to the buyer's exquisite taste. As far as Ferdinand I's artistic sense was concerned he successfully emulated his far more famous brother Charles V and it was doubtless from his father that Maximilian II inherited his love of beautiful objects, a love that led him to become one of the foremost patrons of the armourer's art in the West, a fact which is insufficiently known and appreciated. In this he can certainly be compared with his contemporary, Henry II of France.

At the same time as he obtained the blue and gold garniture, Maximilian received another constructed in exactly the same way. All its surfaces are closely fluted and bordered with gilt etching. Quite obviously he was given yet a third, etched and heavily gilded all over, of which only the helmet is preserved in the Wallace Collection, London (A. 188). Its unusual construction is a match for the other two; the foot tournament helmet, revolving on the collar by means of a grooved beaded edge, can be transformed into a field helmet by adding detachable gorget lames.

Vienna, Waffensammlung, A 576

Curb-bit and stirrups of Maximilian II (1527–76; King of Bohemia, 1549; Roman King, 1562; King of Hungary, 1563; Emperor, 1564)

Knights were riders and the horse plays a dominant part in their history. Around the middle of the second millennium B.C., the Hittites and related peoples of the Near East were among the first to use them for tactical purposes. After the second great migration of nations in the 12th century B.C. the horse was harnessed to the war chariot and emerged as the animal ridden by warriors. At the height of the Middle Ages it was covered with a trapper bearing the owner's heraldic emblems. As protection the horse was eventually to receive plate armour and the iron-faced saddle that belongs to it. Frequently, however, the iron chanfron alone was considered sufficient protection for the charger and may be seen as the equivalent of man's helmet. But a snaffle-bit – or in the case of the unruly charger a curb-bit, which acts as a lever on the horse's mouth – stirrups and spurs always formed part of equestrian equipment. Riding equipment was not counted among the arms but was kept near them in the armouries which, significantly, were in the care of the master of the horse. This provides evidence of the great importance that the ruling class attached to the horse in their court life. The books on horses that were so widely read by the aristocracy dealt with their breeding and illnesses and with breaking and training according to the principles of the Spanish riding school. Other, more specialised "Bit-books" contained accurate illustrations of many different kinds of bits for every conceivable purpose and temperament.

A curb-bit and a pair of stirrups, remnants of an extremely rich set of riding equipment, have been preserved in Vienna. (The spurs that belonged to it were probably attached to the sabatons of the armour and lost with it.) The material is cast bronze and the outside is ornamented with legendary figures cast and chased in relief, whilst the inside is covered with etched ribbons. The entire surface is heavily gilded, with the exception of the tongue-piece of highly polished steel. To judge by the decoration, the work must have been done in Augsburg. These parts are obviously remnants of the garniture to which the similarly decorated helmet in the Wallace Collection (A 188) belonged. This also provides us with the name of its owner and the date of its creation – Maximilian II, then King of Bohemia, owner of the blue and gold and the closely fluted garnitures which were completed by the third golden one. One can imagine the brilliant impression created by this golden garniture, consisting of chanfron, saddle and the bridle illustrated here. The profusion of its endless ribbon pattern and the mass of decorative motives is confined within elegantly drawn contours that are at once gentle and severe.   *Vienna, Waffensammlung, A 594*

37 ANTONIO PICCININO (SWORDSMITH), MILAN, AND A SPANISH GOLDSMITH, c.1550

The golden rapier of Maximilian II (1527–76; Emperor, 1564)

The gallery of the great collector Archduke Ferdinand II contained a rapier that must surely be one of the most beautiful of its kind. The hilt, of heavy cast gold, is adorned with rich and most exquisitely tooled foliage, volutes and angels' heads, most of which are covered with brilliantly coloured enamel. Rosette-shaped nuts enable the hilt to be dismounted and kept — for instance when travelling — in a case. The excellent blade by the Milanese swordsmith Antonio Piccinino proves that the rapier was not only a precious and elegant accessory to a splendid court dress, but that in case of necessity it could serve as a weapon.

Long quillons and cone-shaped pommels of this type were otherwise only known on rapiers of around 1570. Nevertheless, this appears to be a weapon which was recorded in Maximilian II's inventory as early as 1552. The description given there is absolutely accurate. It mentions, moreover, that a dagger once accompanied it, and that both were presented by Wratislaw II of Pernstein in Bohemia to his overlord, Maximilian II, King of Bohemia from 1549. The latter passed on the magnificent gift to his younger brother, Archduke Ferdinand II, Governor of Bohemia, perhaps feeling that by so doing the arms would remain to adorn the court at Prague.

Golden and gilded rapier hilts of this kind were a speciality of Spanish goldsmiths, as is known from examples at Dresden; after all, Spain was the home of the rapier. The master who made the splendid Vienna piece may have come to Bohemia in the retinue of the wife of the knight of Pernstein. She was a Dona Maria Maximiliana Manriquez de Lara of the Mendoza family. Wratislaw was no doubt a generous patron of this artist. His court at Pernstein is reputed to have been magnificent and to have aspired to an almost regal splendour.

Vienna, Waffensammlung, A 588

Wheel-lock rifle of Maximilian II (1527–76; King of Bohemia, 1549; Roman King, 1562; King of Hungary, 1563; Emperor, 1564)

In order to gain a clear understanding of historic arms it is necessary to consider the following aspects in relation to each other: the artistic style of the work, the system and the degree of technical progress of the mechanism, and any heraldic facts. The Vienna ivory rifle with the coat of arms of the King of Hungary and Bohemia, a member of the Hapsburg family, possesses a wheel-lock of the early type which has survived on many specimens made in the decade that began in 1550. This weapon can therefore have belonged only to Maximilian II. He gave notice of his claims to Hungary—which were disputed and where he was only crowned in 1563—by putting the Hungarian before the Bohemian coat of arms which he had been entitled to bear since 1549. The rifle must certainly have been made before 1562, as it does not show the single-headed Roman royal eagle.

Its counterpart comes from the castle of Mährisch-Kromau, the property of the Princes Liechtenstein and to-day is in the Metropolitan Museum of Art, New York (29.151.1). It bears the coat of arms and the initials PDC of its owner, Philip of Croy, Duke of Aerschot, Prince of Chimay (1521–95; sole heir, 1551). This weapon does not yet include among its decoration the collar of the Golden Fleece which, as a member of the Order, Philip had to wear at all times. Both rifles must therefore have been made between 1549 and 1556.

The barrel and lock of the Vienna example are covered with fine gold and silver damascened scrolls. The stock is entirely veneered with carved ivory plaques framed by ebony bands. The reliefs tell the story of Perseus and Olympus. Apart from the royal coat of arms, panels on the underside show the overthrow of Phaeton and the transformation of Daphne. The decorative figures, which are partly enclosed by mounts as though caged, are more likely to have been borrowed from designs engraved on copper by Cornelis Bos of Antwerp than from his fellow-countryman Cornelis Floris. There is no signature to tell us the name of the master who made the rifle but the style of the lock at least indicates Nuremberg as the place of origin of the mechanism.

Vienna, Waffensammlung, D 71

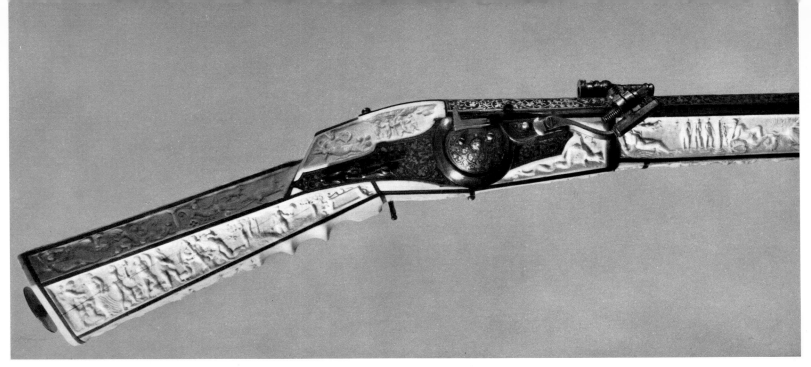

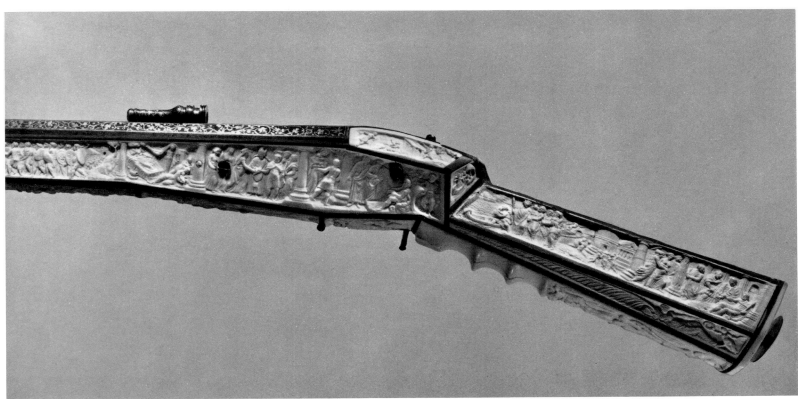

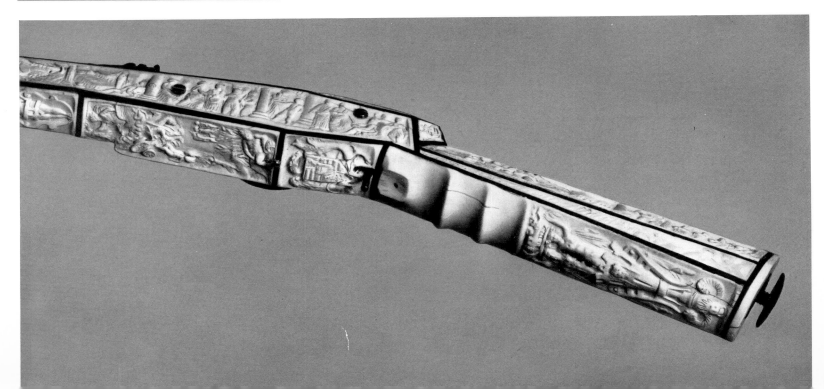

39 KUNZ LOCHNER, NUREMBERG, c. 1555

Armour for horse and man of Sigismond II Augustus, King of Poland (1520–72; King, 1548)

Stockholm presents us with the rare case of a uniformly decorated armour of heavy steel that has been preserved in all its parts. The resulting picture is one of completeness. This is in fact a monument, a genuine equestrian statue of the monarch, which shows us his size, his tastes and what he looked like on horseback. Here we are brought face to face with a life-like original in three dimensions while the portrait can only convey two.

Apart from the Nuremberg guild mark this sumptuous work bears the mark of Konrad Lochner in several places. With Valentin Siebenbürger, Lochner is the most important armourer of his generation in this great centre of production. The Protestant city supplied northern, Protestant Germany, Saxony and the Polish royal residence at Cracow on her old trading routes. When Kunz Lochner made a journey to Poland in 1559 to collect at long last the outstanding purchase price for his work, he followed in the footsteps of Veit Stoss and Hans Dürer. The cast bronzes from Vischer's Nuremberg workshop had gone in the same direction. The king reigning at the time, the last of a line descended from the Lithuanian family of the Grand Dukes of Jagiello, had ordered for his own use a highly decorated and extremely costly armour from Nuremberg. So far it has unfortunately not been possible to ascertain the name of the artist who worked for Lochner and etched the surfaces with an entwined ribbon pattern, which he then gilded and varnished in black, white and red. This "cold enamel" replaced genuine enamel which, owing to its brittleness, was hardly suitable for armour. The decoration of this unusual work follows the Eastern preference for dense, colourful, carpet-like ornament.

The king's brother-in-law, Nikolaus Radziwill, nicknamed "the Black", belonged to the oldest Lithuanian aristocracy and was Baron and Duke of the Holy Roman Empire and Lord High Chancellor of Lithuania. Vying with the monarch and obviously for the same occasion, he had ordered an armour garniture for himself, which was an exact replica of the one belonging to Sigismond Augustus. To-day most of the parts are preserved in Vienna, but fragments have been scattered as far apart as Paris and New York. By way of inheritance the royal garniture passed to Sweden, to Radziwill's Vasa relations who succeeded the Jagiellons on the Polish throne. Its round shield remained in Poland and was in the collection of Prince Krasinski until 1939. *Habent sua fata arma:* the historical study of arms is to a large extent closely related to the piecing together of minute archaeological fragments, and similarly one has to reconstruct the original units from widely dispersed parts. *Stockholm, Kgl. Livrustkammaren, 2603*

40 SAXON, c. 1550

Wheel-lock pistol with ape's-head pommel

LEIPZIG, 1555

The short wheel-lock pistol of the Archduke Ferdinand II (1529—95; Governor of Bohemia, 1547—64)

In 1556, during his campaign against the Turks in western Hungary, the Archduke Ferdinand II carried, when wearing his black velvet riding outfit, a pair of notably long silver saddle pistols. The light cavalry then customarily used pistols in wartime, the so-called "German Black Horsemen," who were armed in this way, being particularly feared. They were mainly recruited in the Protestant North of the Holy Roman Empire.

Ferdinand came by the two pistols through his courtier Henry VI, Burgrave of Meissen, a member of the Plauen family of Governors (1536–72; Burgrave from 1554). He was commander-in-chief of the Archduke's mounted Life Guards during the above-mentioned campaign. One of Henry's almost identical silver pistols is kept in the Vienna Collection. The master HS forged the barrels, which bear the date 1555. The silver mounts covering the entire stock were produced by a Leipzig silversmith whose name is not known but who was greatly influenced by the medals showing the crucifixion which were made by the Leipzig engraver Hans Reinhard in 1544. Side by side with the religious scene of Jesus on the Cross there are lively hunting scenes framed by foliate bands. This points to the possibility that the weapon was used for sport as well as war. Blackened etching covers both the barrel and the lock. It matches the serious character of the equipment, which was kept entirely to black and white.

The pistol of the *Fäustling* type, the pommel of which is in the shape of a silver ape's head, is rather earlier. It, too, originated in the armoury of the Archduke and its barrel and lock-plate are decorated with delicate silver damascened foliage. The warm brown of the walnut stock shines through silver mounts which are partly embossed and partly fretted. Antiquity and Christianity blend in the illustrations: Mucius Scaevola, a satyr and nymph on the one hand, and, on the other, Christ on the Cross with his disciples in contemporary dress. Pistols dating back to before 1560 are very rare and each must be considered as a work of art in itself.

Vienna, Waffensammlung, A 525 and A 439 a

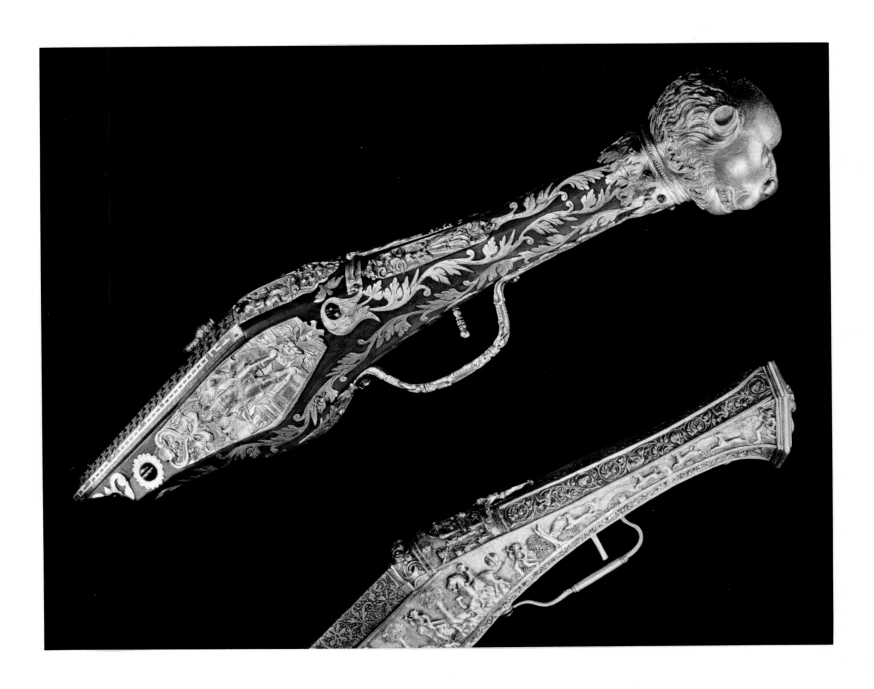

41 FRENCH, c. 1555

Two "cortellaggi" with pistol mechanisms

The history of swords with single-edged curved blades goes back a very long way. The archetypes of pre-Christian times developed quite differently in the East and the West. In the East, in Central Asia, they became the sabre of the equestrian peoples, in the West the heavy fighting knife first of the Teutons and eventually of the foot-soldiers of the Middle Ages. In Italy it appears that the ancient origin of single-edged swords was vaguely remembered during the 15th century. In the mistaken belief that this large knife, the *cortellaggio*, sprang from a Roman source, it was carried with the fantastic, pseudo-antique *armatura alla romana*. The 16th century continued in this error.

The thought of possessing guns which could, by the use of a mechanical ignition lock, be fired at any time must have had a fascinating effect on the soldiers and technicians of the 16th century. Swords, hafted weapons, maces, battle-axes and war hammers were all equipped with pistol mechanisms that were probably of little practical value. They no doubt enjoyed experimenting all the more. The smallest possible mechanism was built into the quillon-blocks of the hilts of the swords illustrated here. It comprises a spring-operated grooved plate and a cock holding pyrites. This concealed pistol, whose barrel was formed by the back of the blade, could be fired by pressure of the thumb.

Both weapons must have been intended for clients of the highest rank, probably for the French court itself. The artistically high standard of their design as well as the fact that the reliefs on the silver mounts show the direct influence of Etienne Delaune, the court craftsman of Henry II of France, give weight to this assumption. They are based on Delaune's engraved plates. Evenly distributed damascening decorates the plain surfaces of hilt and the base of the blade. A fantastically horned lion's head that forms the pommel stems from pseudo-antique concepts, whilst the eagle's head has its origin in ancient tradition to which, in a simplified form, some present-day knife handles still pay tribute. These arms must have been carried with a sumptuous *armatura alla romana* on the occasion of a *joyeuse entrée*, a triumphal procession.

Vienna, Waffensammlung, A 2248 and A 2249

42 FRENCH, c. 1555

The "Medici burgonet"

Some historical arms of the highest quality still pose problems as to the identity of their makers, place of origin, the personages who placed the order and their original owners. One of these pieces is the truly superb burgonet with visor now in New York. This masterpiece derived its name from the portraits of the two Medicis, the Grand Dukes of Tuscany, because the helmet is unmistakably that which appears in paintings of Ferdinand I (c. 1590) and Cosimo II (c. 1620). But who was the previous owner, and how did the helmet get to Florence? Who was the armourer? Was he an Italian who had emigrated to France, as so many of them had done, or was he a native Frenchman? Was the embossing produced in Paris, or might it have been created elsewhere in France?

These questions certainly do not lessen the enjoyment of studying the burgonet. One thing is certain, even if this parade helmet, which may once have formed a representative unit together with a round shield, was not created for King Henry II of France (1519–59; King, 1547), it certainly approaches his personal tastes very closely. The decade beginning in 1550 produced not only masters who rivalled each other on the highest artistic and technical levels, but also the requisite connoisseurs, their clients and patrons. Henry II was one of the really great patrons of the armourer's art, a fact that becomes abundantly clear when one delves more closely into his life.

The designs appear to have been made in Paris by Henry II's draughtsman Etienne Delaune (1518/19–82). These sketches depict combats of Centaurs and Lapithae, quarrelling children, Medusa heads, and the slender ribboning and the wave and pod patterns that surround the whole. Who subsequently produced the perfect, gilded, blued and embossed work, and who etched the pattern of ribbons and arabesques on the lower border that is based on a copper engraving by Jacques Androuet I Ducerceau of 1540? Was the burgonet sent to Florence as a gift from the French king's widow, Catherine de' Medici? Whatever the circumstances, this parade helmet gives evidence of the tremendous accomplishments of French artists who, from 1530 in their "School of Fontainebleau", were exclusively influenced by the style of Raphael's pupils.

New York, Metropolitan Museum of Art, 04. 3. 217 and 22. 140. (From the Duc de Dino Collection)

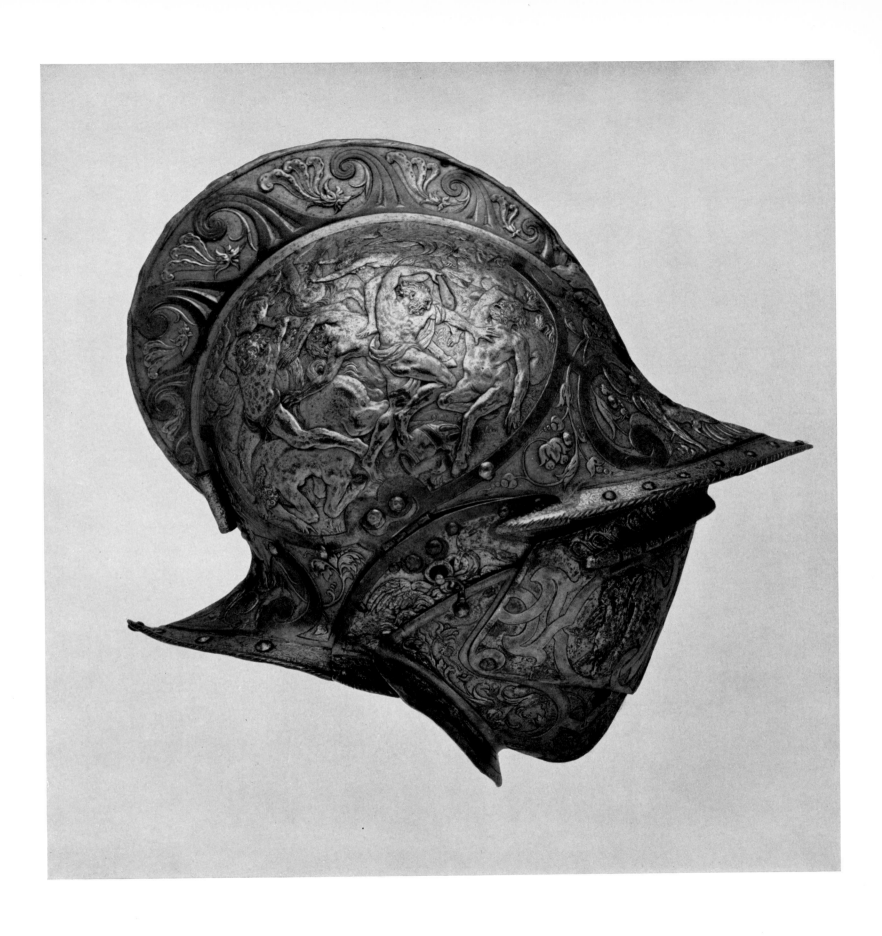

43 LOW GERMAN, c. 1555–60

The half-armour of Johann von Rantzau (1492–1565)

The Holstein knight Johann von Rantzau was one of the most famous war heroes of his time. For this reason his armour was placed in the Archduke Ferdinand II's Heroes' Armoury at the castle of Ambras near Innsbruck even before 1593. The knight was not only an outstanding soldier but also a scientist and art connoisseur, who travelled as far as Santiago de Compostela and Jerusalem. He was one of the first followers of the new doctrine in the North, who at the age of thirty-one became involved in those intrigues around the throne which convulsed the whole of northern Germany, the Hanseatic League, and Scandinavia where the despotic and cruel actions of King Christian II of Denmark (1481–1559; King, 1513), brother-in-law of the Emperor Charles V, caused a general uprising in 1523. The discontented vassals elected his uncle Frederick I (deceased 1533) as their king and Sweden, under Gustav Vasa, broke completely away from the Scandinavian Union.

Johann von Rantzau retained at all times a leading position and remained loyal to the new king and to his successor Christian III (1503–59; King, 1533). In the fighting against the intrigues of the deposed Christian II and his allies, Rantzau commanded the Danish troops and achieved victory after victory. In 1532 Christian II was taken prisoner. Rantzau twice took Copenhagen and once conquered Lübeck, the headquarters of the Hanseatic League. His last and most famous act was the subjugation of the feared peasants of Dithmarschen in 1559, after which he retired to his Breitenburg castle so widely renowned for its art treasures.

During the war in Dithmarschen he may have worn the armour but unfortunately we do not know the highly important workshop in northern Germany where it was made. Did it come from Brunswick, whose armourers supplied Gustav Vasa? Was it made at Münster, or at Cologne, of whose outstanding position as centres of armour production there is considerable documentary evidence? Or is it the product of another workshop of Lower Saxony? The armour is clearly one of a large group, the style of which reveals a connection with Nuremberg, but which shows an excessive inclination towards affected forms and exuberant decoration which seems to float on their dark metal surfaces. This is a German national style, showing no trace of Italian influence and representing the taste of the Protestant "Black Riders", the enemies of the Roman Catholic Emperor. The champions of the Protestant Party are depicted wearing this equipment in paintings by the younger Cranach, Virgil Solis and Jost Amman as well as on tombs in North German churches.   *Vienna, Waffensammlung, A 691*

44 GIOVANNI BATTISTA SERABAGLIO (EMBOSSING ARTIST) AND MARC ANTONIO FAVA (DAMASCENING ARTIST), MILAN, 1559/60

The "Milanese Armour" of the Archduke Ferdinand II (1529–95; Governor of Bohemia, 1547; Lord of the Tyrol, 1564)

In order to represent his elder brother Maximilian II (King from 1549) with due dignity in Prague, Ferdinand II obtained his parade arms not only from Innsbruck and Augsburg but also from Milan. At the beginning of 1560 he made payment to the partners Serabaglio and Fava for an embossed, blued, and gold and silver damascened garniture. It was said of Serabaglio in 1583, *"fu raro e principale nel ferro"* – he was a rare and outstanding master of iron embossing. He was a member of the generation which followed the great initiator Filippo Negroli. The embossed illustrations consisted of increasing numbers of small parts. Entire scenes incorporating many figures were depicted on medallions. The individual representations of bodies and faces became more summary and their expressions duller. The damascener Fava also found room for detailed landscapes and pictures of cities in his ornamental bands which can only be properly appreciated with the aid of a magnifying glass.

To judge by its construction the equipment must have belonged to a high-ranking cavalry officer, for example, a general of light cavalry. The half-armour without lance rest (a *Harnasch*) is formed of transverse lames in the oriental manner, a type that reached Central Europe via Spain, Italy and Hungary, regions that had close contact with the Orient. It included an open burgonet, and pauldrons with mail sleeves and gauntlets. A horseman required spurs. The mace was hung on his light, fretted horse armour with iron-mounted saddle. He carried a spear (see plate 45) in his hand, a rapier or estoc at his side. Both mace and spear served as a sign of rank. Profuse and already confused illustrations of scenes, persons, allegories and legendary figures cover its surfaces with Greco-Roman mythology combined with the heroes' cult of the Old Testament, the Christian virtues presented next to ancient gods. The romantic epic of chivalry of the Italian renaissance still played its part. A strict system based on medieval typology provided the established formulae for the confrontation of Old and New Testament equivalents. Here the system has been transformed into a free play between idealistic and frightening concepts. During this extremely critical period tribute was paid to beauty. The models of the past were projected into the present. The continents and the deeds of their heroes were represented in a work of art designed to adorn a princely wearer.

Vienna, Waffensammlung, A 785

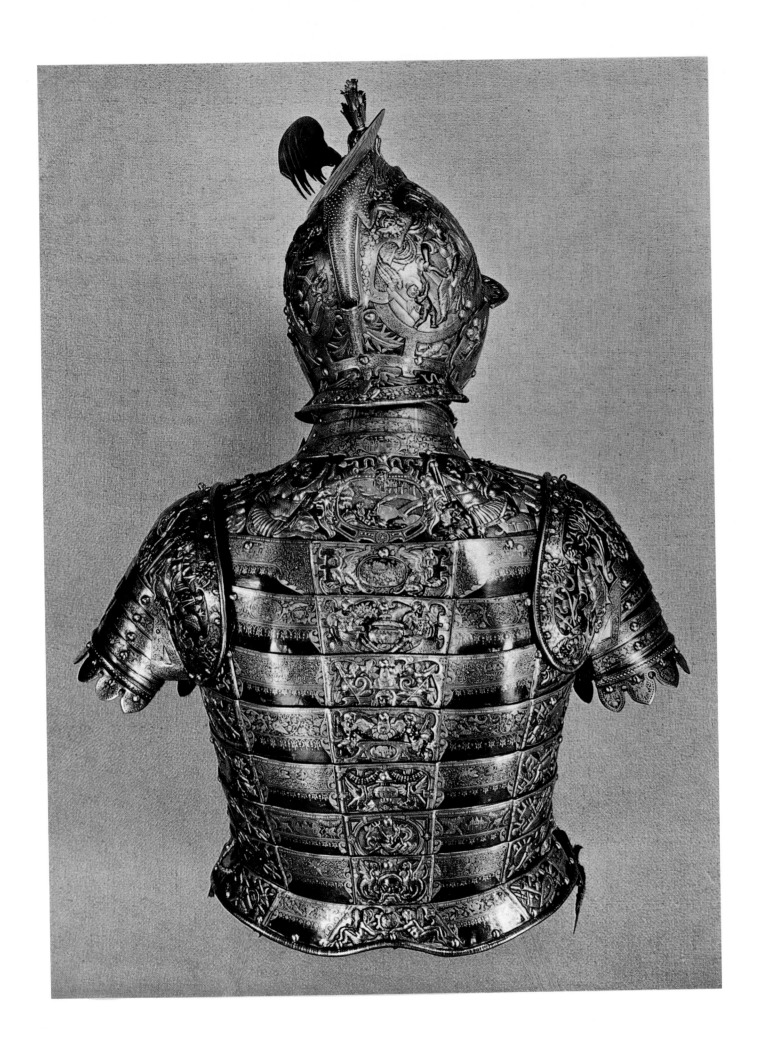

45 GIOVANNI BATTISTA SERABAGLIO, MILAN, 1559/60
Boar spear of the Archduke Ferdinand II (1529-95)

ITALIAN, c. 1555
Folding partisan

A chiselled and damascened spear, with its lugs in the form of two boars' heads, also belonged to the "Milanese Armour" which the Archduke Ferdinand II purchased from the Milanese craftsman Serabaglio in 1560. These heads and two medals depicting the hunting goddess Diana and Adonis, and marked with the initials A and D, indicate that such lugged spears were used for the dangerous boar hunt. But what was the significance of such hunting equipment in association with light armour? We know from contemporary paintings that heavy spears were not only a sign of rank of infantry officers in the imperial army, but that the commanders of light cavalry of the Spanish type were armed with such spears. Titian's painting of Charles V on the battlefield of Mühlberg in 1547 serves as particularly splendid documentary evidence in this context. Just as the pistol, originally intended for war, was also used for hunting, so the spear too was employed as a heavy thrusting weapon and sign of rank in war.

In the first quarter of the 16th century the partisan was still a spear with a broad blade. It was carried by the _partigiani_, the supporters and bodyguards of Italian princes. During the second quarter of the century the weapon was given a longer blade and the crescent-shaped ears which have since become typical. It is depicted like this in the 1544 illustrated inventory of Emperor Charles V's armoury. The head of the very long hafted weapon can be folded to make it easier to accommodate on journeys. The ears are automatically retracted by a simple but sensible mechanism. The Vienna collection possesses an identical piece, its socket and the base of the blade enriched with damascening; the dark lacquered haft decorated in gold paint with oriental arabesques, motives which had enjoyed increasing popularity in the West from about 1540. Two medallions on either side of the blade bear the inscriptions JUL(ius) and C(aesar) I(mperator), the imperial title suggesting that this Vienna weapon once belonged to Charles V's court.   _Vienna, Waffensammlung, A 752 and A 2255_

Crossbow and cranequin of the Archduke Charles II (1540–90; Lord of Styria, 1564)

By the middle of the 16th century firearms, which had by then been considerably improved, finally drove the crossbow from the battlefield. But as a hunting weapon, above all for the stag hunt, and especially as a most lavishly decorated item of sporting equipment, it continued to be highly prized. Rifle competitions and archery were among the most popular amusements for young and old, rich and poor. Archduke, count and artisan entered the range. The *Pritschenmeister*, a mixture of troubadour, conjurer and master of ceremonies, supervised the correct running and safety of the event. In the hope of receiving presents he wrote eulogies and prettily illustrated descriptions of the festive occasion, a great many of which have been preserved.

An exceptionally beautiful ivory inlaid crossbow had its origin in the Viennese imperial court *Jagdkammer*, where it was always associated with a chiselled iron cranequin. Both bear the same archducal coat of arms of the Austrian dynasty. Maximilian II's two brothers must have used this crossbow for hunting, more probably the younger, the Archduke Charles II. According to the date on the cranequin he received it in 1563, the year of Maximilian II's coronation as King of Hungary, possibly for the festivities which took place around this highly significant political occasion. The ivory veneer on the crossbow's stock shows the figures of Mercury and Mars, hunting scenes, scrolls with animals and coats of arms. Some of these decorations are engraved and some are carved in relief. Apart from the large trigger, only fragments have been preserved of the complicated set-trigger mechanism which permitted the most delicate release. The noble harmony of the ivory's matt white with the golden mounts is reminiscent of the elegant decoration on Burgundian weapons of the 15th century. The taste of the upper classes showed a very similar trend at this period when the 16th-century style was fully developed. The steel bow with its waxed hemp cord is tied to the stock with hemp string. Its inner side is finely etched with thirteen coats of arms of the Hapsburg dominions, the outer with tournament scenes; one has to imagine the missing decoration of coloured tassels. The cranequin is chiselled with the coat of arms with its supporting angels, and the toolsmith dated it and stamped it with his mark.

In place of the cumbersome West European windlass-bender, German craftsmen had as early as the 15th century invented a bending mechanism in which a rack is worked by a series of gears, by a principle similar to that of a car jack. The cranequin was attached by a loop to the stock whilst the gear rack and claws, when cranked back, drew the cord to the cocked position and the bow was ready to shoot.   *Vienna, Waffensammlung, D 262 and D 263*

Armour for horse and man of Eric XIV, King of Sweden (1533–77; reigned 1560–68)

When Henry II of France died tragically in a tournament in 1559 he left many parade armours and had dreamt of owning more. A little later a king in the far North, Sweden's Eric XIV of the House of Vasa, had as many and more made for himself, thus matching Henry's possessions as well as realising his dreams. To-day the equipment of Eric XIV still provides proof of his enormous love of ostentation. It did not end well. He had barely come to the throne when he unsuccessfully courted Queen Elizabeth of England. In order to equip himself worthily and royally he looked for a suitable craftsman, whom he found in the person of the goldsmith Eliseus Libaerts of Antwerp. Their names became associated with the highest achievements of the armourer's art. A man's armour, a round shield and a chanfron in Stockholm, a cartouche-shaped parade shield in Skokloster Castle near Uppsala, and two complete armours for horse and man in Dresden give evidence of this unique relationship between king and artist. Although it lasted for only a short time, from 1562 to 1564, it was very fruitful. In 1564, when Libaerts was on his way to the Swedish King in Stockholm, he was taken prisoner on board ship by order of the Danish King, Frederick II, with the two garnitures which Eric XIV had never seen. In 1604 and 1606 respectively, the armours were sold, and left Copenhagen for Dresden, where they remain. His extravagance and cruelty caused Eric to be deposed in 1568 and kept prisoner until his unexplained death in 1577.

The large Dresden garniture with complete horse armour is not only the finest specimen from the artistic point of view, but also the best and most perfectly preserved. Its producer was the above-mentioned goldsmith, who lived in Antwerp from 1557 and who had obviously visited Paris before making it.

In Paris the draughtsman and famous engraver Etienne Delaune (1518/19-82) was then designing a whole series of embossed parade garnitures for horse and man for his own monarch, Henry II (1519–59), among them shields of all forms, round, oval, pointed-oval and cartouche-shaped. He supplied his lord and master with far more designs than could ever be actually produced. Eliseus Libaerts, however, translated Delaune's ideas and designs into three-dimensional reality. We do not know who carried out the actual armourer's work; but a hundred motives in Libaerts' embossings clearly show the French artist's influence, although on the other hand there is a significant divergence from the French towards Flemish art. Apart from the figures in the style of Michelangelo, mention must above all be made of a relationship between the embossing and the etching, the dense scrolls of which completely cover the background to produce a typically German effect. Eric XIV had the chanfron decorated with a representation of Christ the Redeemer, badge of the Order of the Saviour which he had wanted to found as a counterpart of the ancient and great European Orders of the Garter, the Golden Fleece and St Michel. The sequence of the Labours of Hercules on the horse armour indicates that the Scandinavian identified himself with the Greek demi-god who, as the suffering hero, is the classical counterpart of Christ. The Trojan and Argonaut scenes on the man's armour were to constitute a historic link between Eric and his country and the great antiquity of Greece.

Dresden, Historisches Museum, E 7

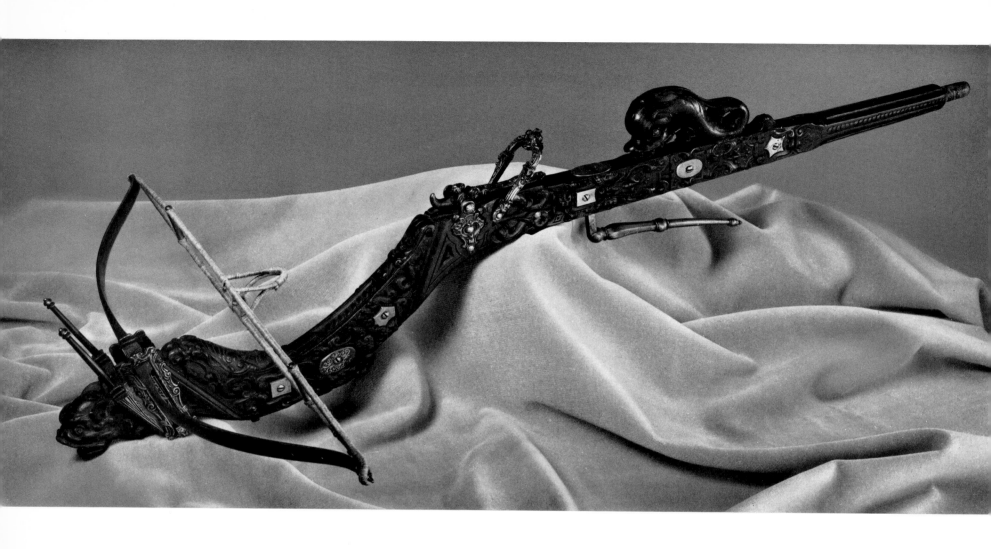

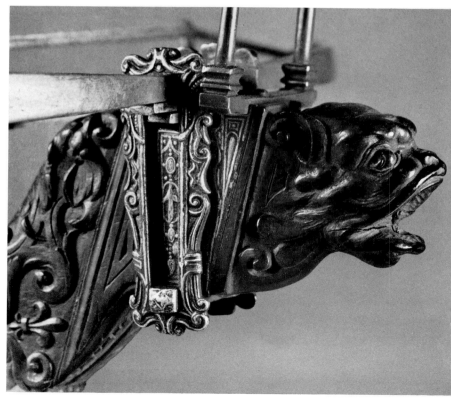

Bullet-crossbow of Queen Catherine de' Medici (1519—89; married, 1533) or of King Charles IX of France (1550-74; King, 1560)

One of the darkest chapters of French history is calamitously linked with the name of Catherine de' Medici, Queen of France. She was widowed in 1559 as a result of a tragic accident at a tournament that caused the death of Henry II. Her son Charles IX, only ten at the time, became sovereign of the French Kingdom in 1560, as a consequence of which the ambitious woman virtually ruled France. She attempted to strengthen her position through the struggle for power between the Roman Catholic Party of the Duke of Guise and the Protestant Huguenots. The violence of the Guises led to the outbreak in 1562 of the civil war that ravaged France for decades. When the Huguenots increasingly gained the upper hand, she schemed their destruction through the massacre that she planned with the help of the Duke of Guise and the approval of King Charles. It was carried out on St Bartholomew's Eve, 1572, when it is believed that 20,000 Huguenots were murdered. But their power was not broken. On the contrary, the enmity increased and the civil war continued.

A crossbow of sorts in Paris is believed to have been the Queen's property. It is a so-called bullet-crossbow, with its cord divided into two parts and fitted with a loop to release small bullets used for hunting birds and small game. The adjustable backsight and the bead foresight, which is fastened between two pegs, made it possible to aim accurately. The delicate projectile weapon, which can be bent manually, is known in the form shown here from North Italian paintings. It must have been a Lombard master who made the Paris royal specimen and created the rich carving of the shaft with scrolls, masks, French lilies and dolphins, its mounts of chiselled and damascened iron. The mirrored initial C and the royal crown that can be seen on the backsight arch may refer to the royal widow Catherine, but might just as well stand for her son Charles (IX), who remained unwed until 1570 and normally used the initial K. But the Dauphin's badge of a dolphin, which is shown several times and is fully sculpted on the column, seems to indicate the young King Charles as owner rather than his mother, because kings liked to continue to use this badge of succession to the throne.

Paris, Musée de l'Armée, L115

49 SOUTH GERMAN, 1558, 1589 and 1554

Guard's spear of the Emperor Ferdinand I (1503-64; Emperor, 1558)
Guard's halberd of Wolfdietrich von Raitenau, Archbishop of Salzburg (reigned 1587-1611)
"Hartschier" glaive of Maximilian II (1527-76; King of Bohemia, 1549; Emperor, 1564)

DUTCH, c. 1560
Embossed pointed-oval shield

A guard of archers who escorted the King of France as Duke of Burgundy in the Middle Ages carried in addition to their bows and arrows knife-like blades mounted on long hafts. It can be shown that this *couteau* existed as long ago as Merovingian times, but was probably of even more ancient, Eastern origin. As the legitimate heir of Burgundy, Charles V adopted the guard of archers with their *couteaux*. His nephew Maximilian II introduced the bastardised German term *Hartschiere* (archers) – later the *Arcièrenleibgarde* – to the Viennese imperial court. The word *couteau* became the German term *Kuse* (glaive).

The Hapsburg guards had previously carried spears, and evidence is available to show that they had done so from the time of Frederick III (Emperor, 1452–93), except during the reign of Ferdinand I (Emperor, 1558–64).

The halberd, a combination of spear and axe, is mentioned in 13th-century literary sources. In the 14th century the Swiss made the weapon famous and feared. At the time of the Emperor Maximilian I it was seen in the hands of the landsknechts, especially as a weapon of troop leaders, from whom it found its way to the guards of the Italian and German princes.

The guard's weapon is distinguished from the mass of ordinary war equipment by its splendid design and particularly by the profuse etching that includes a monogram, emblems and the sovereign's coat of arms. Only three of the many known examples are illustrated here:

A spear, ordered in 1558 on the occasion of Emperor Ferdinand I's coronation; an archer's glaive, dated 1554, owned by his son Maximilian II when still King of Bohemia; and finally a bodyguard's halberd of 1589 that belonged to Wolfdietrich von Raitenau, Archbishop of Salzburg.

The three hafted weapons have here been combined into a "panoply", an arrangement that was not, as is usually assumed, an invention of the 19th century. Not only was the panoply known in the 16th century, as a decorative element in ornamental engravings and on architecture, but it was also commonly hung on the walls of princely residences.

The pointed-oval shield in the Vienna Collection may originally have belonged to such a panoply. Its form and embossed design can clearly be traced back to the artistic circle of the School of Fontainebleau. However, the deep embossing, the abstruseness of the masks and the figures so reminiscent of Michelangelo, all point to some other place of origin, to Antwerp, where the Hapsburgs ruled. The designs by the leading ornamental artist Cornelis Floris of that city, used for surrounding the scenes from the saga of the Argonauts carrying off the Golden Fleece, clearly allude to the exclusive Order so cherished by the House of Hapsburg.

Vienna, Waffensammlung, A 969, A 2039, A 1219 and A 757

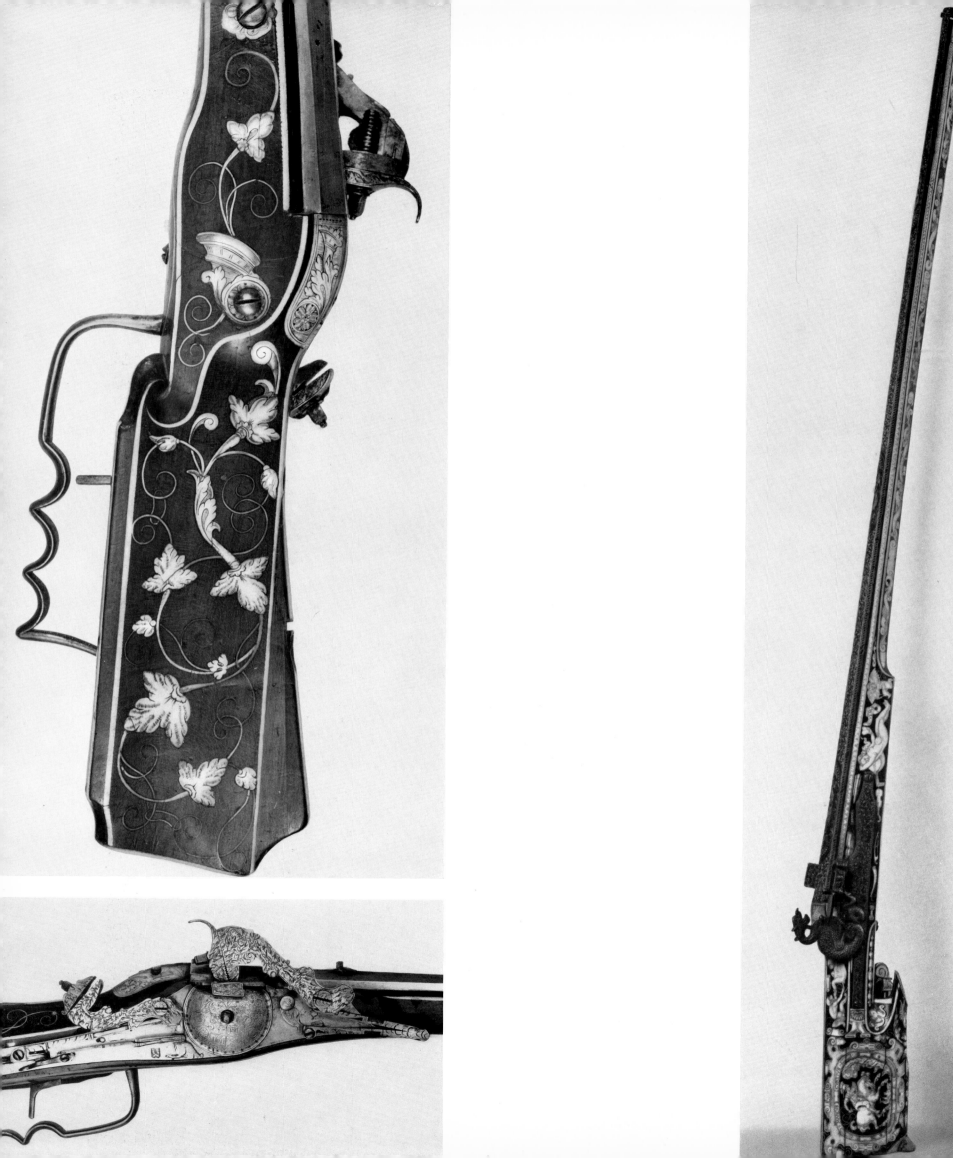

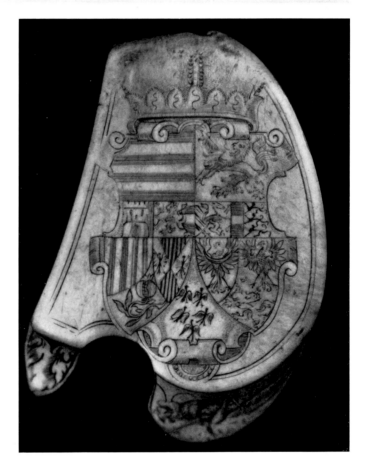

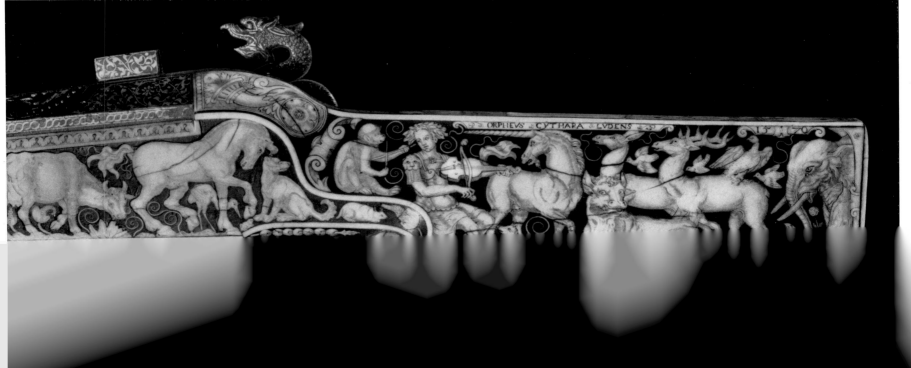

50 WOLFGANG PAUMGARTNER (STOCKMAKER) VIENNA, 1568

Wheel-lock rifle of Johann Jakob von Khuen Belasy, Prince-Archbishop of Salzburg (reigned 1560–86)

HANS PAUMGARTNER (STOCKMAKER), GRAZ, 1570

Matchlock rifle of the Archduke Charles II (1540–90; Lord of Styria, 1564)

Previous Double Page

The barrelsmith stamped his signature and the date *1568*, the locksmith his initials, IG, the stockmaker engraved WP (for Wolf Paumgartner of Vienna), on the hunting gun of the Salzburg Archbishop Khuen Belasy, whose ownership is revealed by his coat of arms on the lock's gilded wheel-cover.

The loosely distributed hop sprigs, cornucopias, and scrolls of inlaid bone on the elegant mahogany stock form a magnificently original and distinctly superior ornament.

Hans Paumgartner, mentioned as gunstockmaker to the court of the Archduke Charles of Styria at Graz, must have been Wolf's brother. His most beautiful work is the mahogany stock of the Vienna gun which he marked HP 1570. It is most profusely and charmingly inlaid with bone, and the chiselled iron of the barrel and of the dragon serpentine holding the match attempt to equal it in the delicacy of their arabesques. The Roman hero Marcus Curtius, a pair of apes, and Venus and Cupid are to be found on the lock side; Orpheus among the animals on the cheek side; Fortune, Charity and a pelican below; and, scattered over-all, musical instruments, the heads of animals and floral scrolls. The composition takes in a little of everything, presenting it in the most charming way conceivable.

Munich, Deutsches Jagdmuseum, and Vienna, Waffensammlung, A 2305

51 FRANZ GROSSSCHEDEL, LANDSHUT, 1571

Foot-combat armour from the "Roseleaf" garniture of the Emperor Maximilian II (1527–76; Emperor, 1564)

In 1572 Maximilian II paid an enormous sum to Franz Grossschedel, armourer to the ducal court in the Bavarian capital of Landshut, for armour for his own use. The Emperor obviously wore this shining garniture, with its gold and black etched ornamental bands displaying rose leaves and thorns, in 1571 for the tournaments on the occasion of the wedding of his brother Charles II of Styria. It was no longer a large garniture with extra pieces for 12 different combinations, as was still in fashion around 1550. The new type of garniture consisted of five complete armours and the horse armour. Maximilian was the only emperor who, in 1571, would be so lavish towards himself and his four sons! Philip II of Spain employed *Maestro Bolfe* (Wolf Grossschedel of Landshut), and Maximilian II used the latter's son Franz who, like Titian, was raised to the nobility in 1566 on account of his artistic prowess. During a period of affected stylistic exaggeration the "Casa de Austria" fostered a classic style of a most elegant simplicity and quietly noble form.

Vienna, Waffensammlung, A 474b

Tilt armour from the "Interlaced" garniture of Rudolph II (1552–1612; Emperor, 1576) and his brother, the Archduke Ernst (1553–95)

Archduke Charles II's marriage to the Bavarian Princess Maria in 1571 must have been of tremendous importance to the Viennese court. It constituted an alliance between two neighbouring great powers under the auspices of the Counter-Reformation. No other festive occasion has presented us with so many objects of the highest quality, so many precious relics. Maria's bridegroom Charles of Styria, a younger brother of the Emperor Maximilian II, the court, and the citizens of the town with their well-equipped guard awaited her in Vienna. A number of etched and dated servants' armours and hafted arms in the Historisches Museum in Vienna serve to remind us of the great event. The Emperor's sons, the Archdukes Rudolph and Ernst, also came to Vienna for the bride's reception, and festivities and tournaments helped to make her stay in Vienna more pleasant before she continued her journey to Graz, her husband's residence.

The "Interlaced" garniture of Rudolph, heir to the throne, and of his eldest brother and escort, Ernst, must have been created on the occasion of this tournament. It bears only its owners' archducal coat of arms. Just one year later, Rudolph was crowned King of Hungary and after another four years he was Roman King. The armourer had to consider not only the habits of the Spanish-educated prince, but also the customs of the place of festivity. In each instance the tilt, tournament and foot-tournament armours were designed on different lines for the two brothers: for the one, in the Italo-Spanish, for the other, in the German style. Parts of the garniture found their way to Paris and Leningrad. No master's mark or signature is to be found anywhere. If it was the work of the Augsburg armourer Anton Peffenhauser, who also supplied the tilt armour, dated 1571, of the bridegroom, Archduke Charles II (Vienna A 885), he excelled even himself with this quite exceptional garniture. In spite of its somewhat compact form, which is due to its period, it must be counted among the most beautiful examples of the armourers' art of the second half of the 16th century. The outstanding etcher also gave of his best. The pattern in the imperial colours of black and gold spreads itself over the surfaces, forming complicated knots, with beautiful foliage and hop sprigs filling the loops of the ribbon. A process begun haltingly around 1550 was now complete: the pattern of oblong bands which had so far been obligatory was now obsolete. Decoration proliferated in an almost baroque way all over the armour, which is not burdened but invigorated by it. Whilst French etchers of the day regarded armour almost exclusively as an item of dress, the German artist still took account of its artistic character and of the sculptural quality of the steel shell which contains the human body. *Vienna, Waffensammlung, A 886*

Half-armour of Henry III of France (1551–89; King of Poland, 1574–75; King of France from 1574)

From Francis I (King from 1515) to Louis XIV (died 1713), the French kings left a series of most important armours which would fill an impressive volume as yet unwritten. In 1530, Francis I founded the first School of Fontainebleau with the aid of Italian artists and so the renaissance was introduced into France. It has gradually become obvious that his son Henry II overshadowed him as a patron of the armourer's art. During his own reign (1547–59) he clearly preferred the employment of Frenchmen who, as a nation, had always been renowned as refined and intelligent artists. They revealed their talents also in the design of arms and armour; French armour began to rid itself of Lombard influence, which had so far been a determining factor, and evolved its own special features. This applied to the armourers' work, to the cut and modelling of plastic forms as well as to the eminently French decoration of plain surfaces. Henry II's armour at the Wartburg near Eisenach (No. 59) is the first to show the signs of this style. Paris has preserved one youth's armour each of Henry II's three sons and successors, Francis II (1559/60), Charles IX (1560–74), and Henry III. They show a logical development of taste and style towards a definite goal which announced the emergence of the baroque. The natural plastic shape of the breastplate altered first to a waist finishing in a deep point and finally became the so-called "peascod". The swelling long tassets were attached directly to the breastplate, together with which they formed extremely broad hips. There are a number of typically French features in the construction of helmet and vambrace. Leg-harness was probably no longer provided. Soon the fashionable wore armour only as a kind of representative steel jacket. Western Europe paid exaggerated tribute to the ideal of slimness and boyish, almost feminine delicacy. Though France's position as leader of fashion was not established by Henry III with his exceedingly extravagant tastes, it was certainly considerably reinforced by him. What is more, France developed – in addition to her unique splinted parade armour – her own special decorative techniques on flat planes. The surfaces were covered over-all with a fine etched pattern and the whole heavily gilded. The etching of the Charles IX armour in Paris (G 120) imitated the stitched diagonal pattern of oblong bands that was in fashion for men between 1560 and 1570. In the case of Henry III's armour it was a dense mesh pattern, the slanting lines of which also relentlessly and rigidly cut across the body's shape. Inside every one of the many small squares, which follow one another in continual rapport, there is a minute star-shaped blossom. Often compared with a wall-paper pattern, an imitation of contemporary interwoven materials, it reminds one, rather surprisingly, of the guilloched print on bank-notes.

Not a single royal emblem occurs on Henry III's armour. Therefore it must have been made before his accession to the throne. The French Revolution so completely destroyed every archive that not one document relating to any royal armour, not a single armourer's name, no place of origin and no exact date has survived. No school of armourers in the West makes research so difficult, with the possible exception of the neighbouring Low German school.
Paris, Musée de l'Armée, G 121

54 LUCIO PICCININO, MILAN, c. 1578

Burgonet, arm defence and mace of the Duke Alexander of Parma and Piacenza (1545—92; Duke, 1586)

In 1579 the famous General Alessandro Farnese wrote from the Dutch battlefield to his uncle Archduke Ferdinand II in the Tyrol that at Namur there was an exceptionally beautiful parade armour of his which was to be sent to the Heroes' Armoury at Innsbruck. This, however, is not described in the inventories of Ambras until 1596. The author of a book in praise of Milan, Paolo Morigia, reported in 1595 that one Lucio Piccinino had produced quite excellent and very rare parade armour of great value for this particular Duke Alexander as well as for other princes. He goes on to say that Lucio not only was the craftsman who embossed the iron (and silver), but that he also acted as his own artist and goldsmith. Twenty years after Giovanni Battista Serabaglio, Piccinino used every available means to achieve an accumulation of florid splendour which would be difficult to surpass. The background is of blued iron above which is raised superabundant embossing. The embossed fleshy parts of the figures are silvered and gilded. The decorative elements are damascened in gold and silver and further enriched with rows of silver pearls. Although the arrangement of the ornament still follows the system of broad ribbons and borders, draperies and festooned fruit hang between the bands. It is due to the latter that the whole tends to seem so immense. If the wearer's joints are covered by the heads of lions or savage beasts, it only indicates compliance with the ancient tradition of the Italian gothic style. This, therefore, was the stage reached in the development of Milanese parade armour by around 1580, and here we come face to face with Lucio Piccinino's late renaissance style. On this basis it is possible to identify his other works in Madrid, London and New York, and it is from this point that his school evolved. In view of his versatility it may be assumed that the extremely precise designs in Vienna, Paris and Hamburg were also Lucio's work.

The decorative technique employed on the general's mace, the symbol of his command, matches perfectly that of the armour. But in place of the embossing it shows deep, masterly iron chiselling. In this case the six flanges of the head have been elaborated into wild monsters' masks.

Vienna, Waffensammlung, A 1153, A 1132 and A 1153b

55 GIOVANNI PAOLO CECHINO (GOLDSMITH) AND FRANCESCO DE SANTA CRUCE (EMBROIDERER), ROME, 1581

The consecrated hat and sword of the Archduke Ferdinand II (1529–95; Lord of the Tyrol, 1564)

Clement VI (1342–52), who resided at Avignon, appears to have been the first pope to award consecrated hats and swords. The presentation, made annually after consultation with the College of Cardinals, was to honour a prominent personality who had worked meritoriously for the protection of the Church. The gifts were consecrated by the pope on Christmas morning and were ceremoniously presented to the chosen person at Christmas Matins during rites, borrowed from the Emperor's coronation, at which the hat was placed on the recipient's head and the sword buckled around his waist. Were he unable to attend, the gift was taken to him by a legate.

The first sword to be preserved was made 100 years after the introduction of the custom and was awarded by Pope Eugene IV to King John II of Castile in 1441. The blade of the ceremonial weapon, which is kept at the Real Armería in Madrid, bears very early etching. From that time on, several such swords have been handed down to us. Particularly well known among them is the sword at the National Museum in Zurich sent by Pope Julius II to the Swiss in 1511 in recognition of their assistance against the French.

That great art collector, the Archduke Ferdinand II, upholder of the Counter-Reformation, was twice distinguished in this way, in 1567 by Pope Pius V and 1581 by Pope Gregory XIII. Not only have both swords been preserved but the two hats as well, and this is an extremely rare occurrence. Each has the traditional and peculiar tall shape characterising the hats of elegant gentlemen in paintings by the Siena masters Simone Martini and Ambrogio Lorenzetti from the first half of the 14th century, at the time when the first awards were made.

Francis, Bishop of Säben, presented the Archduke with Gregory XIII's consecrated offerings in May 1582. The papal embroiderer Francesco de Santa Cruce produced the fine pearl embroidery on the black velvet hat that shows flames and a radiant star, the dove of the Holy Ghost and buttons. The richly embroidered hangings of gold brocade on red silk were also made by him. The Pope's name and the eleventh year of his pontificate (1582) appear on the tongue of the belt. Giovanni Paolo Cechino, a goldsmith mentioned several times on bills of the Vatican court, was the master who created the embossed and pierced scabbard on red silk and the fantastic hilt. Foliage decorates the long grip and the cross-guard, the quillon-block taking the form of a mask. The pommel, in the shape of dragons, bears the dragon coat of arms of the Buoncampagni family from which the Pope came. These arms occur several times in the embroidery on the belt and also appear on the scabbard alongside a medallion showing the Apostles Peter and Paul. Pope Gregory XIII has one outstanding claim to fame. In 1582, the year of Ferdinand's award, he replaced the Julian calendar, that had for so long proved inadequate, by the improved Gregorian, which remains in use until the present day.

Vienna, Waffensammlung, A 989

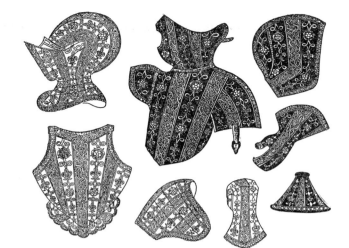

56 JACOB HALDER, GREENWICH, c. 1590

The armour of George Clifford, Earl of Cumberland (1558–1605; Earl, 1570)

In 1515 King Henry VIII of England set up a royal armoury, which employed Netherlandish and German craftsmen and was modelled on the workshops of his ally, the Emperor Maximilian I. About ten years later it found a permanent home near the royal residence of Greenwich and soon developed its own particular style. The Greenwich School was characterised by the most careful design, functional but economic arrangement of garnitures, and a love of technical devices and unusual forms.

About 1555 Jacob Halder came to Greenwich from Augsburg, an appointment that was probably due to the marriage of the Roman Catholic Queen Mary of England to Philip II of Spain in 1554. The English court was now interested in the Augsburg armour and etching that was preferred by the Spaniards, and Halder seems to have mastered this latter technique in addition to his skill as an armourer. When Queen Elizabeth (1558–1603) came to power, Halder, in spite of her opposition to Roman Catholicism, played an increasingly important role. Between 1576 and 1607 he was master armourer and led the workshop to the peak of its artistic achievements. After Mary, Queen of Scots, was beheaded in 1587, the country was threatened by a campaign of revenge on the part of Philip II of Spain; finally, in 1588, the Armada was sent to England, only to be sunk. During this period Halder was called on to produce a great many simpler field armours as equipment for English courtiers. However, both before and after, he continued to create a number of superb armours for the same circle. Sketches of his own creations and those of his predecessors, Erasmus Kirkener and John Kelte, were included by him in the so-called Greenwich Album, which today is one of the treasures of the Victoria and Albert Museum in London.

The armour of the Earl of Cumberland from Appleby Castle must be regarded as Halder's greatest achievement. It is of the highest quality, even though the excessively long and pointed form of the breast may appear strange. This peascod breastplate corresponded to the period's bizarre fashion created by King Henry III of France. The gilded etching against a purplish ground combines different styles in a masterly manner: the alternating bands and emblems – in this case the Virgin Queen's Tudor roses and lilies – had their origin in Italy, whilst the etcher used designs by the Frenchman Jacques I. Androuet Ducerceau (c. 1520 to c. 1585) for the ribbons on the bands themselves. The armour was part of a large garniture "for felde, tilte, tournament and foot", as it was then called. George Clifford may have ordered it for the annual ceremony when, in 1590, he became the Queen's Champion, her symbolic protector. The armour reflects the high standard of culture achieved by Elizabeth's England with which Shakespeare's name is immortally linked.

New York, Metropolitan Museum of Art, 32. 130. 6

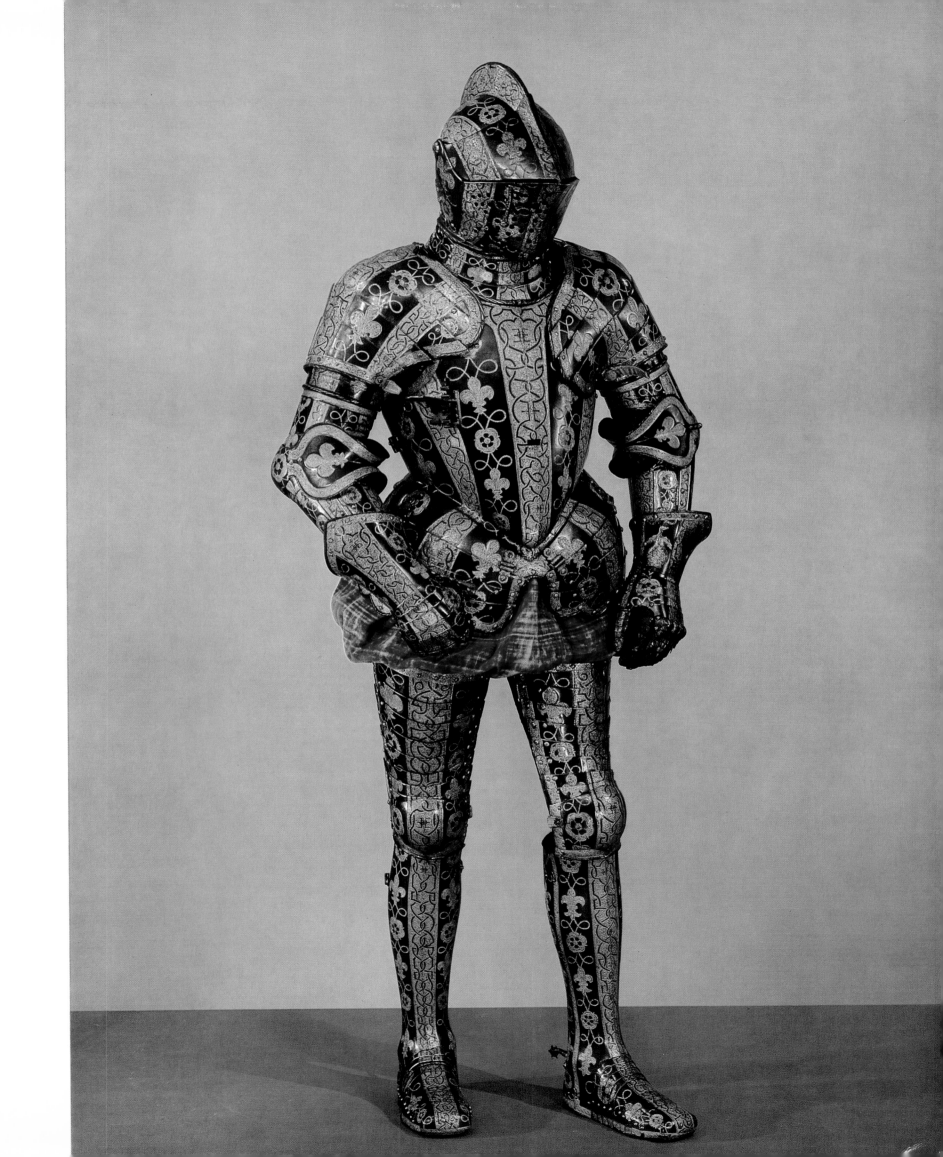

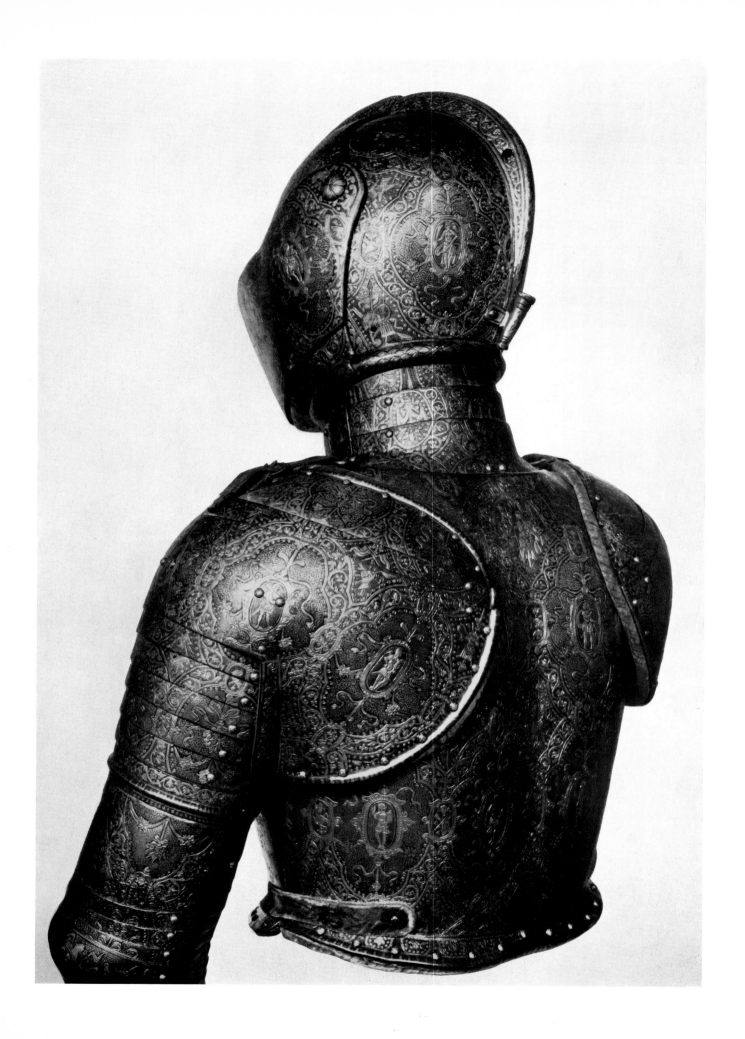

57 MASTER I O, MILAN, c. 1600

Foot-tournament armour, possibly the property of the Emperor Ferdinand II (1578–1637; Emperor, 1619)

The plastic form, the proportions and cut of this all too heavy Vienna half-armour with its repetitive pattern of medallions point to its having been created around 1600. It reaches only to the hips, indicating that blows below the belt were forbidden, and consists of the firmly locking close-helmet, breast- and backplates (the latter always very much lighter), close-fitting pauldrons and gauntlets. Dressed in this way, participants in the tournament fought over a separating barrier in groups of six to twelve, armed with long pikes and broadswords. A prince who was not fit enough to take part in such armed combat earned little respect.

The armourer struck his signature on the breast- and back-plates: within a shield there is a blurred I O placed laterally next to a two-towered castle indicating the Castello Sforzesco. Sword blades by several Milanese swordsmiths stamped with the same ducal castle bear this out. For use in the highest circles the surface of such a sportive costume had, of course, to be richly decorated. Even before 1560 it had occurred to the French to cover armour with an over-all mesh pattern, proof of which can be seen in the Paris boy's armour (G 119) of King Francis II, who died at the age of fourteen (ruled 1559–60). The pattern fascinated clients and craftsmen alike for half a century until the end of the renaissance. Milanese masters like Pompeo della Cesa developed the rhombic net patterns, a style that was taken up by the unidentified Milanese I O, who followed one row of quatrefoil medallions with another, filling the spaces with individual figures of warriors in ovals suspended by ribbons, and with trophies of war. The frames are damascened in gold and silver with dense scrolls of exaggerated delicacy. The fine needle and acid of the etcher were no longer the prevalent tools. More careless and much clumsier techniques of embossing and engraving by mechanical means led towards the baroque, which they were eventually to dominate completely.

There is an identical, though somewhat smaller and very light counterpart (A 1529) of the I O armour in Vienna. It is not difficult to visualise the two archducal brothers of the Styrian branch of the Hapsburg family, the Emperor Ferdinand II and the younger Leopold V (1586–1632), ready to enter the foot-tournament shoulder to shoulder. Their cousin, the Archduke Albrecht VII (1559–1621), wore an armour made by the same master for his wedding to his Spanish cousin and for the award of the Order of the Golden Fleece in 1599. Portraits of Albrecht repeatedly show him in this famous armour, parts of which are now dispersed to Brussels and Cracow.   *Vienna, Waffensammlung, A 1712*

58 PETER OPEL, REGENSBURG, c. 1590

Wheel-lock rifle

If costume and armour are completely covered with ornament and figurative subjects, it goes without saying that the small arms carried with them could never remain undecorated. Here chiselled iron and wood carved in relief take the place of the armour's embossing; engraving with the burin replaces acid etching. Heavy fire-gilding and the excellent work of the minor artist indicate that the owner, who is unfortunately unknown, must have been of princely rank. To give a complete enumeration, the following types of decoration are present: on the barrel are the allegoric figures of Fortitudo (strength), Vanitas (vanity), pomegranate tendrils, and, forming the backsight, a sculpted dragon with hinged wings; Pyramus and Thisbe are chiselled on the lock-plate; the head of a wild beast and a royal head on the cock; on the stock, Actaeon and Endymion and hunting scenes; Leda with the swan on the patch-box cover; Atlas carrying the golden firmament carved in ivory on the butt-plate. The stock-maker placed his initials PO next to the figure of Fortuna at the thumb-rest. The South German cities produced an astonishing number of master gunsmiths and schools whose highly-placed clients required them to have a thorough grounding in the classics.

Vienna, Waffensammlung, D 213

59 HANS STOPLER (BARRELSMITH), WOLFGANG STOPLER (LOCKSMITH),
DAVID LEIMBER (STOCKMAKER), NUREMBERG,
BARREL DATED 1592

Wheel- and matchlock musket of a Count Starhemberg

The rifle decorated in relief has its counterpart in this smooth gun, every part of which is, however, densely inlaid and engraved. At the end of the century, towards the close of the renaissance, the fine lines become increasingly crowded. It is not possible to imagine a rifle that was more extensively marked; Hans Stopler's mark, the inspection or quality mark of the Nuremberg Guild and the date 1592 are on the barrel; Wolfgang Stopler's signature with the Nuremberg inspection mark are on the lock; the initials DL with a lily of David Leimber are on the inside of the stock, covered by the lock-plate; and next to it is the Nuremberg mark for high quality timber stocks. The only thing lacking is some indication of ownership. As the piece comes from the armoury of Count Starhemberg at Eferding Castle to the west of Linz in Upper Austria, it must have been used by one of his ancestors. Nuremberg, the city of ingenious technicians and skilful craftsmen, as well as the home of "Nuremberg Toys" and a classic toy-manufacturing town, at that time supplied small arms to the world. Once again the inlaid illustrations combine antique concepts in the form of a triumphal procession of the gods – among them of course the indispensable goddess Fortuna – with contemporary war and hunting scenes, allegories and legendary figures. The lock mechanism is a combination of the hunting wheel-lock and military matchlock. The heavy musket had to be placed on a rest when firing.

Following Double Page

Sammlung Hans Schedelmann, Salzburg

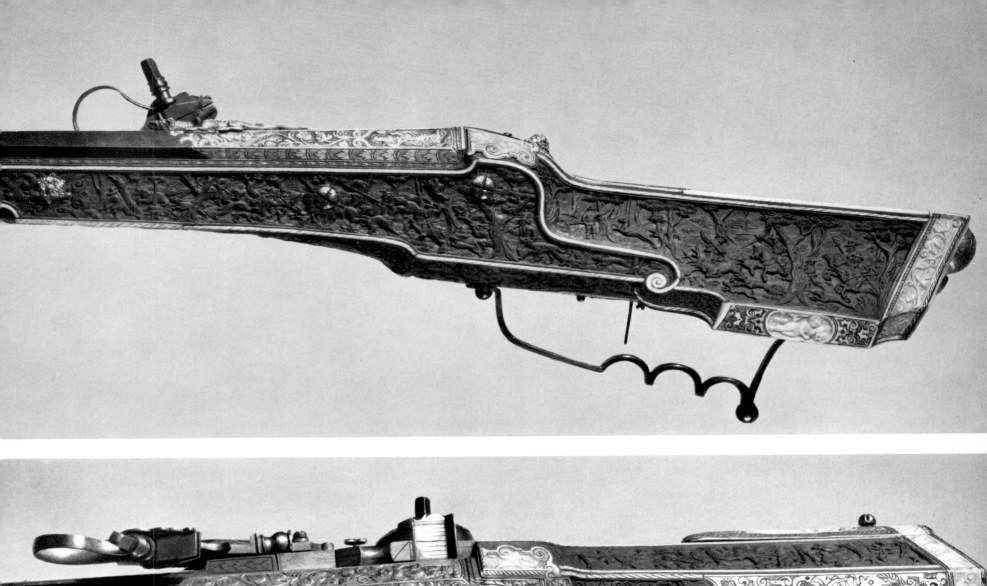

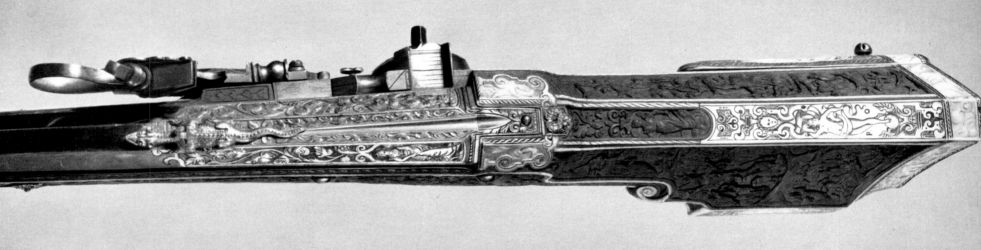

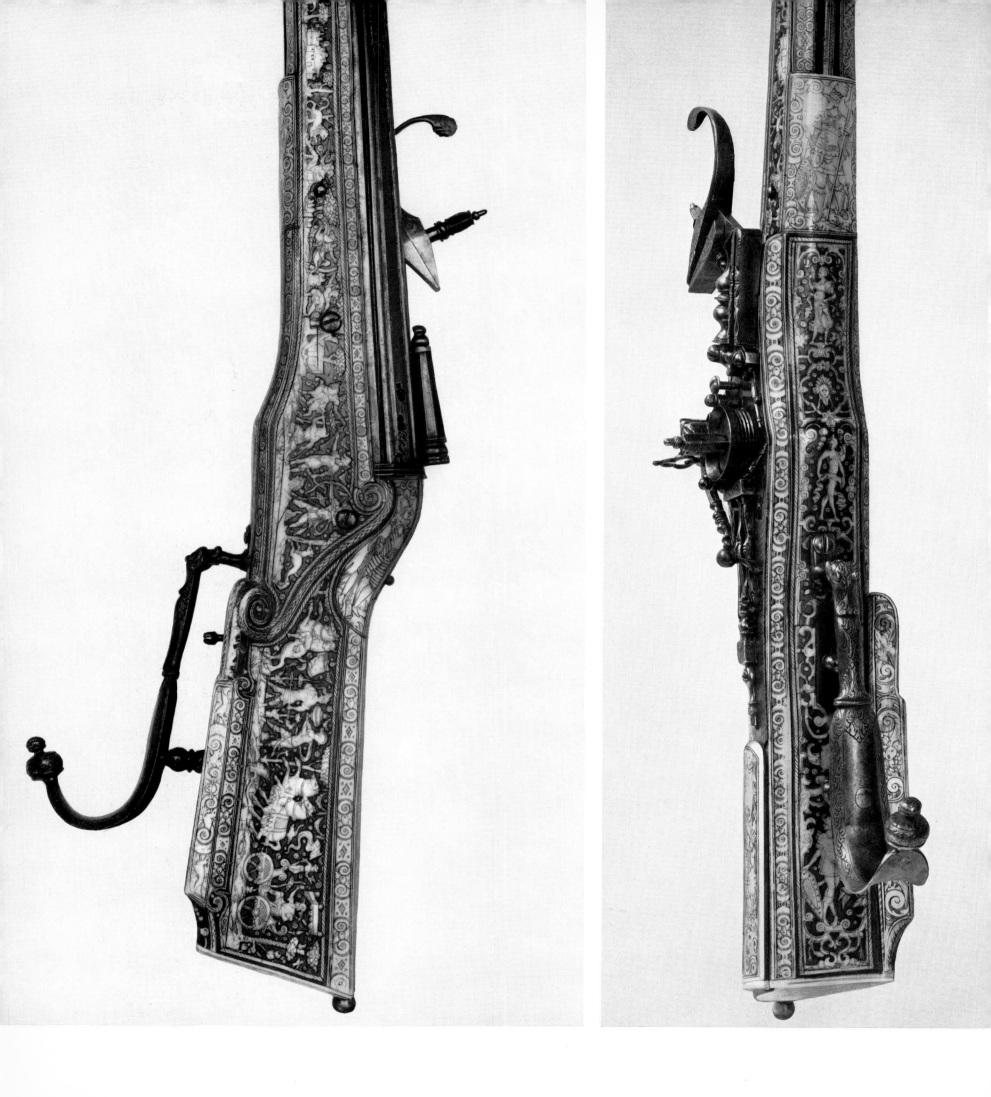

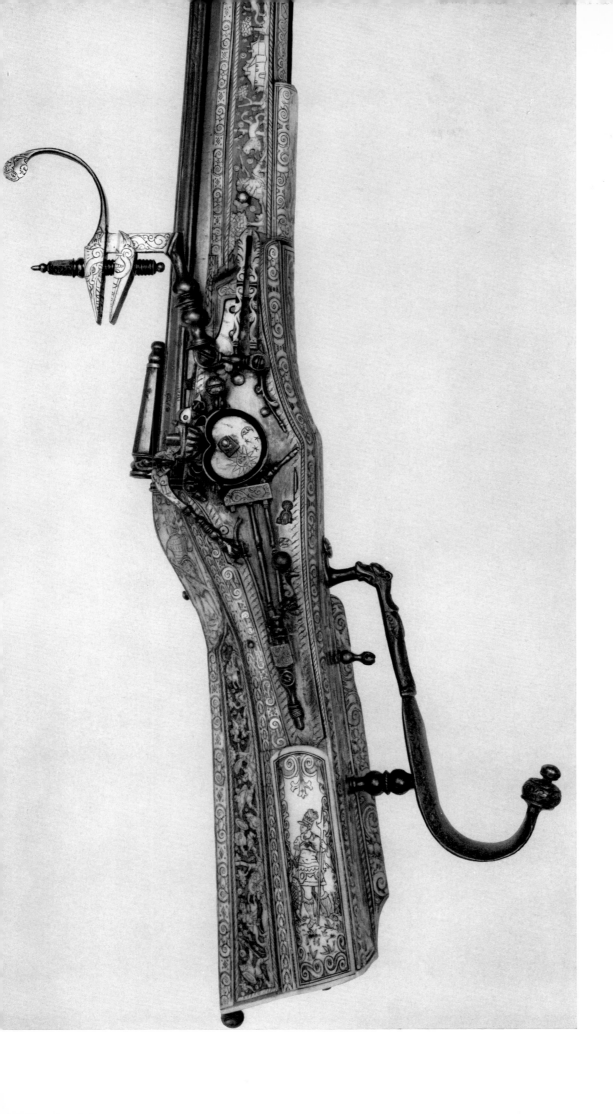

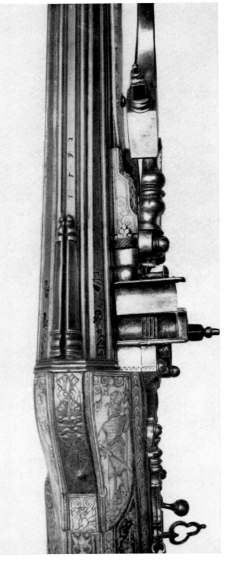

60   DUTCH, 1600–10

Partisan of the Life Guards of Maurice, Prince of Orange (1567–1625; Governor of the Netherlands, 1587)

The Protestant powers in Northern Europe became stronger in the course of the late 16th century. England took the lead under Queen Elizabeth I; the Netherlands, Denmark and Sweden followed. The rebellious Netherlands, supported by England, broke with Spain in 1581. While the southern provinces were reconquered by Duke Alessandro Farnese of Parma for King Philip II between 1578 and 1592, the northern provinces with Holland in the forefront, fought successfully for their freedom. They were commanded by Prince William I (assassinated in 1584) and his son, Prince Maurice of Nassau-Orange, and in 1648 Holland eventually emerged from the conflict as a great European and sea power.

Maurice of Orange was an outstanding, possibly the greatest, military genius of modern times. Stimulated by a study of the writers of antiquity, he initiated a fundamental reform of the army around 1590 and no longer marshalled his order of battle in square masses of troops but in formations without great depth. He produced the drill book required for this, regulated the tactical use of the various arms of the service and unified their armament. Other European powers soon followed his example when it proved its excellence.

Thanks to his successes, the Netherlands gained considerable moral strength and great power in spite of their feudal government. His own position as Governor amounted almost to being king. He was surrounded by a select guard of noblemen in accordance with the French example, each armed with sword and partisan, a broad spear with two upturned hooks at the base of its blade. As was customary in the case of guards' arms, those of the Oranges were richly decorated. Apart from the Prince's half-length portrait with inscription, the etching, partly blackened and partly gilded, still shows fine ribboning, scrolls and trophies borrowed from the ornament created by the Frenchman Ducerceau.

New York, Metropolitan Museum of Art, 27. 226

Parade rapier with chiselled iron hilt

Great things were happening in Italy towards the end of the 16th century. The Il Gesù church had been erected in Rome around 1575 as an example of the new baroque art in building; the brothers Caracci had established a new school of representative religious painting at Bologna; Michelangelo da Caravaggio, the founder of a realistic style of painting that proved to be of pioneering originality, had come to work in Rome and south Italy. While in this way the baroque style with its large-scale dramatic forms displaced the plain art of the late renaissance, which was calculated to appeal to the beholder's finer sensitivities and intellect, it also produced a counter-trend. People with elegant tastes and trained artistic sense, the court circle, were still desirous of having their "own" art as far as painting, sculpture and craftsmanship were concerned. It was to be even more ingenious, still more carefully designed and richer than ever before, a style that particularly suited Dutch artists and German masters. These mannerist fashions of between 1590 and 1620 could be compared to a hothouse plant of fascinating, sparkling yet decadent beauty. The Emperor Rudolph II (1552–1612; Emperor, 1576) who had his court in Prague, was the outstanding patron of this movement. He was one of the greatest art collectors of all time whose character was a curious mixture of noble sentiment and unpredictability, of high education and superstition. Rudolph was afflicted by the tragic inheritance of his great-grandmother, the mad Juana of Castile, and he and his brother, Matthias I (1557–1619; Emperor, 1612), were the last of the main line of the Hapsburgs.

In 1610 Rudolph II presented the Elector Christian II of Saxony with a rapier, whose fine chiselled iron was the work of Daniel Sadeler, an artist who had emigrated from Antwerp and was working for the Emperor in Prague with the rank of "Court Gilder". For this work he re-used draft sketches that had been designed by Etienne Delaune for Henry II of France around the middle of the 16th century, which throws light on the tastes prevailing at that time. A parade rapier in the Vienna Collection – probably once the property of Rudolph II – is closely related to Christian II's rapier which is now in the Dresden Historisches Museum. Once again the style of the figures and ornament can be traced back to Delaune, but in its fineness and density the chiselling surpasses the work of Sadeler. It was created by an unknown master, whose home may also have been in the Netherlands.

Rapier hilts had become more complicated in the last quarter of the 16th century. The basic construction of quillons, arms of the hilt and lower *pas d'âne* was retained with the addition of a side branch of the knuckle bow that curved down to meet the lower *pas d'âne* in an S-shape. Parrying guards branching into three parts on the inside of the hilt balance it. The hand and fingers were thus almost completely enclosed. In the early 17th century and entirely in keeping with the very late renaissance style, the system of protecting bars and arms was extended and became confusing and diverse. Here, too, the baroque was eventually victorious and resulted once more in the development of simpler and more practical forms.

Vienna, Waffensammlung, A 1109

62 EMANUEL SADELER (IRON CHISELLER) AND ADAM VISCHER (STOCKMAKER), MUNICH, 1599

Musket rest, wheel-lock musket, spanner, powder flask and priming flask

CASPAR SPÄT (IRON CHISELLER), MUNICH, AND ELIAS BECKER (STOCKMAKER), AUGSBURG, c. 1635

Wheel-lock gun, spanner, priming flask, and a pair of wheel-lock pistols of Maximilian I of Bavaria (1573–1651; Duke, 1595/97; Elector, 1623)

The first Bavarian Elector dispatched a gift of sixteen of his own most beautiful arms from Munich to arrive at Turin on 1st December 1650. His reason was the marriage by proxy of his eldest son and successor, Prince Ferdinand Maria, to Henriette Adelaide, the sister of the recipient of the presents, Charles Emanuel II of Savoy (1634–75; Duke, 1637). At the time, both bride and bridegroom were fourteen years old. These arms are still one of the most treasured possessions of Turin's Armería Reale. The masters were three Munich iron-chisellers who worked with three stockmakers from Augsburg: Emanuel Sadeler and Adam Vischer, Sadeler's brother Daniel and Hieronymus Borstorffer the Elder, Caspar Spät and Elias Becker the Elder. Only ten of the sixteen objects are illustrated here. The remaining six comprise a rapier (G 99) by Emanuel Sadeler, a rapier (G 98), a wheel-lock rifle (M 11) and a spanner (N' 13) by Daniel Sadeler, a rapier (G 195) and a wheel-lock rifle (M 9) by Caspar Spät.

With these masters and in particular with these their most perfect works, Munich, the ducal and electoral seat, surpassed even Paris as the centre of the finest conceivable craftsmanship in the field of *armes blanches* and even more so in the field of splendid firearms. The most magnificent achievements of the Sadelers, emigrants from Antwerp, were based on French graphic models. They too utilised the engravings by Etienne Delaune (1518/19–82) and every technical means available for artistic decoration was exploited: chiselled, gilded and blued iron; silver and gold damascening; and engraved ivory inlays on the finest of timbers.

It is significant that each of the three stockmakers placed his initials on the largest of his works, the wheel-lock rifle. Caspar Spät marked the barrels of his wheel-lock guns with his initials, CS. The two Sadelers did not leave one single work marked by their hand. Their father Emanuel and his brother Jan had already been cutlers in Antwerp, members of a craft that produced not only knives and sets of cutlery but above all sword and rapier hilts, and their decoration. Only the long blades were the preserve of the swordsmiths. Their uncle, Jan, was the founder of a widely dispersed dynasty of copper-engravers who worked in every part of Central Europe from Antwerp to Rome, including Cologne, Frankfurt, Munich and Augsburg, Prague, Innsbruck and Vienna.

Vienna, Waffensammlung, A 2252; Turin, Armería Reale, M 12, N' 12, N' 22, N' 23 (E. Sadeler) – M 10, N' 15, N' 24, N' 27, N' 28 (C. Spät)

63 DANIEL SADELER OF MUNICH (IRON-CHISELLER) AND DAVID ALTENSTETTER OF AUGSBURG (GOLDSMITH), PRAGUE, 1603–10

Wheel-lock rifle and powder flask of the Emperor Rudolph II (1552–1612; Emperor, 1576)

IMPERIAL COURT WORKSHOP, PRAGUE, c. 1600–10

Hunting implements of the Emperor Rudolph II

Rudolph II, as Emperor with his court in Prague, gathered around his castle on the Hradchin masters of all the arts and made them work for his pleasure. Disliking wars, he evinced no interest even in his own armour which was ordered for him by his father when he was still a young man. The adult ruler had none at all, hunting being his only open-air recreation. Daniel Sadeler from Munich and David Altenstetter from Augsburg were attracted to his court where they created this precious gun and flask. One chiselled the blued iron on the gilded background of barrel and lock; the other made the partly gilded and abundantly enamelled silver mounts (marked DA F) of the stock and powder flask. Arms had increasingly become collectors' pieces, objects to be looked at and shown around to be admired on the occasion of shooting contests. The hunting cutlery was used when the hunt was over. The game was carved with the carving knife, the gilded fork was used to put the meat on the spit and the choicest pieces were offered on the broad-bladed serving knife or *presentoir*. As is known from the innumerable sumptuous vessels which he owned, Rudolph II had a particular liking for semi-precious stones; so, in order to please him, the handles of his unsurpassably noble cutlery set were made of carved agate. The mounts are enamelled, corresponding again to his personal tastes.   *Vienna, Waffensammlung, D 209, 209 a and D 206*

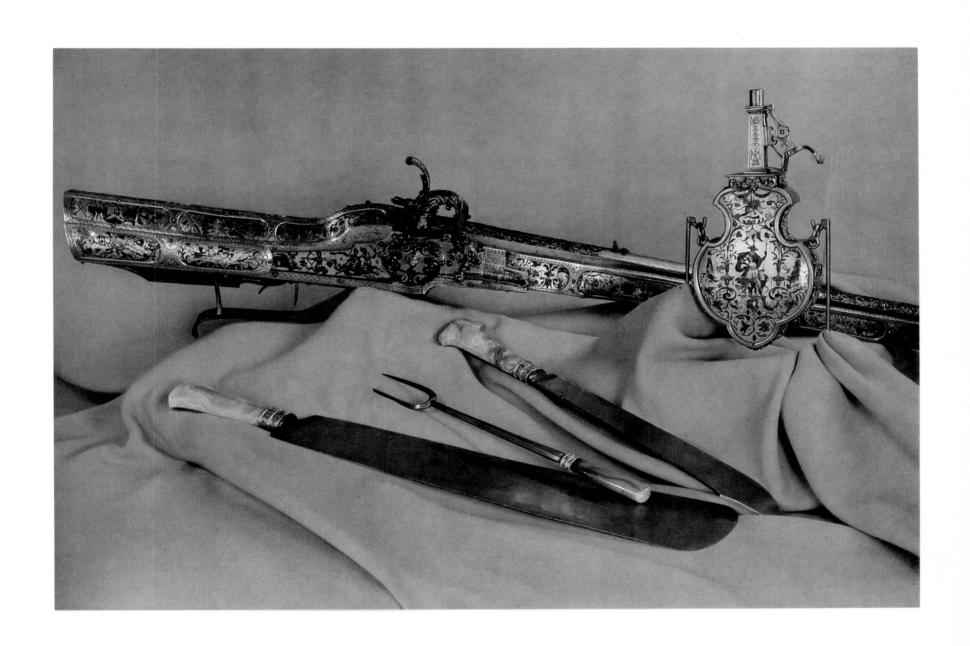

The coronation saddle of Charles IX, King of Sweden (1550–1611; King, 1604)

Coronation day is the climax of a ruler's life. The ceremony is surrounded by symbolic rites and the great occasion demands a display of the utmost splendour. Around 1560 Eric XIV, the son of the first Vasa king Gustav I and the eldest brother of Charles IX, introduced this custom to his out-of-the-way Nordic kingdom. A claim for his position to be recognised by the Western world was associated with the splendour of his coronation regalia, which still constitute the most superb part of the Swedish crown jewels.

But not only the king had to impress the crowds with his magnificence. The equipment of the horse on which he rose above the crowds was also smothered in treasure, all of which was especially made for the festivities. A new saddle for the king's horse was created on each occasion and it was always in accordance with the latest fashion and changing ideals of style. Afterwards it was kept as a memento of the historical occasion. King Gustav Adolf, Charles IX's son and successor, expressly laid down in his Edict of 18th March 1628 that the equipment he had worn at the battle of Dirschau be preserved. This constituted, so to speak, the "Articles of Association" for the Royal Armoury in Stockholm, which thus became a museum for the Swedish nation.

Charles IX used the title of king from 1604 but only had himself crowned in 1607. For the occasion his horse was equipped with an Eastern type saddle and harness, the surviving parts of which bear witness to the fact that arms and armour had become pure works of the goldsmith's art, museum pieces. Ruprecht Miller, a Low German – apart from Antwerp, The Hague and Amsterdam, Hamburg frequently supplied Swedish kings with precious objects, – was the goldsmith who created not only Charles IX's horse armour of 1607, but also, in 1620, the crown for his wife Christine – mother of Gustav Adolf – as well as crown, sceptre and orb for Maria Eleonore, Gustav Adolf's wife. The following items of the horse's finery have been preserved: the two clasps from the chanfron and tail straps, together with the three sockets that held the plumes; the mounts from the low saddle pad which protected the rider's right thigh; the entire cantle; and seven mounted topazes of the harness. Therefore, apart from most of the goldsmith's work the saddle lacks the wooden saddle-tree and all the textile and leather straps. With these objects the far North, successfully rivalling the more favoured regions of the West, has left us a marvellous work, a late mannerist jewel in which scrolls encircling crowns and lions, victory palms and trophies, cut precious stones, Centaurs and Roman warriors in gold and the finest coloured enamel are set on gilded silver foil.

Stockholm, Livrustkammaren, 3858 ff

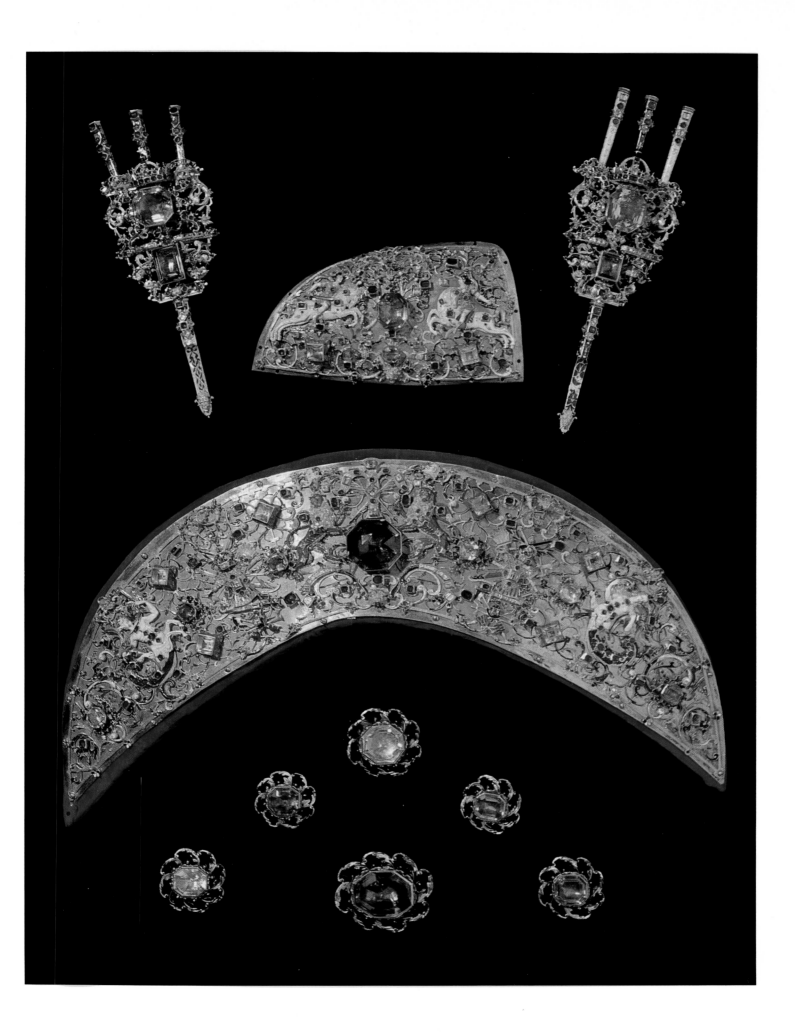

65 GASPARO MOLA, FLORENCE, c. 1610

Burgonet and round shield of a Grand Duke of Tuscany, Ferdinand I (1549–1609) or Cosimo II (1590–1621)

Gasparo Mola was a Lombard from the neighbourhood of Como, like so many Italians exceedingly versatile, working not only as goldsmith, engraver of medals, seal cutter and master coin-designer, but occasionally also as an armourer of distinction. He was employed by the princely mints at Turin, Florence, Modena and ultimately in Papal Rome.

A sword and dagger in Paris and the helmet and shield shown here, part of the few treasured remnants of the rich grand ducal armoury in Florence, were created by him.

The iron surfaces of both helmet and shield are covered by a diaphanous web or frame of gilded silver intended purely as ornament. Tendrils, scrolls and draperies, about which are scattered trophies and legendary figures, form this decorative overlay. Starting at the circumference, the following figural representations can be traced on the shield: classical emperors' heads; the twelve signs of the Zodiac; and the six virtues, four of them secular, Wisdom, Strength, Temperance and Justice, and two spiritual, Faith and Hope. The series is continued on the helmet with Love and on the reverse, alien to this group, Fame blowing a double horn. This arrangement, although not exactly profound, is not confused either, as is all too often the case in the late renaissance. The miniature dragon, a common helmet ornament, and the bird's mask on the peak follow an ancient tradition. The goldsmith's work is of enchanting refinement, the various metals, one upon another, providing extremely attractive colour effects which must have been admired in all their glory at many a court ceremony.

Florence, Museo Nazionale (Bargello), 760 and 761

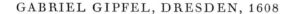

66   GABRIEL GIPFEL, DRESDEN, 1608

Hunting trousse of Christian II, Elector of Saxony (1583—1611; Elector, 1591)

The Saxon court was always inclined to collect objets d'art and beautiful arms. In the case of the Elector Christian II the neighbouring imperial court in Prague, where Rudolph II (Emperor, 1576–1612) accumulated his own unique treasures, appears to have served as a stimulus that furthered this tendency. There was great envy, much exchanging of presents, and tremendous rivalry in the purchase of precious objects.

Towards the end of 1608 Christian II acquired a hunting trousse that, in its sparkling late renaissance magnificence, was intended rather to be looked at than to be used. It consists of hunting dagger, set of knives, bag, hunting horn with straps, "hunting cords" for tying up small game, and a dog's collar. Coloured enamel ornaments, hunting scenes, and emeralds in rectangular settings form an overlay on the once green velvet or golden metal background. The simple hunting sword hilt follows the form of Dutch originals. The blade of the cleaver, used for breaking up the game, is etched with the Saxon coat of arms, the date and the prince's initials CDAHZSC (Christian der Andere, Herzog zu Sachsen, Churfürst = The Other Christian, Duke of Saxony, Elector). However, the initials refer to the person who placed the order and not to the eventual owner because the trousse was presented by the Elector at Christmas to his elder brother John George I (1585–1656; Elector, 1611).

Dresden, Historisches Museum, M 264

Pallasch with scabbard from the "Hungarian" parade garniture of the Duke Maximilian I of Bavaria (1573–1651; Duke, 1597; Elector, 1623)

From the 15th century on, the all too powerful Turkish Empire continued to exert increasing pressure on Central Europe. In 1529, a Moslem army camped for the first time before the gates of Vienna and during the 16th century there were constant invasions of Austria by the Turks with frequent counter-thrusts by the imperial troops into a disputed Hungary that was divided into two camps. Temporary calm came only at the beginning of the 17th century. The Eastern part of Central Europe had learned not only to fear its unrelenting enemy, but also to appreciate some of his qualities. The Janissaries' courage was considered exemplary. Islam's highly developed ornamental art, created as it was without recourse to pictures, the brilliant jewels that enriched its splendid possessions, all fascinated leading circles. In Turkish or Hungarian costume the Archduke Ferdinand II and his retinue organised "Hussar Tournaments" in Prague and Vienna around the middle of the 16th century, and for these festivals the Viennese goldsmith Nikolaus Gross supplied arms in Hungaro-Turkish style.

This fashion also reached the courts of Dresden and Munich. The saddle and bridle, mace, and the sword from the Bavarian National Museum shown here originate from the armoury of the Duke Maximilian I of Bavaria. Dresden owns almost identical counterparts, probably ordered by the Elector Christian II of Saxony (died 1611) in 1610 on the occasion of his visit to the Emperor Rudolph II in Prague. His successor John George I presumably accepted and paid for the garniture from the Prague goldsmith Johann Michel in his stead around 1613/14. From this we can also identify the master and date of the Munich garniture.

The sword illustrated here is a so-called "pallasch", a broadsword with straight blade related to the war knife carried by the Hungarians and Croats, who were loyal to the emperor, in addition to a slender "estoc" and an Oriental sabre. Eventually the pallasch became accepted as a cavalry weapon by nearly every army in Europe. The pommel and the double-angled quillons follow the hilt type of European war knives, whilst the long scabbard clamps are in the Eastern style. The parts are shaped in the form of a lion's head, a lion's claw, dragons and dragons' tails of gilded silver richly encrusted with Bohemian garnets, amethysts, topazes and rock crystal. Apart from the jewels, both hilt and scabbard are decorated with the colourful Hungarian filigree enamel which we have already noticed on the Dresden Electoral Sword of 200 years earlier. The flat blade, marked with the Wolf of Passau, has gold and silver damascening at its base in an arrangement that clearly shows the influence of the painting on Turkish flags.

Although the decoration of the garniture was based to such a marked degree on Eastern models, with its confusing division into many small parts, its iridescent colours, the many-layered, transparent structure of overlaid ornament, it nevertheless largely corresponds to such purely European works in the late renaissance style as the burgonet and shield of Gasparo Mola in Florence.

Munich, Bayerisches Nationalmuseum, N 2526 and N 2527

The gilt rapier of Christian II, Elector of Saxony (1583–1611; Elector, 1591)

Next to the imperial court, those of Bavaria and Saxony in particular led the field in pomp, splendour and patronage. The Dresden armoury was unable to compete with the imperial one with regard to the possession of armour, but it had a unique collection of swords and daggers of the highest quality the equal of which could hardly be found elsewhere.

Among the gems of the Dresden swords is a rapier with gilded and blue enamelled hilt of cast brass which, according to the inventory, was presented by the Saxon Court Marshal Christoph von Loos to the Elector Christian II in 1610. Every part of the hilt has in this case been transformed into a minor work of art. The pommel takes the form of a woman's head crowned with feathers; the guard is shaped like a serpent-headed female figure; the lower guard is fashioned as a siren with outspread wings flanked by two dragons' heads. It is quite impossible to be sure whether its maker intended it as the combination of slanted *pas d'âne* with two recurved quillons common at the time, or whether this was the beginning of the large inclined shell-guard.

The fantastic repertoire of the artists of Fontainebleau and the ornament engravers of Antwerp was being used most freely at this time. *Dresden, Historisches Museum*

Wheel-lock rifle of Sigismund III Vasa (1556–1632; King of Poland, 1587–1632; of Sweden, 1592–99)

As a work of art this splendid rifle reflects the taste of the very last stage of the renaissance. Plain surfaces enclose the heavy, compact form, the weight being as far as possible balanced by the finest and most close decoration. Neither the barrelsmith nor the maker of the etched lock left his mark but the master of the inlaid stock, who is unfortunately unidentified, signed it with the initials HL. For no apparent reason he included the figures of gaily tumbling putti and amoretti among a surging pattern of scrolls and tendrils. On the underside of the stock he placed fretted female figures on a silk ground, among them representations of the Virtues.

Following Double Page

The weapon becomes a historical document thanks to the engraved royal arms on its butt-plate. The Polish and Lithuanian coats of arms lead, while those of Sweden and the Vasa family take second place. The gun belonged to the Roman Catholic Sigismund III, who was deposed by his uncle Charles IX in Protestant Sweden and against whom, from 1601 to 1611, he fought a violent war the story of which is recorded on the lock-plate. It shows how Poles armed in the Eastern fashion, winged horsemen with their typical bird's wings, targe-shield and sabre, routed Swedish cavalry equipped with pistols in the style of the West. Only historical reasons can account for the fact that the gun ended up in Vienna. Sigismund was successively married to two Styrian princesses, cousins of the Emperor Rudolph II. Apparently the gun and its counterpart (Vienna, D 67) were presents from Constance to her husband – she was Queen of Poland from 1605 – and were returned to Austria with her dowry after the King's death.

Vienna, Waffensammlung, D 68

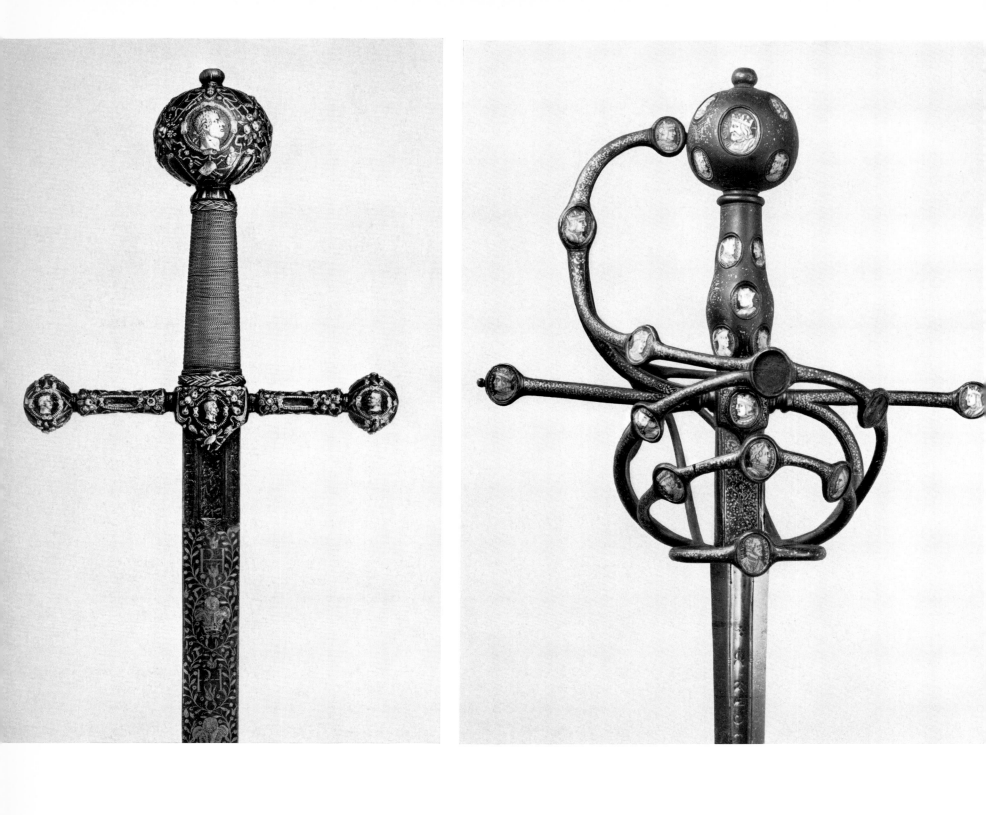

Sword of Henry, Prince of Wales (1594-1612)

ILLUSTRISSIMI GENEROSISSIMIQUE PRI. HENRICI
MAGNÆ BRITANNIÆ ET HYBERNIÆ PRINCIPIS.
Vera Effigies.

In 1607 when Louis XIII was still Dauphin he sent Henry, Prince of Wales and heir to the throne of Great Britain, a present in token of his friendship. The gift consisted of a brace of pistols, a sword, and a gilded and enamelled armour for horse and rider of which the pistols and the armour have been lost. The latter was probably an embossed and heavily gilded piece with applied colour enamel in the style of the oval shield of King Charles IX (1550–74) in the Louvre. Such later developments of Henry II's fine parade arms, though in a considerably coarser style, were made until well into the 17th century. The sword in the Wallace Collection is probably the only relic of Louis' gift. The blade bears the mark of the Solingen smith Clemens Horn. The gold ornament on the blued base of the blade shows a great likeness to those on Henry IV's rapier and dagger; on it, framed by laurel branches, are repeated the monogram PH of Prince Henry, who died tragically young. Emperors' heads are inlaid in silver against the dark chiselled steel of the simple cross-shaped hilt. The remaining silver damascening, representing festooned fruit and trophies of arms, is no longer flush with the surface but in bold relief, in a picturesque decorative style that is also found on German and English arms of about 1610–20.

The French royal swordsmith Pierre Vernier and the damascener Jean Petit, who both worked at the Louvre, may have created the sword for Prince Henry. On the other hand, evidence produced by Claude Blair, as yet unpublished, suggests that the sword is English, perhaps by Robert South, royal cutler. Its form, unusually simple for the period, suggests that it may have been intended as a sporting weapon for the tournament, as the medieval sword with the cross-hilt survived in this sphere and for ceremonial purposes.   *London, Wallace Collection, A 511*

PARIS, AFTER 1614

Rapier of Louis XIII, King of France (1601-43)

The House of Orleans died with King Henry III in 1589. Henry of Navarre (1553–1610), a Bourbon, ascended the French throne as Henry IV the same year, after the Edict of Nantes ended the civil war between Roman Catholics and Huguenots. A year later, in 1590, he courted Maria de' Medici, who, as Queen, was to bring the country as little good fortune as her predecessor of the same family. On the occasion of his wedding on 13th December 1600, Paris presented the King with a damascened rapier and dagger with inscriptions and little inlaid oval plaques of mother-of-pearl (Paris, J 380 and London, Wallace Collection, A 790).

A very similar counterpart, though with a richer hilt, is the rapier of his son, King Louis XIII. The weapon is dated 1614 on the Toledo blade made by Silvester Nieto. Its similarity and the date lead to the assumption that it was not only made in the same workshop but was also presented by the same person on the same occasion. In 1615 the 14 year-old King married the Spanish Princess Anne and, like his father, he may then have received this rapier from the city of Paris. It is finely damascened, but bears no inscriptions, to compensate for which the mother-of-pearl plaques are carved with the portraits and names of every French king up to and including Henry IV. The combination of inlaid precious metal wire with mother-of-pearl and the use of royal or imperial heads became extremely fashionable among French craftsmen at that time.   *Paris, Musée de l'Armée, J 381*

71 FRENCH, c. 1620

Pair of wheel-lock pistols

This unique pair of equestrian pistols inscribed AGRISOLE on the lower edge of the lock-plate
– made to be carried in saddle holsters – is practically unsurpassed in ingenuity and refinement
of design. One is inclined to assume that this inscription stands for a master's name, but it may
only identify their place of origin ''at Grisole'', as there is a small place called Grisolles to the
north of Toulouse. The early flintlock musket of one Phelipeau de Vrillière at Windsor Castle
(316) bears the comparable inscription ''Faict. A. Turene'' (made at Turenne, a tiny village
between Toulouse and Limoges). Although the Agrisole pistols show no other marks, are un-
dated and give no indication of their owner, their form, decoration and the construction of their
mechanism establish an obvious link with the best French work of around 1620.

The barrel is chiselled with delicate scrolls and the imperial double eagle is, surprisingly, placed
right at the top, followed by Judith, Juno, a Roman general, Venus and St George, each under
a canopy. They are clearly based on copper engravings by Etienne Delaune (1518/19–82).
Nobody else influenced gunsmiths of all kinds with his decorative patterns for so long as did
this court artist of King Henry II of France. The gently rounded and heavily gilded reliefs are
placed against a roughened dark background. The lock of pure French type and all the mounts
are ornamented by the same hand in a similar manner. The profusion of three-dimensional
figures shows the greatest possible likeness to the work of Jean Henequin at Metz in Lorraine:
the wheel-lock rifle he made for Louis XIII of France dated 1621 (Munich National Museum,
1733) and his engraved pattern book for gun locks of the same time. At the base of the cock,
which takes the shape of a dragon's head, crouches a bagpipe-playing ape. Nude male figures
are placed above the cock spring, leaning against it. The wheel retainer is a king, armed in
antique style, with sceptre and crown. Heads sprout, and tiny figures of the most delicate and
charming kind rest everywhere.

Eight medallions around the superbly elegant pommels point to the French kingdom. The
head of Henry IV of France (1553–1610; King, 1589) can be clearly recognised on the underside and probably also that of his son, Louis XIII (1601–43; King 1610). The Agrisole pistols
would have been worthy of a place in his armoury, which was equipped with arms of the
highest refinement. On all his small arms the King's original inventory number was stamped
on the underside of the stock in front of the trigger guard. This, however, is not the case with
the Agrisole pistols. Were they perhaps a present from Louis XIII to some highly distinguished
personage indicated by the double eagle right at the top of the barrel?

Vienna, Waffensammlung, A 2241

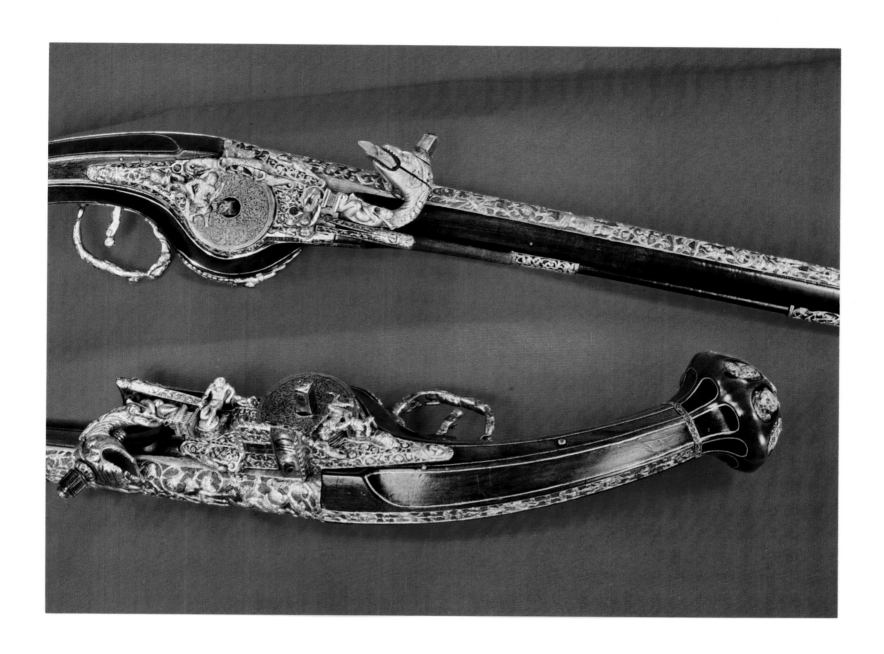

72 EUGUI NEAR PAMPLONA (NAVARRE, PYRENEES), 1620

Round shield from an armour garniture of Philip III, King of Spain (1578–1621; King, 1598)

An extremely heavy parade armour, reaching to the knees and of exotic appearance, together with a second helmet, chanfron and saddle (A 350–A 353) are to be found at the Real Armería, Madrid. From old inventories we learn the place and date of its production: Pamplona, March 1620. The workshops in the disputed Basque border territory between Spain and France from which the iron ore came, were in fact situated at the small village of Eugui, high in the mountains. The neighbouring city of Pamplona undertook the marketing of its products. There is no doubt that King Philip III of Spain was the purchaser. In 1613/14 he ordered three similar boy's armours for his sons Philip IV, later to become Velazquez's patron, Charles and Ferdinand. He himself owned a half-armour from Eugui-Pamplona. It reached to the hips, had the enormous total weight of 152 lb, and bore the Philippus-monogram PHS III. The date of its manufacture is not recorded.

On the basis of some emblematic illustration, it has been argued that Philip III intended to present this three-quarter armour of 1620 to his brother-in-law and ally, Charles Emanuel II of Savoy (1562–1630; Duke, 1580). This would mean that it was never used or that it was returned from Turin to Madrid before 1652, when it was mentioned in the inventory. The evidence is not convincing and this must be another armour that belonged to the King himself. It is not known when and how the round shield or rondache, which belonged to the garniture, left Madrid. Recently it was found in Linz, where it now hangs in the arms hall of the old Austrian Hapsburg residence on the Schlossberg. A master in the south-west corner of Europe once again adopted and summarised ideas from south, north and east. His was one of the last workshops to operate just before armour production ceased to be a flourishing and independent craft. The classic banded decoration found on German renaissance armours supplied the ornamental scheme. The frame of wavy lines with lilies goes back to the gilded brass borders of late gothic armour. From 1540 onwards, the motive of medallions within ornamental bands was used hundreds of times by German, French and Italian etchers. The S-pattern, the arrangement of the motives as if strung on a continuous bar, points to the Milanese master IO of c. 1600. The very fine gold damascening, the three-dimensional silver damascening and the pearled lines are reminiscent of Milan. An oriental feeling pervades the whole. This is not only due to the Eastern character of the legendary figures, monsters and dragons in iron bas-relief on the medals. All the works of this workshop (in Madrid, Paris and Malta) leave an overriding impression of something exotic. The mozarabic, the Mohammedan ornamental art of past centuries, survived in this decorative movement, and it is significant in this context that the clumsy figurative illustrations are on the level of folk art.

Linz, Oberösterreichisches Landesmuseum, C 1997

73 FRENCH, c.1630–40

Parade rapier of Christian (V),
Crown Prince of Denmark (1603–47)

Under King Christian IV (1577–1648; King, 1588) Denmark experienced not only the zenith of its political power but also of its culture. The battle between the Emperor and the Protestants that broke out in Bohemia in 1618 was the beginning of the Thirty Years War. When the cause of the German Lutheran Party appeared to be lost, Christian IV took over its leadership in 1625 and obtained the support of England and France against the Emperor. In 1629 the war came to a disastrous end for Denmark and her leading role had to be ceded to the new great power, Sweden.

In the course of his anti-Hapsburg policies, Louis XIII and the omnipotent Cardinal Richelieu not only supported the enemies of Ferdinand II (1578–1637; Emperor, 1619) with money and arms, but they also endeavoured to ensure their continued assistance by means of valuable presents. In this way French influence and art arrived in the Scandinavian countries. The parade rapier of King Christian IV's son, Crown Prince Christian (V), is quite obviously French. Similarly superb pastel-coloured enamel on gold is otherwise found only on some French parade hilts. The wedding in 1634 of the Crown Prince – who incidentally never reigned – may have been the reason why the rapier was made. The radically simplified form of the hilt is in keeping with Dutch tastes, traceable in the last resort to the reforms of the great Maurice of Orange. The artistic medium, however, is French. The favourite animal motive of the French late renaissance, the serpent-dragon with its swollen, scaled and winged body, forms the knuckle bow and quillon. The grip ends in a lion's-head pommel which is constructed of peculiar gristly shapes and pendant lobes of skin. Just as in the middle of the 16th century in Antwerp, ornamental engravings emerged now in 1630–40 showing unpleasant decorative elements that appear to have been inspired by corpses in the anatomical theatres, by mucus membrane and internal organs. This trend is the last manifestation of the late renaissance and is appropriately known to German art historians as *Knorpelstil*, or "cartilage style". Although normally not particularly attractive, it has in this example of the minor arts at any rate presented us with one very charming work. *Copenhagen, Rosenborg Castle, 17*

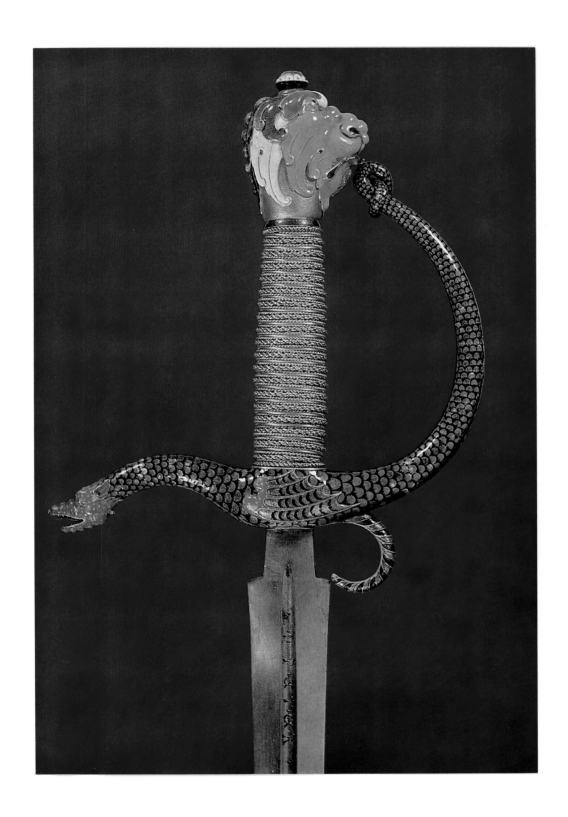

74 HANS SCHMIDT, FERLACH, 1628

Silver wheel-lock rifle of Leopold V, Archduke of Austria (1586–1632; Lord of the Tyrol, 1618)

It is well known that the traditional and still flourishing gunsmith manufactory at Ferlach in Carinthia dates back to 1550–60. Until recently, however, it was not possible to name even one single work from the early Ferlach period. We owe a debt of gratitude to Karl Dinklage for his original research at the Carinthian Provincial Archive, groundwork that now enables us to recognise real masterpieces of the gunsmith's craft of the second quarter of the 17th century as Ferlach achievements. *See also following double page*

The master in charge, artist, organiser and "*Verleger*", that is the wholesaler, was, as we now know, the ingenious gunstockmaker Hans Schmidt of Riedlingen on the Upper Danube in Swabia, a subject of the Hapsburg Regent of the Tyrolean-Swabian estates. In 1628 he manufactured for his master, as the records put it, a *Zielrohr*; that is, a target weapon as opposed to one for deerstalking. It was an exceedingly laborious task and a planned companion piece was never made. The master said that he would not undertake such toil again. Later, however, probably in 1645, he produced a simplified version for the Lord of the Manor of Ferlach, Count Siegmund Ludwig von Dietrichstein (1610–98) (Vienna D 108). Hans Schmidt died in 1669, an honoured and wealthy man.

The silver gun of Leopold V, Emperor Ferdinand II's younger brother, bears not only the master's initials HSCH, but also his coat of arms which is identical with his seal on a letter at the Carinthian Provincial Archive. Thus a great treasure, perhaps the most superb wheel-lock rifle ever made, has been acknowledged as Austrian work.

The wheel-lock alone shows, apart from the masterly engraving of the lock-plate, two outstanding details; the cock in the shape of a fantastic bird's head and a miniature lion apparently seeking to arrest the whirring wheel with his teeth. But the greatest profusion of the magnificent decoration is spread over the stock and the accompanying circular powder flask. On the black wood background are inlaid little plaques, scrolls and pegs of silver, all shaped and engraved by the hand of Hans Schmidt, to form entire scenes amid landscapes. Every form of the chase is illustrated most charmingly on the stock, and the flask shows verses of Psalm 144 and the parable of the Good Shepherd. All the figures are presented in the heavy costume of the early baroque. The name, coat of arms and portrait of its noble owner occupy pride of place. The masterly execution of the work justifies the high esteem in which Hans Schmidt was held.

Vienna, Waffensammlung, D 93 and 93a

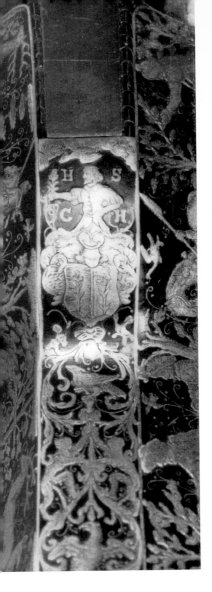

LEOPOLDVS·DEI·GRA·ARCHI...

75 GERMAN, 1630–40

The armour of Johann, Count Sporck, General of the Imperial Cavalry (1601–79)

The army reforms introduced by Prince Maurice of Orange during the Netherlands' fight for freedom against Spain revolutionised warfare throughout Europe around 1590. Not only Dutch tactics but also her armament were copied. The heavy cavalry soldier now wore armour in the Dutch style with close burgonet, tassets reaching to the knee, and strong riding boots replacing greaves and sabatons. After 1600, only those members of the nobility who wished to represent themselves as knights of tradition still wore greaves and sabatons.

Louis XIII of France (King, 1610–43) had already revealed in his boyhood an inclination towards knightly sports and beautiful armours. Contrary to all the signs of the times he dreamt of a revival of the *gens d'armes*, heavily armoured lancers enrolled from the aristocracy, who even then were being replaced increasingly by the cuirassiers, armoured cavalry whose prime weapon was the pistol. Nevertheless we owe it to his interest that tournament armour experienced a final brief international flowering, and that the armourers based their work for the aristocracy on French models whose typical features, such as borders enlivened by filed ornaments or the direct attachment of the tassets to the breastplate, were copied everywhere. Apart from Louis XIII's armours in Paris itself, there is an armour in Vienna, which is one of the most beautiful examples of this very late armourer's art. Its owner was General of the Imperial Cavalry Johann, Count Sporck, an old warrior who had proved himself during the Thirty Years War and who in 1664, as an old man under Montecuccoli, successfully fought against the Turks at St Gotthard. The heavy, dark blue armour is decorated only with wavy gilded borders, ornamental rivets and red velvet pickadils. Its proportions emphasise, as did the dress of the period, the thickset body ideal of Rubens' day. The old soldier, proud of his steel parade costume, had himself portrayed in it on his tomb in the deanery church at Lysa (Lissa) on the river Elbe.

Although people continued to have themselves painted wearing armour, its time had passed by the end of the Thirty Years War. The heavy cavalry retained only the burgonet and cuirass, the officer only the gorget, the so-called *Feuermantel*, as a sign of rank. Firearms, which had already displaced the lance, held the field. Henceforth the craftsmen's entire ingenuity was concentrated on firearms and the indispensable sword.

Vienna, Heeresgeschichtliches Museum, NI. 81

ILL.ᵐᵉ ATQVE EXCELL.ᵐᵉ D.D. IOANNES À TSERCLAS S.R.I. COMES, BARO DE TILLY ET MARBAIS &c. SAC. CAES. MAIT. NEC NON SER. ELECTORIS AC BAVARIÆ DVCIS. LOCVM TENENS GENERALIS, CONSILIARIVS ET RESPECTIVE CAMERARIVS.

Philipp Sadeler fecit et excudit.

76 LAZARINO COMINAZZO (BARRELSMITH) AND
FRANCESCO GARATTA (LOCKSMITH AND IRON-CHISELLER),
BRESCIA, c.1650

Pair of wheel-lock pistols, probably of
Ernst Salentin, Altgraf of Salm-Dyck (1621–84)

Around the middle of the 17th century, armour as a symbol of chivalry faded into the background. The rapier, too, became unimportant compared with the brilliant role it had played
during the renaissance. Its colour was now a drab grey-black and its form greatly simplified.
It gradually became clear that firearms were the weapons that stood in the forefront of any
new development, on which all attention centred, which occupied all artists and forged a link
between them. The whole of Europe now produced rifles and pistols of outstanding quality.
Even in the smallest village, technical experiments were proceeding and there was great
rivalry in the art of decoration. Prince and aristocrat used pistols on horseback, in combat and
for the hunt. This explains the tremendous demand and the fact that so many masterpieces
have been preserved.

One of the oldest and most renowned places in which the craft of the gunsmith flourished is
Brescia and the near-by Gardone di Val Trompia in the mountains. Members of the Cominazzo
dynasty became the most famous barrelsmiths and there is evidence that they flourished from
the 15th century until 1877. About a dozen masters of this name worked throughout the 17th century. However, the fact must not be overlooked that the most coveted characteristic of Brescian
pistols and carbines was the work of other masters, namely the inlays that were sunk into the
stock, usually with the appearance of lace cut out of iron and then engraved. The barrels bear
the signature LAZARINO COMINAZZO, but inside the lock-plates are the initials FG with the
lily of Francesco Garatta, who signed the delicate decorative work. In this case, an exceptional
one, the inlays are of shining gilt brass, the burr-walnut stocks lending warmth to the strong
colours. The mark of the princely Salm-Reiferscheidt armoury and the number 25 are stamped on the lower edge of the butt. The pistols made the long journey from the old Westphalian
moated Dyck Castle to the Pacific coast.

Norman Blank Collection, Beverley Hills (California, USA)

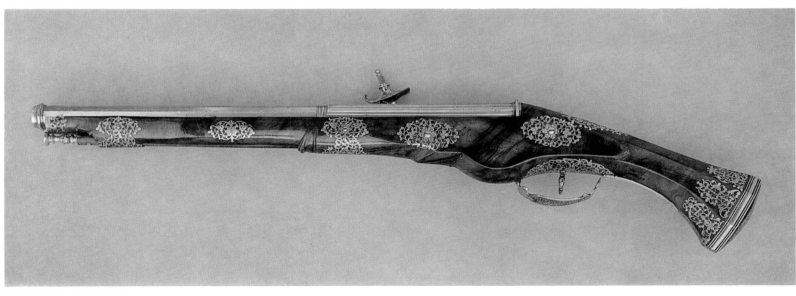

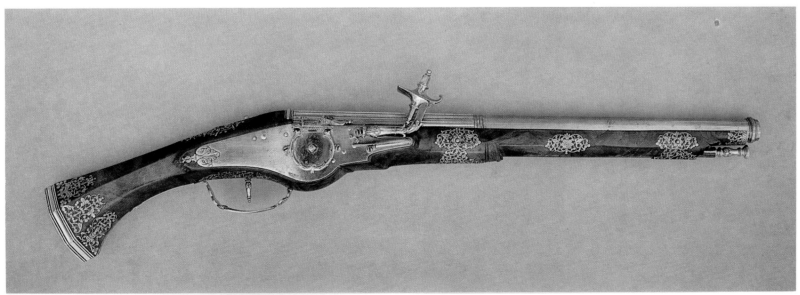

Baldric and rapier of Charles X Gustav, King of Sweden (1622–60; King, 1654)

Religious zeal and the concept of a great empire on the Baltic caused the Swedish King Gustavus Adolphus (1594–1632; King, 1611) to intervene in the German religious war. Dashing from victory to victory, the great King met his death near Lützen in 1632, leaving only a daughter as heir to the throne. She was the highly educated Christine of Sweden, who renounced her claim to the crown in 1654 after having spent some time in France, which she so admired. Eventually she became a Roman Catholic convert and died in Rome in 1689. It was during her reign that French cultural influence replaced the previously prevalent German tastes. A greatly experienced soldier took Christine's place on the throne, her cousin from the family of Pfalz-Zweibrücken who became King Charles X Gustav.

On the occasion of his coronation and wedding in 1654 he had a magnificent wardrobe made for himself, the major part of which has been preserved. At the time, the French court of Louis XIV (King, 1643–1715) was the model which everybody tried to emulate in all things. It is not surprising therefore that most of the clothes and materials were ordered in Paris. At no other time in European history was men's dress so bulky and effeminate as around 1650 to 1660, the beginning of the late baroque, when it consisted of a huge hat, turn-down collar, short horseman's cloak, *Rheingrafenhose* open at the lower end, buckled shoes or boots; everything trimmed with cord, rosettes and lace. Dutch paintings, such as those by Terborch, show us what they looked like. Part of the costume was the sword belt, which as a rule was no longer buckled around the waist but ran as a broad band from the right shoulder to the left hip like those on which the Turks carried their sabres.

Charles X's baldric is covered with close golden embroidery in relief, entirely in accordance with the heavy baroque style. Sculptural groups of fighting animals, the conglomeration of which is reminiscent of such scenes by Peter Paul Rubens, intermingle with tendrils, blossoms and foliage. The rapier's iron chiselling is designed in similar high relief with the same *horror vacui*. Military arms and courtier's arms were now of different design. The former retained its strong hilt, whilst the courtier's rapier only possessed its rudiments: short quillons, two small arms of the hilt and two horizontally arranged shells. From now until well into the 19th century the courtier's rapier retained this type of hilt, usually also equipped with a knuckle bow.

Stockholm, Livrustkammaren, 3440

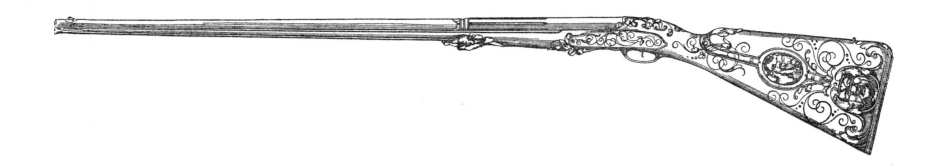

78 LE CONTE (GUNSMITH) AND JEAN BERAIN THE ELDER (STOCKMAKER), PARIS, c.1660

Flintlock "Wender" gun of Louis XIV, King of France (1638–1715; King, 1643)

The most richly decorated gun in French gunmaking history was presented by the Sun King's ambassador to the young King of Sweden, Charles IX (1655–97; King, 1660) at Stockholm Castle on 12th December 1673. Many other arms of most perfect design were included in this gift, which was of great political significance. The gun bears the French King's initials LDGR (Ludovicus Dei Gratia Rex) on the upper edge of the stock. It is due to the alliance with France, which had proved so successful during the Thirty Years War, that Swedish collections are so richly endowed with major works of French gunsmiths and textile designers.

From the technical point of view the gun presents an example of the many experiments to increase the rate of fire of the cumbersome muzzle-loader. Several types of repeating guns had emerged as far back as the 15th century. There already were breech-loaders in the early 16th century when wheel-lock guns were first produced. In the 17th century, which was the age of technology and the natural sciences, amazing progress was made in developing the magazine rifle. But lack of mechanical precision made mass production impossible and resulted in surprising though individual solutions which were constantly changing and were confined to the favoured classes who formed the highest strata of society. In the case of the gun illustrated here two barrels lie one above the other *(Bockbüchse)* and can be revolved *(Wender)*. Each barrel has its own priming pan but a common cock fires both.

Artistically, the gun belongs to the pre-classic era of parade arms craft under Louis XIV, a period that lasted from 1655 to 1665 and is characterised by the signed pieces and the engraved pattern book of Thuraine and Le Hollandois, the pseudonym of Adrian Reynier. The otherwise unknown gunsmith Le Conte signed his name on the lock-plate. The barrels are gold damascened with hunting scenes and figure medallions showing Minerva. Every part of the lock is either chiselled or engraved with figures and scrolls, the cock screw taking the form of a magnificent lion's head. The fretted silver inlay on which one finds the signature "Berain fecit" is of the most delicate. The signature is that of Jean Bérain the Elder (1639–1711), one of the most versatile decorative artists of his time who, in 1659, published an engraved pattern book of designs for gun ornaments. In him the decorative skill of Etienne Delaune (1518/19–82) was once more revived. Nearly all the motives and the method of their arrangement go back to Delaune's originals: apes, birds and serpents within scrolls; Minerva and Mars reclining on weapons, as well as Apollo, amoretti and grotesque masks on medallions. A work like this was designed and made to be the subject of inexhaustible critical observation.

Stockholm, Livrustkammaren, 3888

79 FRENCH, c. 1680

Spontoon of the Guards of King Louis XIV of France (1638–1715; King, 1643)

Under the "Sun-King", Louis XIV, France became the most active military power in Europe. Louis' campaigns against the Holy Roman Empire and Holland, his war to secure the Bourbons' succession in Spain, his endeavours to establish colonial power, are all well known. The structure of his army was copied everywhere, as were the magnificence of his castles and the splendour of his court.

A bodyguard, the *Gardes de la Manche* formed by 24 aristocrats, was at the King's disposal. Two of its members took turns in carrying out their duties dressed in a white, gold-embroidered tunic, and carrying a rapier and "spontoon", a shortened variety of the partisan, which also served as a badge of officer's rank in the army.

The spontoons of the royal guard are worked in burnished and heavily gilt pierced steel. Above the socket adorned with lilies and crown the globe rests in a flower-cup and is covered with French lilies. The King in the role of triumphant victor being crowned by Fame and surrounded by trophies is enthroned on a quadriga whose steeds have trampled down eagle and lion, the heraldic beasts of the Hapsburgs. Louis' symbol, the sun, rises above all this with the motto "Nec pluribus impar," which freely translated means "And the equal of several opponents." In this way the illustrations reveal in the baroque's dramatic way something of the King's political concepts.   *Paris, Musée de l'Armée, K 496*

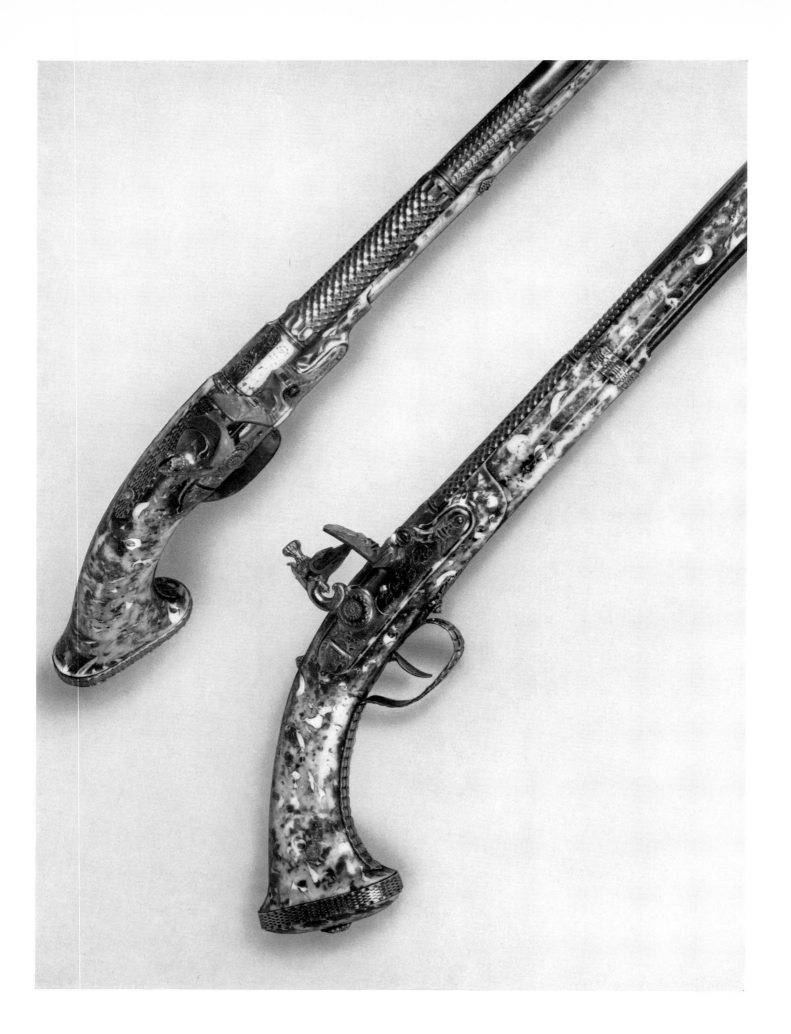

80 CHRISTOPH TREFFLER, WEST GERMANY, c.1660

Pair of flintlock pistols

New ages developed their own special preferences for characteristic raw materials that reached the West via the newly-opened trade routes, particularly from the new colonial territories in the East. Tortoise-shell and ivory are the fashionable materials which characterise the middle of the 17th century and subsequent decades. By about 1650 to 1660 the baroque had achieved a classic firmness and clarity. The age of Louis XIV of France (1638–1715; King, 1643) had dawned, an age that was to give a tremendous fillip to the gunsmith's craft. Paris exerted its influence in the first place on her border territories, the Netherlands, Lorraine, the Rhineland and Alsace, but later it made itself strongly felt throughout Germany. Comprehensive research into this highly impressive movement is still in its infancy.

The master who made the Vienna pistols with their brown speckled ivory stocks is only revealed by the engraved signature on the lock-plate. He was the otherwise quite unknown Christoph Treffler, who did not give his place of origin. We must deduce the date when they were made from the features of the style. Purchaser and owner have to be sought in the very highest circles. The barrels and locks, with the exception of the steel springs and the battery on which the falling cock struck fire, are of heavily gilded bronze, the mounts of massive silver. Sparse engraving with a few leaves and blossoms constitutes the only figurative decoration. Apart from this the whole is dominated by a purely ornamental scale and trellis pattern of charming purity. Each screw in the shape of a rosette, to be interpreted either as a flower or the sun, is a masterpiece of decoration. Whose were the favoured hands that were allowed to use arms of such amazing precision?   *Vienna, Waffensammlung, A 1472 and A 1473*

Flintlock gun, with cameos, of the Emperor Ferdinand III (1608–57; Emperor, 1637) or Emperor Leopold I (1640–1705; Emperor, 1658)

The flintlock, also called the French lock, was invented in the first decade of the 17th century. The inventor, or at least the maker of the earliest preserved flintlock guns, was Marin le Bourgeoys of Lisieux in Normandy (deceased 1634). Henry IV and above all his son Louis XIII of France (1601–43) were the owners of the first and at the same time the most beautiful small arms with the new mechanism, which soon conquered all Europe where they continued in almost exclusive use until the early 19th century. Parallel to this the old lock types maintained their position with a certain pertinacity in a number of other nations, the wheel-lock among the Germans, the snaphance lock among the Italians, the Miquelet lock among the Spaniards. In the end they all gave way to the flintlock, just as the national type of butt – be it the German or the Spanish form or the musket stock – gave way to the classic French gun butt of the 17th century, which today still rules supreme.

The flintlock of the splendid Vienna piece is marked "in achen". The stock is uniquely decorated with carved cameos of the 16th century or with copies of them. The unknown gunsmith must therefore have worked quite close to the French border under the direct influence of the French. Above the chamber the plain, blued barrel is ornamentally carved. The lock is rather simply engraved. The wooden stock was probably supplied plain to Vienna where it received its unusual, in fact extremely odd, decoration consisting of hard stones cut in relief, called in Italian "cameo", that are surrounded by mother-of-pearl plaques, mounted semi-precious stones and countless seed pearls and enamel studs. This decoration is typical of the style of the "cabinet specimens" exemplified by the goblets, bowls, necklaces and other jewellery of the emperors in the 17th century and of the imperial workshops which supplied their art collections. This curious weapon was surely intended less for practical use than as a rarity, made specifically as a cabinet specimen to be exhibited and admired.

Vienna, Waffensammlung, D 237

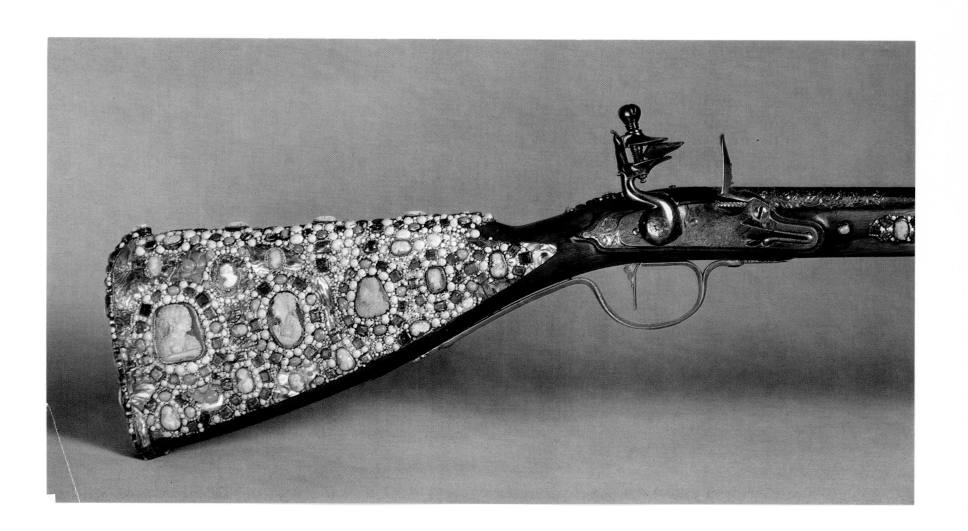

Pair of wheel-lock pistols

Between 1650 and 1670 the production of extravagant pistols with stocks carved from one piece of ivory flourished in the Dutch town of Maastricht in the Duchy of Limburg. Ivory had played a dominating part in small religious sculpture during the early and late Middle Ages. As far back as the early 17th century it had, in Augsburg and more especially in the Netherlands, already been incorporated into ceremonial goblets with rich gold mounts. Now it again became a precious and fashionable material. A whole school spread from Maastricht where masters such as Johan Louroux, Jacob Kosters and De la Pierre marked their works. Their style of ivory stock was copied at Sedan as well as in Aix-la-Chapelle and even in Vienna. It has since been possible to establish that the master "La Marre à Vienne" was Jacob la Mort de la Marre from Paris, who worked as royal gunsmith in Vienna from about 1680 to 1700.

The pistols are always of the same type. The butt ends in a masterly carved head of a warrior with characteristic features and fashionable moustache, but with a helmet of antique appearance, with dragons and plumes of feathers spreading above it. On the back of the butt and around the opening for the ramrod are striking grotesque heads. The lockplates and the section of the barrels over the chamber are chiselled and engraved with hunting scenes. At the side of the wheel one can read MAASTRICHT. Wheel-lock mechanisms were still being constructed there around this time and not only in Germany. The Netherlands have on several occasions made valuable contributions to the gunsmith's craft of the West and research into this is by no means complete, but these ivory pistols constitute a well-known achievement. The destruction of Maastricht by Louis XIV of France in 1673 put a sudden end to the Dutch national school.

New York, Metropolitan Museum of Art, 14. 25. 1432

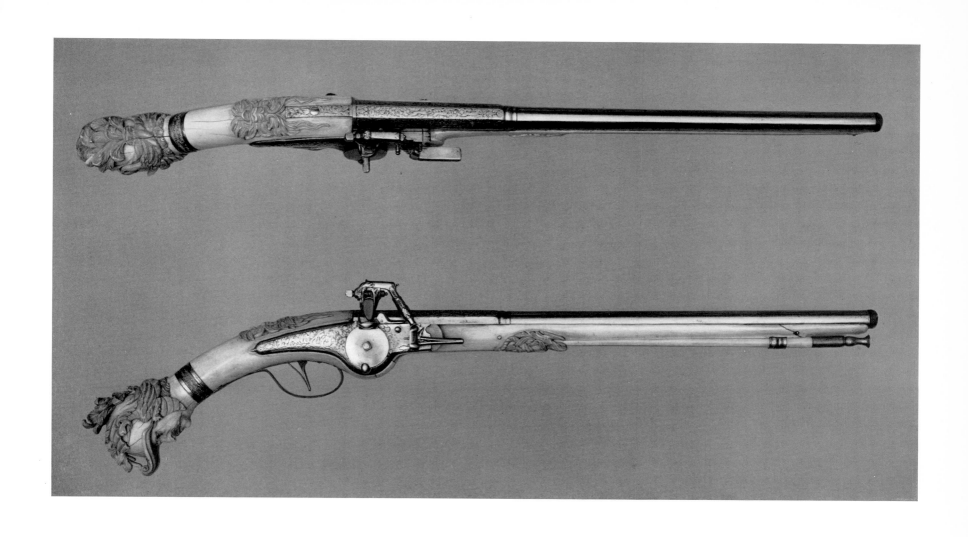

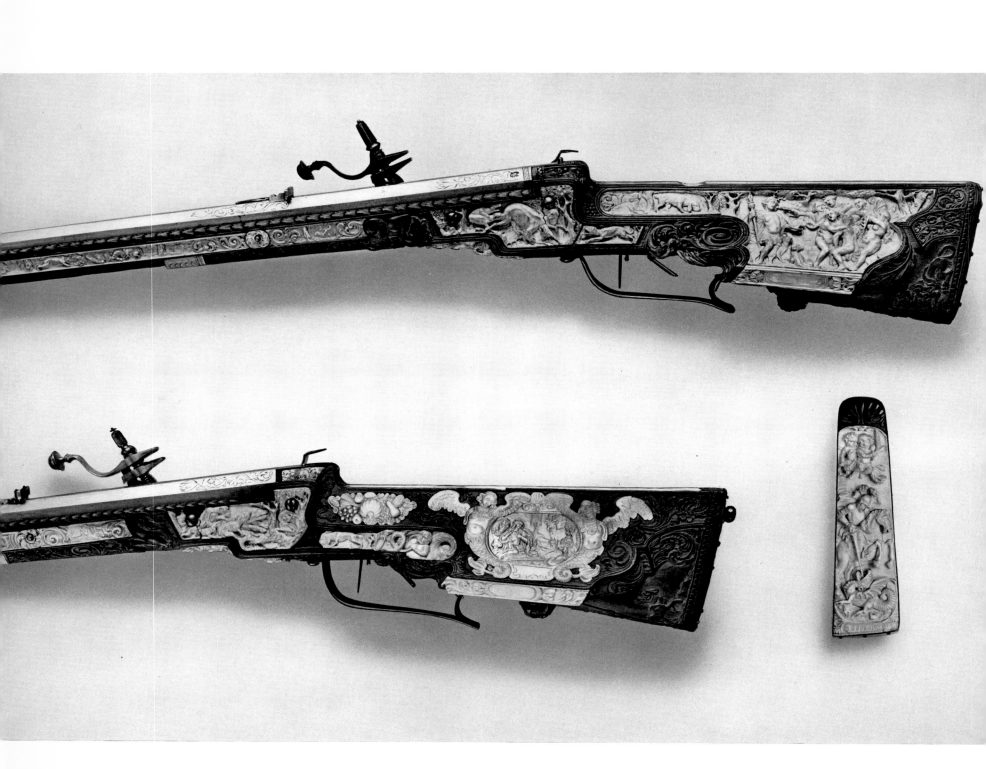

83 JOHANN HAAS (GUNSMITH) AND
JOHANN MICHAEL MAUCHER (CARVER AND GUNSTOCKMAKER), SCHWÄBISCH-GMÜND, 1682 AND 1671 RESPECTIVELY

Two wheel-lock rifles, the first of which was made for a Duke of Württemberg

The political disunity of Germany had decisive consequences on the arts. The need for recognition was met by the purchase of works of art and by promotion and patronage which spread to the courts of even the smallest principalities. Not only the famous capitals and the independent free towns of the empire, but quite a number of smaller towns and villages established, for instance, gunsmiths' workshops of astonishingly high quality. Schwäbisch-Gmünd was made famous by the Maucher family of craftsmen whose most important member was Johann Michael, a carver not only of goblets, bowls and groups of figures, but also of gunstocks the dark timber of which was carved and inlaid with ivory reliefs and engraved mother-of-pearl plaques. These are dispersed between Chicago and Dresden, London and Graz, while Munich has a whole series, as well as pistols and powder flasks. The two dated rifles in Munich illustrated here fully reveal the intricate profusion and the opulent richness of their style.

The barrels bear the mark HVG (Haas von Gmünd) of Johann Haas and the unicorn mark of the Gmünd Guild. The stocks are carved with the initials MM of Michael Maucher, whose skill can best be seen on the cheek rests of the butt. The upper rifle, with the Württemberg coat of arms, shows Diana and Actaeon, hunting scenes in ivory, and a lion and ape with dense foliage carved in the wood. The lower has hunts and a horn-blowing child in ivory on the stock; St George on the patchbox cover; the legend of St Hubert, framed by winged mermaids, and a wreath of fruit in carved mother-of-pearl on the cheek rest. There is little evidence of a carefully considered scheme. Hunting scenes intermingle with fabulous animals, Greek mythology with saintly legend. What is decisive is the decorative effect of the whole, which inspires admiration by its display of such virtuosity. Patterns for Michael Maucher's illustrations have so far been found in the works of Jost Amman of Frankfurt and Adriaen Collaert of Antwerp, both prolific engravers in the late 16th century, to whom craftsmen still turned a hundred years later. *Munich, Bayerisches Nationalmuseum, W 623 and W 627*

84 MICHAEL GULL (GUNSMITH), VIENNA, c.1670

Wheel-lock rifle with ivory stock and powder flask of the Emperor Leopold I (1640–1705; Emperor, 1658)

The octagonal barrel is "rifled", that is, provided with shallow grooves to improve the accuracy of the bullet, is adorned with carved floral scrolls above the chamber, and bears the signature and the punched mark of Michael Gull, who became a master in Vienna in 1647 and later made interesting breech-loaders. The lockplate, with arms, trophies and a stag hunt, and the cock are decorated in the manner of the school of iron-chiselling of Eger in Bohemia. The Hapsburg lion fighting a dolphin – symbolising the French enemy – attracts immediate attention. The fretted gilt double eagle on the wheel cover indicates the imperial owner, the Emperor Leopold I, who throughout his reign had to conduct a murderous war on two fronts against the Turks and the French. Trigger-guard and butt-plate are also heavily gilded. The hair-trigger mechanism with its needle-shaped second trigger to give the utmost accuracy in shooting is considered a Viennese invention.

The gunsmith collaborated with a previously unknown ivory-carver, one of several employed by Leopold I at his court with the title of *Kammerbeinstecher*. This artist carved the solid stock from an elephant's tusk and on its butt he worked combats between hounds and game. The stock still has the traditional clumsy German butt shape, following the trend of German high baroque art which relied on heavy and ample treatment for its effect.

That the powder flask belongs to this gun can be deduced not only from the material, which is ivory, and from the animal group arranged around it, but also from the white and bottle-green enamel, which is to be found at the end of the gunstock underneath the muzzle as well as on the flask's spout and the central cover which conceals a small watch. Such tricks gave pleasure to other princes of the 17th century too, among them a Duke of Brunswick or Pomerania and an Elector of Saxony.   *Vienna, Waffensammlung, D 239 and D 146*

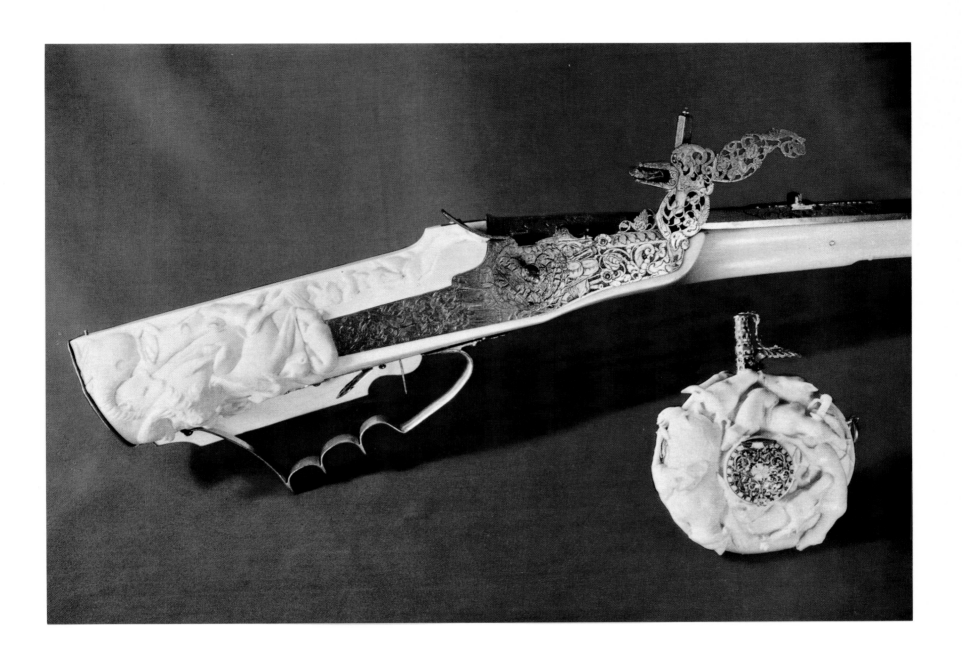

85   FRENCH, c. 1700

Burgonet and oval shield of Louis XIV, King of France (1638–1715; King, 1643)

Louis XIV's parade garniture may have been produced for an occasion of state, but it is much more likely that it was intended to be used in one of the pompous theatrical performances at Versailles in which the King himself played the lead. This garniture was part of an antique costume, in which the ruler would appear as Caesar or—as in this instance—as Perseus in the face of whose Medusa head the enemy was petrified. The inheritance of the renaissance with its ideals of ancient art and demeanour continued to hold sway. Louis XIV's helmet and shield are the last examples of a series of such parade garnitures that began with works made by the Milanese Filippo Negroli for the Emperor Charles V.

In the course of time, however, the exterior of such pseudo-antique accessories changed. Helmet and shield were no longer covered with the embossed reliefs which were so long cultivated in France, but were now adorned with gilded and engraved bronze appliqués on a chemically blued silver background. The figurative motives, although lively in expression and movement, were designed on a large scale and arranged so as to be easily appreciated. The ornamental decoration serves as a frame. The profoundly neo-classical sentiments of French art brought order and balance to the superabundance of the Italian late baroque, which nevertheless lies behind everything. The art of Gianlorenzo Bernini is the artistic and spiritual forebear of the dramatic Medusa head.

New York, Metropolitan Museum of Art, 04. 3. 259/60, from the Duke de Dino Collection

86 GIOVANNI BATTISTA FRANCINO THE YOUNGER (BARRELSMITH), BRESCIA, AND MATTEO ACQUA FRESCA (LOCKSMITH AND IRON-CHISELLER), BARGI NEAR BOLOGNA, c.1690

Pair of pistols with snaphance locks

The signature of the Lombard master GIO BTTA FRANCINO is to be found on the underside of the barrels. He supplied undecorated barrels from Brescia. At "Bargi nel Bolognese", the inscription on another work, indicates that M. Acqua Fresca decorated them in complete harmony with his lock and stock. In accordance with the French style, which had emerged before 1670, the octagonal barrel changes at the breech into sixteen facets and is of circular section at the muzzle. All these facets and round forms demand flat cutting and fine engraving. Barrel No. 1 shows a cavalier in contemporary dress by which the pieces can be dated. On barrel No. 2, a lady with mirror, Sapientia or Vanitas, Wisdom or Vanity, turns towards him. Two busts facing each other on the thumb-plate correspond to these. The lady's hair is dressed high on her head and the gentleman wears the heavy Allonge wig which became fashionable in France around 1680.

Most carefully balanced engraving and outstandingly beautiful chiselling cover the lock and mounts, while the noble ebony stocks are inlaid with silver scrolls. Gently swelling forms in wave-like patterns, profusion with restraint — these are the ideals achieved by the maker. The eye takes in the rounded forms of the pommels with their chased masks and fine engraving, and every detail of the locks' numerous imaginative and fantastic heads and masks, which display great ingenuity and sense of design in a difficult medium. A skilful master endeavoured to emulate his Paris models, the French royal gunsmiths like Bertrand Piraube "aux galleries du Louvre à Paris" (worked 1650–1715), and did so with a certain measure of success.

The lock takes the form of the (Dutch) snaphance, which dates far back into the 16th century and was the imperfect predecessor of the French flintlock. Here pan cover and steel are still separate units, whilst in the case of the ingeniously designed flintlock they were made in one piece, the so-called battery.   *Reginald T. Gwynn Collection, Epsom, Surrey, England*

87 ARMAND BONGARDE, DÜSSELDORF, 1690/91

Set of parade arms: flintlock gun, pair of flintlock pistols and small sword of the Elector Johann Wilhelm of the Palatinate (1658–1716 Elector, 1690)

In 1744 the inventory of the Mannheim Treasury described this set of arms as follows: "A beautiful musket, a pair of pistols, a small sword and cane made of steel and inlaid with gold: masterpieces of Bongarde of Düsseldorf." In 1764 it was already being mentioned in the records of the Electoral Treasury in Munich, to which the last Elector Palatine, Charles Theodore (1724–99), had them transferred. Crown Prince Rupprecht of Bavaria, who was greatly interested in the arts, earned our gratitude by presenting them to the Bavarian National Museum in 1913. They were probably produced on 4th June 1691, on the occasion of the second marriage of Johann Wilhelm of the Palatinate, a member of the Neuburg family, to Maria Anna, daughter of the Grand Duke Cosimo III of Tuscany. On the musket barrel there is the full-length figure of the Elector in pseudo-antique costume, and above it cherubs carry his hat. His half-length figure is repeated on the butt-plate of the musket and on the pistols where it is accompanied by the double eagle of the Holy Roman Empire, whose fief he held. Portraits of the joint rulers face each other on the pommel of the small sword. The gilded and chased iron is of superb refinement and may easily stand comparison with the work of the best engravers of medals and die-cutters. This applies to the entire decoration of barrels, locks and mounts with allegories, prisoners and trophies, with putti and masks, and to the small sword, the shells of which are adorned with well-composed battle scenes. The gilded and engraved blade has been pierced to receive inset pearls and corals.

The master signed the lock of the musket and the pistol barrels BONGARDE A DUSSEL-DORP. Nothing is known about his life prior to his marriage in Düsseldorf in 1678. From the coronation of his sovereign in 1690 until his death in 1727 he held the office of Electoral master armourer and court gunsmith. Outside France he was one of the earliest and at the same time purest and most brilliant representatives and disseminators of the classic Paris style in gun-making during the later reign of King Louis XIV.

Munich, Bayerisches Nationalmuseum, 13/583, 13/1031, 13/1032 and 13/129

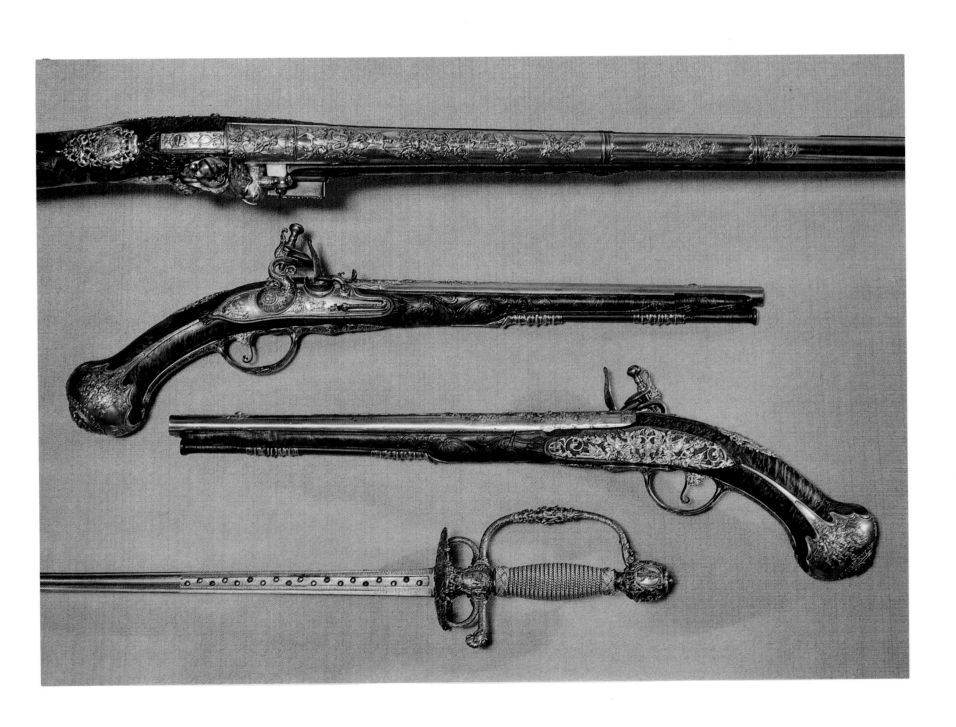

Flintlock gun with tortoise-shell veneered stock of the Emperor Charles VI (1685–1740; Emperor, 1711)

The Archduke Charles – Charles III of Spain – resided in Barcelona from 1704 until the death in 1711 of his elder brother the Emperor Joseph I (succeeded in 1705). In 1706 he spent a short time in Madrid. When the Spanish War of Succession ended in 1714 Spain was ruled by the Bourbons, whilst the Austrian line of the Hapsburgs reigned in the Spanish subject territories of the Netherlands, Milan, and for a limited number of years Sardinia, Naples and Sicily. Due to the Emperor Charles VI's having first ruled in Spain, a strong Spanish influence made itself felt in various fields in Austria. A considerable number of Spanish (and Neapolitan) examples of the gunsmith's craft give evidence of this, primarily in the Vienna imperial armoury but in other Austrian princely armouries too.

This incomparable gun with flintlock of typically Spanish design is the most magnificent example of Spanish work. It is superbly decorated in pure gold and tortoise-shell, with cameos inset. Barrel and lock bear the mark of the Madrid court gunsmith Diego Ventura, and on the lock EN MADRID AN 1722. Philip V of the Bourbon line (1683–1746; King, 1700–24) reigned in Madrid as King of Spain at that time. The stockmaker-goldsmith, maybe a Neapolitan, is unidentified. He ornamented the stock, which is veneered with tortoise-shell and engraved gold inlays of the late baroque that include an apotheosis of Charles VI and a view of Naples on the butt-plate. From 1707 to 1748 Naples was administered by Viceroys of the Austrian Hapsburgs (Sicily was under them from 1720 to 1734). Large mythological cameos have been set into the butt. One is a copy of a work by the Milanese Alessandro Masnago of around 1600, then in the imperial art collection. The upper edge of the butt bears a portrait cameo, the screwplate and the underside three such cameos each.

SOUTH GERMAN, c. 1725–40

Hunting sword with tortoise-shell grip

One might almost believe that this elegant hunting weapon was made, later, to match the tortoise-shell gun of Charles VI. The style of its decoration reveals the tastes of the late baroque on the eve of the triumph of the rococo. Here too the delicate inlays on the tortoise-shell grip veneer are of reddish gold and convey the impression of Chinese art. Pommel cap, quillons and shell-guard are of richly designed gilt brass, a bear hunt on the shell. The fine blade is etched with hunting scenes.   *Vienna, Waffensammlung, A 1758 and A 1688*

Linstock of an artillery officer of the Viennese Citizens' Bombardier Corps

Right into the 19th century Vienna loyally fulfilled its obligation to raise a citizens' army for the City's protection and defence, a duty that dated back to the Middle Ages. Her Students', Butchers', Bakers' and Shoemakers' Companies proved their worth during the defence of the imperial capital against the Turks in 1683. As a result of their victorious battles the imperial commanders Louis William of Baden, Charles V of Lorraine and above all Prince Eugene of Savoy eliminated the Turkish threat for ever and Austria became a leading continental power. Though the Emperor lost his claim to the Spanish crown to the Bourbons during the War of Succession that lasted from 1701 to 1714, Austria felt no ill-effect from the defeat. Liberated from the constant Turkish threat, both town and country became prosperous again. Compared with Italy, the art of the advanced and late baroque emerged in Austria with a delay of half a century. Majestic convents, magnificent palaces and Vienna's festival gardens tell the story.

The artillery officer used the linstock for firing the gun and, if absolutely necessary, to defend himself in close combat; it also served as his badge of rank. The magnificent example from the Vienna Citizens' Armoury belonged, according to its engraved coat of arms, to a wealthy landowning citizen who had been raised to the lower ranks of the aristocracy. For the benefit of his city he took lessons from imperial officers in the art of gunnery during his free weekends because the Citizens' Guard included a Bombardier Corps. On ceremonial occasions he paraded with the other citizens fit for military service in uniform and bearing arms which they had supplied themselves. It may have been the triumphal entrance of the newly-elected Emperor Charles VI (1685–1740) in 1711 that caused him to have the bronze and gilded linstock made by a Viennese founder and engraved with his coat of arms, which unfortunately has not been identified. The two match-holders in the form of eagles' heads allude to the imperial arms. The socket of the linstock head takes the shape of a small bust of the war-goddess Bellona. Chiselled in stone, one can imagine it standing in the gardens of Schloss Belvedere. Its charming coquetry is a typical example of Austrian, especially Viennese, baroque.

Vienna, Historisches Museum der Stadt

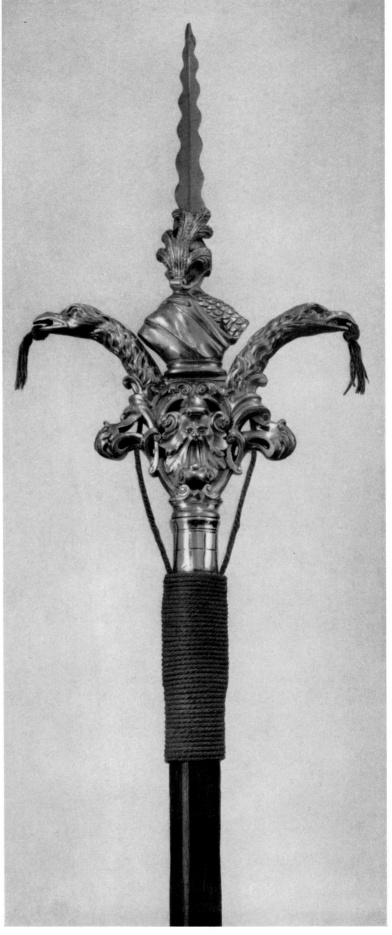

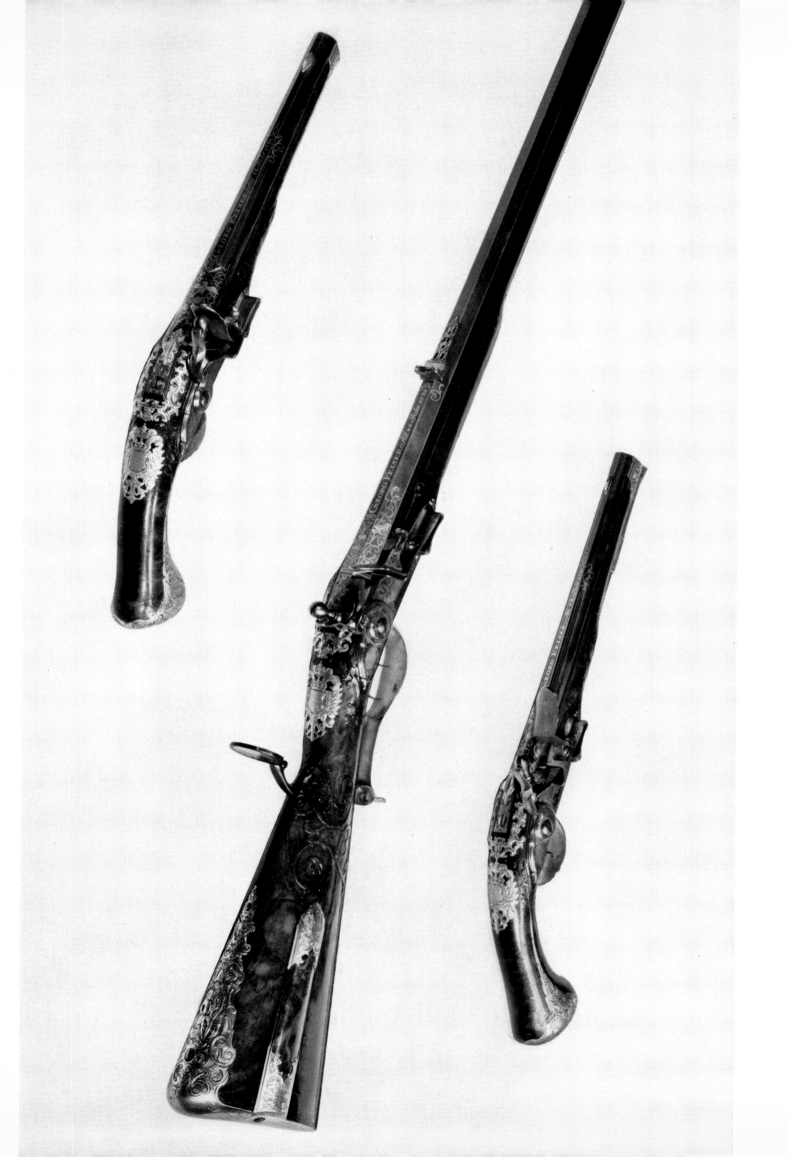

90 GEORG KEISER, VIENNA, 1731

Flintlock rifle and pistols of the Emperor Charles VI (1685–1740; Emperor, 1711)

During the reign of the Emperor Leopold I, four masters, among them the outstanding Michael Gull, founded the Viennese Guild of Gunsmiths in 1661 and thus became independent of the Locksmiths' Guild. Under Leopold's younger son, Charles VI, the Guild reached its zenith and by 1738 it comprised 14 masters, the most important of whom, Georg Keiser, had immigrated from Eger in Bohemia. Their best achievements are to be found in the imperial gunroom which was established at the court to supply the arms used for hunting and for rifle competitions. The members of the Guild constituted a Viennese School which not only worked zealously for the ruling family but also supplied its princely dignitaries. There is no aristocratic family of Austria, Bohemia or Hungary which did not own baroque Viennese small arms. These Viennese gunsmiths were bound by strict Guild rules to make without assistance all the metal parts of a gun: the barrel, lock, hair-trigger and mounts of their masterpiece. Their clever pupils worked in many small provincial towns of Lower Austria, and important closely related workshops were situated in Salzburg, Karlsbad, Prague and Pressburg.

Georg Keiser became a master in 1674. He signed his last known work, three flintlocks pistols (Vienna HGK 291), "Alt 91 Jahr" (Aged 91 years) in 1738. Thus he practised his skills for at least 64 years, a feat which is unlikely to have been surpassed by anyone else in his craft. It is not known in which year he died, but the year of his birth may be deduced from six works which he made for the Emperor Charles VI: a pair each of flintlock rifles and flintlock pistols, which are illustrated here and are marked "Alt 84 Jahr 1731" (Aged 84 years, 1731), and wheel-lock rifles with German butts, marked "Alt 85 Jahr 1732" (Vienna D 337 f). All of them may be part of a large set. The deeply blued barrels bear the master's name and the above-mentioned inscriptions in gold damascening. The locks are tastefully engraved with hunting scenes. The master equipped the ornamentally carved dark walnut stocks with heavy silver mounts which were cast, chiselled and then damascened. Among other things, they include the owner's multipartite coat of arms impaling the imperial double eagle. A set lens, a monocle, is mounted on a hinged arm on the butt for Charles VI, who was near-sighted. A pair of long flintlock guns with the silver coat of arms of Prince Eugene of Savoy-Carignan (1663–1736), the greatest Austrian general, and marked "Alt 87 Jahr" by Georg Keiser in 1734 are the true counterparts of his Emperor's arms (Vienna HGK 148).

In the minor art of firearms, there emerges an extremely attractive aspect of true Austrian late baroque. It was the period in which Fischer von Erlach and Lukas von Hildebrandt built palaces and churches for the Emperor and his Marshal of the Empire, thus establishing an imperial style and making Vienna a centre of European architecture. This leading role is reflected in all Viennese arts and crafts. In spite of their profusion of form and colour, these astonishing late works of Georg Keiser are examples of strict concentration, displaying in spite of all their magnificence a noble restraint. They are included here as an example of the tremendous scope of the gunsmiths' craft at its highest levels in the German-speaking cultural areas during the 18th century. *Vienna, Waffensammlung, A 1760/62/63*

91 VIENNESE SILVERSMITH AND EMBROIDERER, 1732

Red and silver hawking equipment of Christoph Wilhelm, Count Thürheim (1661–1738), the Emperor's master falconer in Upper Austria

According to ancient custom, a Hapsburg, on taking up his reign in his patrimonial dominions, accepted the homage of his vassals and confirmed their rights at a special ceremony. The Emperor Charles VI (1685–1740; Overlord and Emperor, 1711), father of the Empress Maria Theresa, visited Upper Austria late in his reign. In 1732, surrounded by government officials employed at the courts, he accepted the homage of the local vassals at Linz on the Danube. In his capacity as master falconer of the emperor's patrimonial estates, Count Christoph Wilhelm Thürheim, already an old man, was one of the hereditary servants who held office in the royal household. His title, which had its origin in the Persian-Turkish orient, required its bearer to superintend the Emperor's falcon hunts.

For the festive occasion in 1732, Count Thürheim had this splendid falconry outfit made by a silversmith and an embroiderer in Vienna. It consists of falcon hood, lure for recalling the bird, pouch for the falcon's food, and part of the hanger for a hunting sword. The frame of the bag, normally left plain, is here adorned with a finely sculpted medallion of a hooded hunting falcon. The now faded red silk of the set is decorated with profuse silver embroidery and covered with thick silver fringes and swags. Green and gold falconry equipment of this type had been acquired in 1706 for the oath of fealty ceremony of the Emperor Joseph I (1678 to 1711; Emperor, 1705). These two sets provide convincing evidence of the high standard reached by the Viennese artisans; their work was worthy of comparison with the brilliant achievements of the gunmakers, whose trade then flourished in the city.
Vienna, Waffensammlung, A 2289

Court sword of chiselled iron

Franz Mazenkopf was born at Prutz on the river Inn in the Tyrol in 1705. In Vienna he was taught the gunsmith's craft, which had just begun to flourish there, and settled in Prague around 1730. His gilt pseudo-Spanish marks show Fortuna and the bust of a bald man with the initials FMK. As a result of the outstanding quality of his chiselled iron mounts for rifles and pistols the Archbishop of Salzburg, Leopold Anton von Firmian (1722–44), called him to his court to work as a medallist. Evidence is available that records Mazenkopf's presence in Salzburg from 1738 and he still worked there in 1755 after serving three of Firmian's successors as engraver of coins and medals. His son of the same name succeeded to his office. The master died on 2nd May 1776, one of the outstanding craftsmen in his field. Guns and pistols that he made in Prague, two small swords produced in Salzburg, and one each in Turin and Vienna, have been preserved and testify to his superb skill. The hilt of the Vienna small-sword is in the form developed in the middle of the 17th century with knuckle bow, two arms of the hilt and flat shells. The fine, partly gilded and chiselled iron displays the coat of arms and emblems of the Hungarian and Bohemian kingdoms on the pommel. The grip shows on one side a medallion of Maria Theresa supported by Athena and Hercules, and Justice on the other; on the shells is a combat between Pandours. The knuckle bow bears a three-dimensional figure of a prisoner. The completely symmetrical structure of the decoration does not yet reveal any signs of the emergent rococo; only the trellis on the shells is an element of the late baroque. The slender blade is pierced in several places and etched and gilt at its base. The date can be deduced on the one hand from the figurative motives alluding to war and on the other from the illustration of Maria Theresa as Queen of Hungary and Bohemia, but not yet as Empress (1717–80; succeeded in 1740; Empress, 1745). After the death of her father, the Emperor Charles VI, in 1740, Maria Theresa faced a hostile world. King Frederick II of Prussia (1740–86) tried to deprive her of Silesia, an aim eventually achieved in 1763 after three wars of varying fortune, in which France, England and Russia participated. Moreover, with her husband Francis I of Lorraine she had to fight for his succession to the title of Emperor in the Austrian War of Succession (1740–48). In 1745 they succeeded in obtaining his recognition against the claims of the Elector Charles Albert of Bavaria (Charles VII as Emperor from 1740 to 45). So the small-sword must have its origin in this belligerent period. It was once thought to be a weapon of the Emperor Francis I Stephen (1708–65; Emperor, 1745) himself, but the frog-button of the scabbard, in the form of an escutcheon, provides evidence to the contrary. The coat of arms has been erased, but the crown above it has only five points, proving that the weapon belonged to a minor aristocrat who must have served the Austrian cause well for the Archbishop to have such an elaborate sword made for him by his master medallist. *Vienna, Waffensammlung, A 2036*

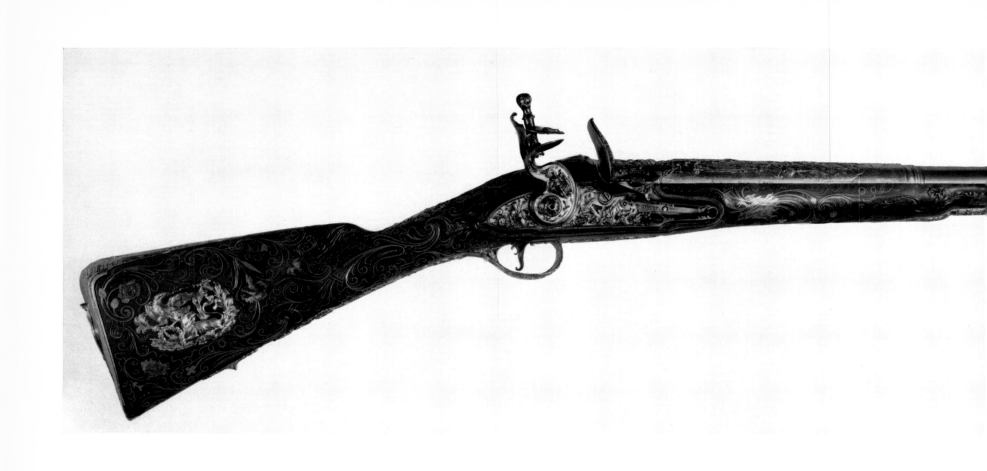

Airgun of George II, King of England (1683–1760; King, 1727)

Compressed air supplied the power for guns, in the so-called airgun, as long ago as the 16th century. Like the crossbow it was long outlawed because of its smokeless and silent method of operation: so, to camouflage its illegality, superfluous wheel- or flintlocks were attached to the outside of the actions. This is the case with the truly magnificent royal London specimen, made by the Suhl gunsmith, mechanic, iron-chiseller and engraver, J. G. Kolb or Kolbe, who returned to his native country after having worked in London in the seventeen-thirties. The actual inner barrel of the rifle is covered by an external brass cylinder. Compressed air contained in the intervening space is pumped into it by a pump in the butt. Pressure on the trigger not only releases the useless cock with its flint, but also, through a valve, as much air as is required for one shot.

The decoration is incredibly profuse. Over the marked barrel there is a silver sleeve with Mars among trophies. Cock, lockplate and side-plate are perfectly chiselled in iron and carry the artist's name KOLBE. Extraordinary, too, is the decoration of the walnut stock with its engraved, silver-wire scrolls and flowers of the same metal entirely in accordance with the exemplary Parisian rococo small arms of the period, and silver plaques with, in relief, figures and symbols from mythology.   *London, Victoria and Albert Museum, 494–1894 (Crown Copyright)*

JOHANN CHRISTOPH STOCKMAR,
HEIDERSBACH NEAR SUHL IN THURINGIA, c. 1745

Flintlock gun, probably of Ernst August I, Duke of Saxe-Weimar-Eisenach (1688–1748; Duke, 1728)

Electors and Dukes of the Wettin family were sympathetic patrons of the arts in the province of Saxony-Thuringia. One branch of this family which occupied the Polish throne from 1677 had always distinguished itself by keeping in close touch with German, Italian, French, and Spanish art centres. The import of works of high quality stimulated it to peak achievements of its own and to the development of extraordinary splendour that was no doubt boosted by the lavish expenditure on similar projects by its neighbours to the east. The chiselling on the barrel and lock of the London Stockmar gun has been colourfully and extensively enriched by means of polishing, bluing and gilding parts. The pale root-walnut stock shows all the refinements of the rococo with its glowing asymmetrical ornaments. The mounts are of chased silver shells set on a gilded background. Inlaid scrolls and foliage of silver, and rows of gilded silver stars, alternate with ivory buttons and even deer-teeth to form together a fairy web covering the surface. The master signed the side flat of the barrel and the owner is revealed on other parts of the hunting set (rifle and pair of pistols, A 1119 and A 1203/04) which display the initials EA and EA D (D standing for Dux=Duke) and the Saxon coat of arms in pure gold. In the absence of the Polish royal arms of the same period, the owner can never have been a member of the main Electoral line, as was hitherto believed, but only a descendant of one of the many ducal branches of the Wettin family reigning over Thuringia.
London, Wallace Collection, A 1120

Two rococo hunting swords

By ancient tradition a sword-like weapon was rarely worn for the chase, but usually a long knife was carried, the so-called hunting sword that achieved its final form in the 17th century. One can see the original bird's-head shape in the thickened form of the pommel. An ordinary curved parrying guard, together with a one-sided shell and, occasionally, a knuckle bow form the hilt fitted to the rather short single-edged blade, with which the game was dealt its coup de grâce.

Hunting was one of the favourite pastimes of the aristocracy and the princely courts. During the baroque in particular this became an ardent passion to the great regret of the rural population who expressed their dislike by dressing the devil in huntsman's costume in their fairy-tales. Ingenious efforts went into the production of the costliest hunting equipment.

The hunting swords from the armoury of the Bavarian Electors in Munich are among the most beautiful specimens of their kind. Ivory and gilt bronze form a noble harmony of white and gold. The hilts are most artistically carved with beasts of the chase. The exuberant ornamental art with its radiating shell-like forms is a clear expression of the rococo, the baroque's final, vigorous, light-hearted phase. With its prominent artists, the brothers Asam, Bavaria then stood in the forefront of the producers of the most superb works in the fields of palace and church architecture, sculpture, decorative painting and skilled crafts.

Munich, Bayerisches Nationalmuseum, 2712 and 2711

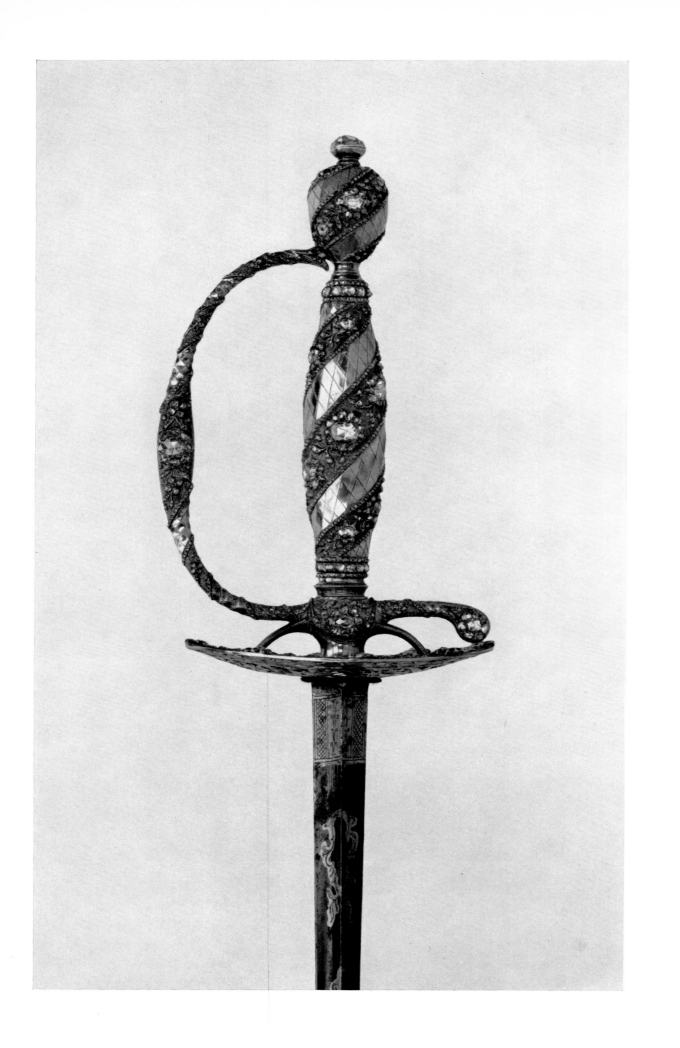

95 PARIS, 1766

Court sword set with diamonds of Christian VII, King of Denmark (1749–1808; King, 1766)

Even in the 17th century the attitude of English and French art towards the Italian baroque was somewhat cool. Italy herself became a little more sedate around 1700, and about 1770 the last phase of the baroque was replaced by a new neo-classical movement, directly influenced by Augustan and Greek antiquity.

The diamond court sword from Rosenborg Castle constitutes a particularly beautiful example of the transitional period. It was part of the regalia ordered in Paris for Christian VII's coronation in 1766. The diamonds and gold of its setting still carry on the colour combination of white and gold, which the rococo held in such high esteem. The asymmetrical ornaments of rococo have, however, been replaced by simpler motives – roses, hanging garlands and vases; the pommel too takes the shape of a vase. The polished gold ground is divided into lozenges, over which is chased an intertwined gold band containing blossoms and foliage of cut diamonds whose cold fire was particularly cherished during the classical revival.

This artistic trend fell on fertile ground in Denmark; it was the home of a number of leading artists in the field, among them the sculptor Barthel Thorwaldsen and the architect Theophil Hansen.   *Copenhagen, Rosenborg Castle, 48*

Pair of flintlock pistols of General Sir Henry Clinton (1738–95)

The fringe countries of Europe again and again prove to be of particular interest in the historical study of arms. There, national peculiarities developed with occasionally unusual but sometimes very attractive results. Small-arms from Sweden, Moscow, Teschen, Sardinia, Ripoll in Aragon or, for instance, Scotland, repeatedly present new and unusual aspects that occasionally reach unexpected heights of achievement. The history of the Scottish pistol dates back to the early 17th century when it developed its own form of stock. Its flintlock always displays local technical attributes and its ornament reveals a pertinacious conservatism and revival of traditional ancient Celtic motives.

With this pair of Clinton pistols the basic national attitude has been maintained, but a step has been taken into the field of highly developed European skilled handicrafts. The pistols were certainly created for an important festive occasion and would appear to have been a present from the British sovereign, George III (1738–1820; King, 1760), to his meritorious General. Sir Henry had fought for his King against George Washington in North America, where he eventually became commander-in-chief. He died when Commanding Officer at Gibraltar. Four enamel medallions recount the connections with the donor's portrait on the barrel, and the coat of arms of the recipient and owner in its customary place on the back of the butt. On the left of the pommel is the emblem of the Scottish Order of the Thistle and, on the right, that of the Order of the Bath. The owner was one of their knights and the King their sovereign. The blued barrels are adorned with gold scrolls; locks and belt-hook are of engraved iron. The typically Scottish stocks of metal, in this case copper, show similar decorative patterns and are heavily gilded. The triggers and pricker-buttons are of solid gold. Not only the pistols have been preserved in immaculate condition, but also their original velvet bags and inlaid case.

W. Keith Neil, Collection Warminster, Wiltshire, England

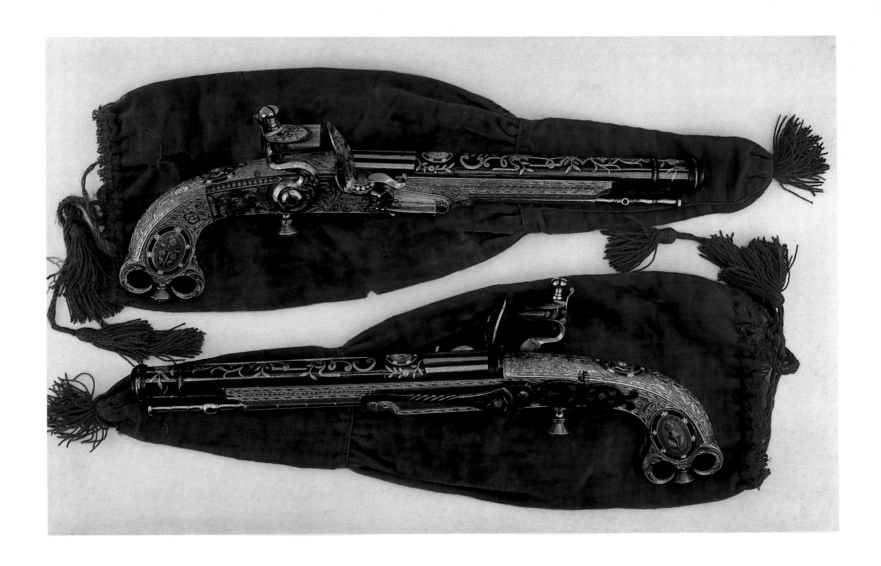

97 NICOLAS NOEL BOUTET, VERSAILLES, c.1810–15, AND LEOPOLD BERNARD, PARIS, c.1835

Flintlock double gun of Napoleon I, Emperor of the French (1768–1821; Emperor, 1804–14/15)–with alternative barrels and percussion locks

In politics around 1800 a Talleyrand or a Fouquet could survive any change of regime and in his field the same applied to N. N. Boutet (1761–1833). One might call him the last genius of the small-arms craft before the onset of the machine age and mass production. As gunsmith, goldsmith and designer he served in turn Louis XVI of France; the Revolution from 1792 as director of the arms factory at Versailles; the Directory; Napoleon I; Louis XVIII, and the royal princes. He proved indispensable to them all. His extravagant rifles and his swords of honour, highly prized gifts which are now dispersed in collections all over the world, are creations characterised by the classicism of the Louis Seize and Empire styles. From both technical and artistic viewpoints his work is remarkable for precision, perfect clarity and fineness. In it, magnificence never oversteps the limits of dignity. But one must not overlook the fact that during the 18 years in which Boutet was in charge, more than 145,000 army rifles were made at the Versailles factory.

One of his late works, which is of special value owing to the precious materials used in its construction, is among a number that found their way to New York. The rib between the plain side-by-side barrels is marked MANUFACTURE DE VERSAILLES and the locks BOUTET A VERSAILLES. The engraved and gilded chiselling of the blued steel surfaces displays tendrils and blossoms, a dog and a wolf. Above all, the stock is unusually profusely worked. It is partly carved and densely inlaid with gold scrolls among which play birds, hares and squirrels. The solid gold mounts include an embossed cartouche with oriental weapons at the small of the butt and a cowering dragon at its end.

No emblem identifies Napoleon I as the owner of this extraordinary work and, so far as its history is concerned, one can deduce that it was produced around 1815, possibly during the Hundred Days, before the Emperor was finally overthrown and exiled. A subsequent owner commissioned Leopold Bernard in Paris, Nicolas Bernard's son, to add spare barrels, with nipples for mercury fulminate percussion caps, and percussion locks. (In France Leopold Bernard produced the first damascus barrel based on oriental patterns in 1804.) The mechanism is a development of the system for which the Scotsman, A. J. Forsyth, applied for the first percussion lock patent in London in 1807. The additional parts are intended as alternative pieces and the character of their decoration is in close harmony with Boutet's work which, technically, they brought up to date.   *New York, Metropolitan Museum, 42. 50. 7.*

Bibliographical Abbreviations:

Fillitz	H. Fillitz, *Katalog der Weltlichen und Geistlichen Schatzkammer, Kunsthistorisches Museum*, Vienna, 3rd ed. 1961.
Gamber, Thun	O. Gamber, Der Turnierharnisch zur Zeit Maximilians I. und das Thunsche Skizzenbuch, *JKS*, vol. 53, 1957.
Gamber, Maximilian I	O. Gamber in: *Maximilian I.*, Exhibition Catalogue, Vienna, 1959.
Gamber, Blankwaffen	O. Gamber, Die mittelalterlichen Blankwaffen der Wiener Waffensammlung, in *JKS*, vol. 57, 1961.
Grosz-Thomas	A. Grosz – B. Thomas, *Katalog der Waffensammlung der Neuen Burg*, Vienna, 1936.
Haenel	E. A. Haenel, *Kostbare Waffen aus der Dresdner Rüstkammer*, Leipzig, 1923.
Hayward	J. F. Hayward, *The Art of the Gunmaker*, vol. 1, London, 1962.
JKS	*Jahrbuch der Kunsthistorischen Sammlungen (des Allerhöchsten Kaiserhauses) in Wien.*
Mann	Sir James Mann, Wallace Collection Catalogues: *European Arms and Armour*, 2 volumes, London, 1962.
Mariaux	Général Mariaux, *Le Musée de l'Armée, armes et armures*, vol. 2, Paris, 1927.
Niox	Général Niox, *Le Musée de l'Armée, armes et armures*, vol. 1, Paris, 1917.
Schedelmann	H. Schedelmann, *Die Wiener Büchsenmacher und Büchsenschäfter*, Berlin, 1944.
Schepelern	H. D. Schepelern in: Hoff – Schepelern – Boesen, *Royal Arms at Rosenborg*, Copenhagen, 1956.
Thomas-Gamber, Innsbruck	B. Thomas – O. Gamber, *Die Innsbrucker Plattnerkunst*, Exhibition Catalogue, Innsbruck, 1954.
Thomas-Gamber, Milan	B. Thomas – O. Gamber, *L'arte milanese dell'armatura*, *Storia di Milano*, vol. 11, Milan, 1958.
Valencia	V. Conde de Valencia de Don Juan, *Catálogo de la Real Armería*, Madrid, 1898.

I Carl Goebel, painter in water colours and lithographer, Vienna, 1824–99. Grandson of the sculptor Josef Klieber; successor to P. Fendi and J. Kriehuber as a painter of genre pictures and fashionable portraits.
Leo Grünstein, article on Goebel in: Thieme-Becker, *Allgemeines Lexikon der bildenden Künstler*, vol. 14, Leipzig, 1921, pp. 300 ff.

1 Fillitz, p. 56, No. 172.

2 H. Schneider, Neues zum Reiterschild von Seedorf in: *Zeitschrift für Schweizerische Archäologie und Kunstgeschichte*, vol. 12, Basle, 1951, pp. 116 ff.

3 Petrajuolo Negroni da Ello, called Missaglia, probably an armourer. Milan, died before 1429.
Oswald Graf Trapp, *Die Churburger Rüstkammer*, London, 1929, pp. 19 ff. and p. 313. – O. Gamber in: Thomas-Gamber, Milan, pp. 718 and 742, ill. p. 705.

4 Thomas-Gamber in: *Europäische Kunst um 1400*, Exhibition Catalogue, Vienna, 1962, No. 543.

5 J. Hampel, Das Kurschwert Friedrichs des Streitbaren von Sachsen in: *Zeitschrift für historische Waffenkunde*, vol. 1, Dresden, 1897–99, pp. 81 ff. – Haenel, ill. 40 a.

6 Tomaso Missaglia, son of Pietro (see note on pl. 3), armourer at Milan. Mentioned 1430, died 1452. Antonio Missaglia, son of Tomaso, armourer at Milan, mentioned 1441, died 1496.
O. Gamber in: Thomas-Gamber, Milan, pp. 719 ff., pp. 747 and 750, ill. pp. 715 and 726.

7 Fillitz, p. 46, No. 148. Gamber, Blankwaffen, p. 36, ill. 33.

8 Gamber, Maximilian I, No. 481.

9 Mariaux, pl. 61/2.

10 Lorenz Helmschmid, son of the armourer Jörg. Armourer at Augsburg, mentioned in 1467, died in 1515. Worked for the Emperor Frederick III and his Counsellor Pruschenk from 1477 and from 1480 for Maximilian I, whose servant and court armourer he became in 1491; with his brother Jörg H. he made jousting and tilt armour for Maximilian I and received considerable payments from him in 1500. He was also employed by Duke Christoph of Bavaria in 1483 and worked for Marshal Jörg Goldacker in 1507.
Gamber, Thun, p. 44, ill. 36.

11 Lorenz Helmschmid, see note on pl. 10.
Gamber, Maximilian I, No. 487.

12 Niox, pl. 52.

13 Hanns Sumersperger, royal cutler at Hall in the Tyrol, mentioned 1492–98.
B. Thomas-A. Lhotsky, Die Prunkschwerter Kaiser Maximilians I. in Wien und Kopenhagen, in: *Vaabenhistoriske Aarbøger*, vol. 6, Copenhagen, 1950/51, pp. 105 ff. B. Thomas, The Hunting Knives of the Emperor Maximilian I, in: *The Metropolitan Museum of Art Bulletin*, vol. 13, No. 6, Feb. 1955, pp. 201 ff.

14 Ercole de' Fideli, originally Salomone da Sesso, goldsmith and blade etcher at Ferrara and Rome. C. 1465–1518/19. Worked for the Gonzaga family, Cesare Borgia and the Papal Court.
Gamber, Blankwaffen, p. 34, ill. 29.

15 B. Dean, A Lion-Headed Helmet, in: *Bulletin of the Metropolitan Museum of Art*, vol. 18, New York, 1923, pp. 224 ff.

16a Konrad Seusenhofer, armourer at Innsbruck. Mentioned from 1500; appointed Maximilian I's court armourer for six years in 1504 and for life in 1509; died in 1517. Worked for the Emperor himself, whose gifts of honour to court dignitaries and

allies he produced, as well as mass military equipment; was in charge of an extensive workshop.
Thomas-Gamber, Innsbruck, pp. 20–22, 66, No. 62.

16b Wilhelm von Worms the Elder, son of the armourer Hans. Armourer at Nuremberg. Mentioned in 1501, Councillor in 1529, died in 1537. Father-in-law of the armourer Valentin Siebenburger.
B. Thomas, Nürnberger Plattnerkunst in Wien, in: *Anzeiger des Germanischen Nationalmuseums*, Nuremberg, 1963, p. 95.

17 Gamber, Maximilian I, Nos. 596–599.

18 Gamber, Maximilian I, No. 613.

19 Kolman Helmschmid, son of Lorenz. Armourer at Augsburg, 1471–1532; master, 1492. Worked for the Emperors Maximilian I and Charles V, the Duke of Mantua, the Elector of Brandenburg. The background to the illustration is the tapestry "The Triumphal Procession of Don João de Castro through Goa in India, 1547" from the Vienna Tapestry Collection; worked in Brussels after a design by Pieter Coecke van Aelst, Antwerp, 1547–50.
Gamber, Maximilian I, No. 616.

20 C. Blair in: *Archaeologia*, vol. 99, Oxford, 1964, pp. 1 ff.

21 Kolman Helmschmid, see note on pl. 19.
B. Thomas, Waffen der Gotik in Niederösterreich, in: *Gotik in Niederösterreich*, Vienna, 1963, pp. 222 ff.

22 Grosz-Thomas, I/66, I/52/24, I/48.

23 O. Gamber in: Thomas-Gamber, Milan, p. 756, ill. p. 761.

24 Kolman Helmschmid, see note on pl. 19.
Valencia, pp. 16 ff., ill. 21

25 Desiderius Helmschmid, son of the armourer Kolman. Armourer at Augsburg, 1513–79 (?). Worked for the Emperor Charles V and his son Philip II of Spain.
Valencia, pp. 46 ff., ill. 9.

26 Mariaux, pl. 3.

27 Ch. Buttin, L'armure de Henri II dauphin, in: *Aréthuse*, No. 25, Paris, 1929.

28 Filippo Barini, called Negroli, armourer and embosser in Milan. Dated works from 1532 to 1545. Worked for the Emperor Charles V, Francis I of France, Francesco I Maria della Rovere of Urbino.
B. Thomas in: Thomas-Gamber, Milan, pp. 760 f., 765 f., ill. pp. 783, 785, 787.

29 Peter Pech, c. 1503–94; master watchmaker, 1542; master locksmith, 1543 in Munich; ducal master gunsmith, 1569. Worked for Charles V and the Bavarian court.
S. V. Grancsay, A Wheellock Pistol made for the Emperor Charles V, in: *The Metropolitan Museum of Art Bulletin*, vol. 6, New York, Dec. 1947, pp. 117 ff.

30 Desiderius Helmschmid, see note on pl. 25.
Valencia, pp. 68 ff. B. Thomas in: *Exhibition of Armour from Austria*, Exhibition Catalogue, Tower of London, 1949, No. 18.
F. Klauner, Spanische Portraits des 16. Jahrhunderts, in: *JKS*, vol. 57, 1961, pp. 128 ff.

31 Bartolomeo Campi, goldsmith, embosser, and military engineer at Pesaro, Urbino, Siena, Venice, Paris and the Netherlands, 1500/10–73. Patronised by princes.
Valencia, pp. 64 ff., pl. 11.

32 (On style) R. Wegeli, Der Schweizerdegen, in: *Jahresbericht des Historischen Museums in Bern*, 1910, appendix, pp. 4 ff.

33a Jörg Seusenhofer, son of the armourer Hans, armourer at Innsbruck, mentioned in 1528, died in 1580. Court armourer to Ferdinand I and worked for him, his family and court dignitaries, as well as for Francis I of France.
Thomas-Gamber, Innsbruck, pp. 74 and 77, ill. 68–75.

33b Matthäus Frauenpreiss the Younger, son of the armourer Matthäus the Elder, armourer at Augsburg, c. 1530–1604. Worked for Maximilian II, the Archduke Ferdinand II, Spanish and Bohemian noblemen.
O. Gamber, Die Harnischgarnitur, in: *Livrustkammaren*, vol. 7, Stockholm, 1955–57, pp. 84 ff.

34 Desiderius Helmschmid, see note on pl. 25. – Jörg Sigman, goldsmith and embosser in Augsburg, c. 1527–1601; journeyman working for D. Helmschmid, 1548–50; master, 1552.
Valencia, pp. 79 ff., pl. 13; S. V. Grancsay, A Helmet made for Philip II of Spain, in: *The Metropolitan Museum of Art Bulletin*, vol. 13, New York, May 1955, pp. 272 ff.

35 B. Thomas, Die Harnische Maximilians II. von 1550, in: *Zeitschrift des deutschen Vereins für Kunstwissenschaft*, vol. 9, Berlin, 1942, pp. 91 ff.

36 Grosz-Thomas, II/36/13.

37 Antonio Piccinino, bladesmith in Milan. 1509–89. Father of the bladesmith Federico and of the embosser Lucio P.
H. Seitz, The Vienna Rapier with the Golden Hilt, in: *Livrustkammaren*, vol. 4, Stockholm, 1946–48, pp. 361 ff. The identification with the old inventories of the collection and the resulting date are here presented for the first time.

38 Hayward, pp. 77, 282, ill. 12c.

39 Kunz Lochner, armourer at Nuremberg, c. 1510–67. Mentioned for the first time in 1543; worked for the Hapsburgs, the Wettin family and the Polish court.
B. Thomas, Die Wiener und Stockholmer Lochner-Rüstung, in: *Nationalmusei Arsbok*, Stockholm, 1947–48, pp. 61 ff.

40 T. Lenk, To the History of the Pistols of the 16th Century, in: *Livrustkammaren*, vol. 4, Stockholm, 1946–48, pp. 349 ff.

41 Hayward, pp. 98 f.

42 B. Thomas, Die Münchner Waffenvorzeichnungen des Etienne Delaune, in: *JKS*, vol. 58, 1962, pp. 145 f., ill. 125.

43 B. Thomas, Die Rantzau-Harnische in der Wiener Waffensammlung, in: *Nordelbingen*, vol. 13, Heide i. H., 1937, pp. 244 ff.

44 Giovanni Batt. Serabaglio, embossing artist at Milan. Mentioned in bills of 1560; in the Ambras inventory of 1583; called an important artist by Lomazzo in 1584 and by Morigia in 1592.
Thomas, in Thomas-Gamber, Milan, pp. 782 ff., ill. p. 698.

45 Serabaglio, see note on pl. 44.

46 Grosz-Thomas, VIII/1/1.

47 Eliseus Libaerts, goldsmith at Antwerp, mentioned there 1557–64; was in royal service in Copenhagen 1564–69; there is also evidence of his work as an engraver of medals.
R. Baron Cederström and K. E. Steneberg, *Skoklosterskölden (The Skokloster Shield)*, Stockholm, 1945, especially pp. 42 f., ill. 8.

48 Mariaux, pl. 59.

49 Grosz-Thomas, III/83, V/112, II/30/1.

50 Hans Paumgartner, gunstockmaker at Graz. Dated works, 1563–86; mentioned at the shooting competitions in 1565, 1568, 1577, 1588 and in the inventory of Archduke Charles' estate in 1590. B. Thomas, Formenadel der Renaissance, in: *Wiener Kurier*, 8 May 1954, p. 14.

51 Franz Grossschedel, son and successor to the armourer Wolfgang. Armourer at Landshut, citizen in 1556, died 1579/81. Worked for the Wittelsbach family, Augustus of Saxony and Maximilian II. B. Thomas, in: *La Toison d'or*, Exhibition Catalogue, Bruges, 1962, No. 128.

52 Grosz-Thomas, V/32–39. Its date and the reason for its manufacture are presented here for the first time.

53 Niox, pl. 20.

54 Lucio Piccinino, son of the bladesmith Antonio. Embossing and damascening artist at Milan. Mentioned in 1595 as working for Alessandro Farnese, Duke of Parma. B. Thomas in Thomas-Gamber, Milan, pp. 788 ff., ill. p. 809.

55 H. Modern, Geweihte Schwerter und Hüte, in: *JKS*, vol. 22, 1901, pp. 127 ff.

56 Jacob Halder of Augsburg, called Master Jacobe, armourer at Greenwich. Mentioned 1553/54, Master Workman 1576–1607. Exhibition Catalogue, *Exhibition of Armour Made ... at Greenwich*, Tower of London, 1951, Nos. 21, 84, 87, ills. 24–26.

57 B. Thomas in: Thomas-Gamber, Milan, pp. 820–825, ill. p. 827.

58 Peter Opel, gunstockmaker at Regensburg. Mentioned 1575/86/96. Hayward, p. 290, ill. 40 c.

59 Hans and Wolf Stopler, barrel- and locksmith respectively at Nuremberg. Active around 1550–1600 or else 1570–1600. David Leimber, stockmaker at Nuremberg. Worked for Maximilian II. Johan F. Støckel, *Haandskydevaabens bedømmelse*, vol. 1, Copenhagen, 1938, p. 295.

60 S. V. Grancsay, A State Partisan of Maurice of Nassau, in: *Bulletin of the Metropolitan Museum of Art*, vol. 23, New York, Feb. 1928, pp. 50 ff.

61 Grosz-Thomas, V/68/7.

62 Emanuel (II) Sadeler, iron-chiseller in Munich. Mentioned 1595, died 1610. Caspar Spät, iron-chiseller in Munich. Mentioned 1635, died 1691. H. Stöcklein, *Meister des Eisenschnittes*, Esslingen, 1922.

63 Daniel Sadeler, iron-chiseller in Prague (1602 until probably 1610) and in Munich (from 1610), died 1632. David Altenstetter, goldsmith at Augsburg. Colmar 1547–1617 Augsburg. See Stöcklein, op. cit., p. 60. The hunting knives: Grosz-Thomas, V/19/9.

64 S. V. Palme and T. Lenk in: *Historiska Bilder*, vol. 1, Stockholm, 1948, pp. 201, 207, 222 f., 229.

65 Gasparo Mola, goldsmith, engraver of medals, master coiner. Coldrè near Como c. 1580–1640 Rome. Worked at Turin in 1607, in Florence in 1608 and 1609, in Rome 1625–40. B. Thomas in: Thomas-Gamber, Milan, pp. 795 f., ill. pp. 812, 814.

66 Gabriel Gipfel, goldsmith from Nuremberg. 1591 in Dresden, 1608 court goldsmith; worked until approx. 1615/20. Haenel, pl. 78. E. Watzdorf, Kursächsische Jagdwaffen von Gabriel Gipfel in der Dresdner Rüstkammer, in: *Zeitschrift für historische Waffen- und Kostümkunde*, Berlin, 1935/36, pp. 4 ff.

67 Compare Haenel, pl. 61 a.

68 Haenel, pl. 59 d.

69 B. Thomas, Eine Radschloßbüchse Sigmunds III. in Wien, in:
Livrustkammaren, vol. 1, Stockholm, 1937–39, pp. 93 ff.

70 Mann, p. 263, pl. 113. Mariaux, pl. 14. J. F. Hayward, Claude Sa-
vigny …, in *Livrustkammaren*, vol. 7, Stockholm, 1955-57, pp.
13–17.

71 Hayward, pp. 140, 285, pl. 19 a, 19 b.

72 B. Thomas in: Thomas-Gamber, Milan, pp. 825 f.

73 Schepelern, cat. No. 17, pl. 27/1.

74 Hans Schmidt, gunsmith at Ferlach; born at Riedlingen on the
Danube; in the service of the Hapsburg court from 1626; raised
to the nobility in 1657; died 1668/69.
B. Thomas, Die silberne Jagdbüchse Leopolds V. von Österreich,
in: *Notring Jahrbuch (Vienna)*, 1960, pl. 35.

75 H. Zatschek and others, *Das Heeresgeschichtliche Museum in Wien*,
Graz-Leipzig, 1960, p. 36, pl. 3. – O. J. Blažiček, *Baroque Sculpture
in Bohemia* (in Czech), Prague, 1958, p. 79, pl. 39.

76 A. Gaibi, Biografiske undersø gelser om familien Cominazzi, in
Vaabenhistoriske Aarbøger, vol. 11 a, Copenhagen, 1962, pp. 5 ff.
M. v. Ehrenthal, *Die Waffensammlung des Fürsten Salm-Reiffer-
scheidt zu Schloss Dyck*, Leipzig, 1906, p. 146, No. 493, pl. 4.

77 G. Ekstrand, Karl X. Gustavs dräkter, Stockholm, *Livrustkammaren*, 1959, pl. 47.

78 Jean (Louis) Bérain the Elder, son and grandson of gunsmiths
from Bar in Lorraine. St Michiel 1637–1711 Paris. Architect,
designer and ornamental engraver; 1674 private and cabinet
designer to Louis XIV.

T. Lenk, *Flintlåset*, Stockholm, 1939, pp. 78 ff., 138 ff., 176,
pl. 59/60, 117 f.

79 Mariaux, pl. 66.

80 Grosz-Thomas, VIII/11/11 f.

81 Grosz-Thomas, VIII/4/4.

82 T. Lenk, *Flintlåset*, Stockholm, 1939, pp. 75 ff., 168.

83 Johann Haas, gunsmith at Schwäbisch-Gmünd, 1655–1704. Jo-
hann Michael Maucher, gunstockmaker and ivory and wood-carver
at Schwäbisch-Gmünd; born 1645, died Würzburg, 1701. Worked
first at Schwäbisch-Gmünd, later in Augsburg and from 1693 in
Würzburg.
E. Petrasch, Über einige Jagdwaffen mit Elfenbeinschnitzerei im
Badischen Landesmuseum, in: *Waffen- und Kostümkunde*, vol. 2,
No. 1, Munich 1960, pp. 11 ff.

84 Michael Gull, gunsmith in Vienna. Master in 1647, died in 1679.
One of the four founders of the independent Viennese Gunsmiths'
Guild.
Schedelmann, pp. 7 f., 72, pl. 1.

85 S. V. Grancsay, *Mediaeval and Renaissance Arms and Armor from
the Metropolitan Museum of Art*, Exhibition Catalogue, Los
Angeles County Museum, 1953, No. 12.

86 *The Art of the Armourer*, Arms and Armour Society, Exhibition
Catalogue, London, Victoria and Albert Museum, 1963, No. 227.

87 Armand Bongarde, gunsmith and iron-chiseller at Düsseldorf.
Mentioned in 1678; from 1690 until his death in 1727, electoral
master armourer and court gunsmith.
H. Stöcklein, Das Meisterwerk des Armand Bongard, in: *Belvedere*,
vol. 1, Vienna, 1922, pp. 95 ff., pl. 44.

88 Diego Ventura, court gunsmith in Madrid. Worked from about 1720 to 1762.
Grosz-Thomas, VIII/4/12, VI/62/22.

89 O.Gamber in: *Das Wiener Bürgerliche Zeughaus 1600–1840, Ausstellungskatalog Historisches Museum der Stadt Wien*, 1962, p.41, No.111, pl.14.

90 Georg Keiser from Eger, presumably the son of the local gunsmith Kaspar. Gunsmith in Vienna; born 1647, master 1674, still active 1740.
Schedelmann, p.11, ill.12f., 64.

91 (B.Thomas) Die österreichische jagdhistorische Schau, Berlin, 1937, in: *Österreichs Weidwerk*, vol.11, No.4, Vienna, 1938, p.126.

92 Franz Mazenkopf, gunsmith and iron-chiseller in Prague c.1740; later, coiner for the Salzburg archbishops.
J.F.Hayward, A Court Sword by Franz Matzenkopf, in: *The Connoisseur*, vol.126, No.517 (August), London, 1950, pp.28ff., 76.

93 Johann Georg Kolbe, gunsmith, iron-chiseller and engraver from Suhl. Mentioned in London 1735–53; later again at Suhl.
J.F.Hayward, *European Firearms*, Victoria and Albert Museum, London, 1955, p.52, No.78, pl. 31–33.
Johann Christoph Stockmar, gunsmith and iron-chiseller at Heidersbach near Suhl. Mentioned 1731–50; worked for the Wettin family.
Mann, pp.525f., pl.175.

94 (On style) Sälzle-Schedelmann, *Jagdbrevier*, Heidelberg-Munich, 1959, pp.66, 67, 87, 111.

95 Schepelern, Cat. No.48, pl.30/1.

96 W.K.Neal, *An Exhibition of Firearms*, Exhibition Catalogue, Longleat, 1962, No.81, cover ill.

97 Nicolas Noël Boutet, court gunsmith at Versailles; from 1818 in Paris; from 1792 Director of the national arms factory at Versailles.
S.V.Grancsay, Napoleon's Gunmaker, in: *The American Rifleman*, vol.69, No.7 (July), Washington, 1948, pp.35ff.

Page 9

Albrecht Dürer, Nuremberg, 1515: Knight attacking a landsknecht. Sketch in the margin of Emperor Maximilian I's prayer book in the Munich Staatsbibliothek, fol. 55, verso.

Page 11

Jörg Sorg the Younger, Augsburg, 1551: Christ on the Cross; rubbing from the etched decoration of the armour of Fernando Alvarez, Duke of Alba, in Vienna, Waffensammlung, A 420.

Page 12

Augsburg etcher, 1571: Rubbing from the etched decoration of the Vienna braided pattern garniture of Archduke Rudolph II; cf. pl. 52.

Pages 14/15

Hans Burgkmair, Augsburg, 1516/18: Six groups of five knights each equipped for different kinds of tournament, i.e. the tilt in leg-harness, the *Wulstrennen*, the *Feldrennen*, the *Fussturnier*, the *Pfannenrennen*, and the Italian tilt. Woodcuts in "The Triumphal Procession" of the Emperor Maximilian I, fol. 48, 56, 54, 42, 53, 45.

Page 17

Albrecht Dürer, Nuremberg, 1523: The artist's coat of arms, woodcut, B. 160.

Pages 20/21

Jost Amman, Nuremberg: Six woodcuts from the book *Eygentliche Beschreibung aller Stände auff Erden*, published in Frankfurt in 1568 and depicting the workshops of various kinds of weapon-makers.

Page 23

Leonhard Beck, Augsburg, 1513/18: Siege of a city. Woodcut in the historical romance of the Emperor Maximilian I, *Der Weisskunig*, fol. 564, verso.

Page 25

Hans Burgkmair, Augsburg, 1514/16: The Emperor Maximilian I visiting his court armourer Konrad Seusenhofer in his Innsbruck workshop where work is being carried out on a *Rennzeug*, a tournament armour for the *Rennen*. Woodcut in the *Weisskunig*, fol. 184, verso.

Page 26

Augsburg, c. 1750: "A Perspective View of the Lower Part of an Armoury," copper engraving.

Page 28

Inspection marks on pieces of armour from Augsburg, Nuremberg, and Landshut.

Page 29

The maker's marks of the armourers Lorenz Helmschmid, Kolman and Desiderius Helmschmid, Matthäus Frauenpreiss the Younger in Augsburg; Jörg Seusenhofer in Innsbruck; Wilhelm von Worms the Elder, Kunz Lochner, Valentin Siebenbürger in Nuremberg.

Page 30

Albrecht Dürer, Nuremberg, c. 1498: Three views of a helm (tournament helmet for the old German joust) made by Lorenz or Jörg Helmschmid of Augsburg. Water colour in the Cabinet des dessins, Louvre, Paris.

Page 31

Lucas Cranach the Younger, Wittenberg, 1544: Guests of the Elector John Frederick of Saxony at a staghunt near Torgau on the river Elbe. Vienna, Gemäldegalerie, 856.

Page 32

Philippe Cordier Daubigny, Paris, 1635 (the date has been changed to 1665): Pattern for the decoration of a wheel-lock; copper engraving.

Facing plate 5
Zürich, c. 1310: Wolfram von Eschenbach, from the *Manesse-* or *Große Heidelberger Lieder-Handschrift* (C). University Library, Heidelberg.

Facing plate 9
Franco-Flemish, c. 1470/80: Pavise for foot combat. The knight, dressed in a Milanese armour, kneels between his lady and Death; above him the epigram "vous ou la mort;" at his feet a pole-axe. British Museum, London, 63,5–1,1.

Facing plate 17
Leonhard Beck, Augsburg, 1513/18: Maximilian I at a falcon hunt. Woodcut in the *Weisskunig*, fol. 158, verso.

Facing plate 21
The style of Daniel Hopfer, Augsburg, c. 1520: Rubbing from the etched decoration on the armour of Jörg Frundsberg in the Waffensammlung, Vienna, A 375.

Facing plate 22
Master LS, Augsburg, c. 1540: Portrait of a member of the Rehlingen family, wearing an armour dated 1527 with an etched pattern entirely in the style of Daniel Hopfer of Augsburg.

Facing plate 23
Milanese etcher, c. 1530: Rubbing from the etched pattern on the armour of Alessandro Vitelli in the Waffensammlung, Vienna, A 350.

Facing plate 28
Filippo Orsoni, Mantua, 1554: "Helmet in the Ancient Roman Style" from his pattern book, page B VIII. Victoria and Albert Museum, London, E. 1777–1929.

Facing plate 30
Ulrich Holzmann, Augsburg, 1546: Rubbing from the etched pattern on the Viennese armour of Philip II of Spain (cf. plate).

Facing plate 33
Jörg Sorg the Younger, Augsburg, 1563: The Viennese armour of Maximilian II of 1549/50 (cf. right-hand photograph), as depicted by the etcher in his pattern book. Stuttgart, Staatsbibliothek, cod. milit. fol. 24, 4, verso.

Facing plate 40
Jost Amman, Nuremberg, c. 1570: German arquebusier on horseback. Woodcut.

Facing plate 42
Jean Goujon; Paris, 1549: Henry II, King of France, on his triumphant entry into Paris in 1549. From the woodcut sequence published by Jacques Roffet.

Facing plate 49
Jörg Sorg the Younger, Augsburg, 1550: Rubbing from the etched pattern on the vamplate in the Waffensammlung, Vienna, A 641, belonging to the armour garniture of Maximilian II by Matthäus Frauenpreiss the Younger, Augsburg, 1549/50 (cf. plate 33, right-hand photograph).

Facing plate 51
Landshut or Munich etcher, 1571: Rubbing from the etched pattern on the Vienna roseleaf garniture of the Emperor Maximilian II (cf. plate).

Facing plate 54
Presumably by Lucio Piccinino himself, Milan, c. 1578: preliminary sketch of the left pauldron of the parade armour of Alessandro Farnese (cf. plate). Vienna, Sammlung für Plastik und Kunstgewerbe, 5345.

Facing plate 56
Jacob Halder, Greenwich, c. 1590/1600: The double-pieces for the New York armour of George Clifford (cf. plate), depicted by the etcher in his pattern book, the so-called *Jacobe Album*. London, Victoria and Albert Museum, D. 607–1894, page 21.

Facing plate 60
Dutch, c. 1600–10: Portrait of Maurice of Orange, taken from the etched decoration of the guard's partisan (cf. plate).

Facing plate 62
Hans Krumper, Munich, c. 1630: Bronze bust of Maximilian I, Elector of Bavaria. Munich, Residenzmuseum, F. V. III-A 292.

Facing plate 63
Ägidius Sadeler based on Hans von Achen, Augsburg, 1603: Portrait of the Emperor Rudolph II. Copper engraving.

Facing plate 66
Dominicus Custos, Augsburg, 1604: Portrait of Christian II, Elector of Saxony, Copper engraving.

Facing plate 70
Dutch, c. 1610/12: Henry Prince of Wales, portrait in foot-tournament armour with pike and sword. Copper engraving.

Facing plate 71
Crispyn de Passe the Younger, Paris, 1624: Portrait of Louis XIII, King of France. Copper engraving.

Facing plate 74
Hans Schmidt, Ferlach in Carinthia, 1628: Detail of the silver inlays on the stock of the rifle of the Archduke Leopold V (cf. plate).

Facing plate 75
Philipp Sadeler, Munich, c. 1630: Portrait of the imperial and Bavarian Lt.-Gen. Johannes Tserclaes Count Tilly. Copper engraving.

Facing plate 78
Jean (Louis) Bérain the Elder, Paris, 1659: Design for the decoration of a flintlock rifle, from a pattern book. Copper engraving.

Facing plate 82
Philippe Cordier Daubigny, Paris, 1635 and 1637 (the dates have been changed to 1665 and 1667): Patterns for the decoration of a wheel-lock, a wheel-lock key and a lock counterplate. Copper engravings.

Facing plate 83
Signatures of the gunstockmaker Johann Michael Maucher of Schwäbisch-Gmünd.

Facing plate 86
Matteo Aqua Fresca, Bargi near Bologna, c. 1690: Lock counterplate of the pair of pistols shown in the plate.

Facing plate 87
Heinrich Raab (engraver), publ. David Funck, Nuremberg, c. 1700: Reproduction of a design for the decoration of a flintlock pistol from the pattern book of Claude Simonin, Paris, 1685. Copper engraving.

Facing plate 90
Publ. Johann Christoph Weigel, Nuremberg, before 1725: Reproduction of the title page of Nicolas Guérard's pattern book of firearms decoration, Paris, early 18th century. Copper engraving.

Front paper
Master of the Housebook, Middle Rhine, c. 1480: Tournament scene: preparing for a German tilt. Fol. 20, verso, and 21 of the so-called *Mittelalterliches Hausbuch*, pen and ink drawing. Wolfegg (Württemberg), collection of the Prince zu Waldburg-Wolfegg.

End paper
Jean (Louis) Bérain the Elder, Paris 1659: Designs for the decoration of flintlock firearms, from a pattern book. Copper engraving.

Dust Jacket
cf. plates 54 and 81.

AIRGUN

A gun or rifle operated by compressed air instead of a powder charge: invented in Germany, early examples date from the late 16th century.

ARMES BLANCHES

A generic term used by collectors to include all forms of swords and daggers.

ARMOURER

The craftsman who forged the various parts of an armour from steel plates and rivetted them together.

ARMOUR GARNITURE

This consists of an armour (or armours) and its "double-pieces", the reinforcing plates used to adapt the basic unit for various uses in the field and several forms of military sport.

BALDRIC

A broad belt worn diagonally across the body from the right shoulder to carry the sword in a hanger at the left hip.

BARBUTA

An open helmet which originated in Italy in the 14th century; often tall with a pointed apex in its earlier forms. Later it was more rounded with its lower edge brought forward at the cheeks to leave a small face opening.

BASCINET

A form of head defence, generally egg-shaped with a pointed apex, which evolved in the 14th century when it was usually fitted with a pivoted visor either of rounded profile or pointed – the "houndskull"– and a protective curtain of mail at its lower edge.

BASES

Fabric skirts, generally knee-length and pleated, commonly worn with armour in the early 16th century. Their equivalents in steel are found on some armours.

BEVOR

A plate defence for the lower part of the face and neck, first introduced towards the end of the thirteenth century. It was used with open helmets or as a reinforcing piece on some close helmets.

BOAR SPEAR

A spear fitted with a transverse lug below the blade. Originally used to hunt boar, bears, and other large game, the boar spear was also used by infantry and as an insignia of rank.

BRIGANDINE

A flexible defensive jacket of fabric with overlapping scales rivetted to the inside. The outer surface is often covered with rich velvet and shows the heads of the rivets.

BURGONET

An open helmet worn by mounted officers and light horsemen in the 16th and early 17th centuries. It usually had a peak and hinged ear-pieces.

BUTT

The thickened rear end of a firearm stock, shaped to be rested against the cheek or shoulder.

BUTT-PLATE

A plate usually of metal, ivory or horn, fitted to the end of a firearm butt to protect the wood.

CANTLE
The hind part of a saddle.

CAPACETE
An open helmet usually worn with a deep bevor: popular in Spain in the 15th century. Its skull has been described as resembling "half an almond shell, usually with a small curved stalk at the apex, and a down-turned brim curving up to form a point at front and rear".

CAP-À-PIE ARMOUR
Complete armour, made to protect the wearer from head to toe.

CHANFRON
A head defence of plate for a horse, introduced in the 14th century. The complete chanfron has side-pieces to protect the cheeks. In the 16th and 17th centuries the half-chanfron, covering the forehead but extending only half-way down the nose, was used.

CHASED WORK
The fine after-treatment with special tools of a casting, or of embossed or chiselled iron.

CORTELLAGGIO (COLTELLAGGIO)
A falchion; a large single-edged sword, usually widening toward the point and of flattened triangular section.

CRANEQUIN
A form of crossbow winder common in Germany. It used a claw-ended rack and pinion to give considerable mechanical advantage in drawing the cord to the point on the stock where it was held by the lock.

CUIRASS
The combined back- and breastplates.

CUISSE
Plate defence for the thigh, introduced in the 14th century when it was usually made in one piece, shaped to the limb with the knee-cop permanently attached. With the development of plate armour came much more elaborate constructions.

DAMASCENING
A decorative technique in which gold or silver was used to enrich the darkened surface of metalwork. In "struck" damascening, fretted designs in gold and silver were hammered into the roughened steel surface. The patterns were cut into the steel with an engraving tool in "beaten" damascening, the gold and silver then being hammered into the grooves.

DOUBLE-PIECES
Supplementary pieces of a suit of armour to adapt the basic unit for use in the field, the tournament, on horseback or on foot.

EMBOSSING
The decoration of metal in relief by working it out of the plane with hammers and assorted chisels.

ENGRAVING
The mechanical application of ornament to metal, using a steel burin or graver to cut the patterns in the surface.

ESTOC
A special form of thrusting sword with a very stiff blade of triangular or square section. It first appeared in the second quarter of the 15th century and is usually fitted with a simple cross guard and a heavy pommel.

ETCHING

A chemical method of applying ornament. The metal surface is covered with an acid-resistant varnish with the pattern being either left clear or scratched through to the metal with a needle. Applied acid eats into the uncovered surface to leave a pattern that can be blackened, gilded or coloured.

FAULD

A laminated extension of the breastplate to protect the lower abdomen.

FELDKÜRISS

Equestrian armour with lance-rest and laminated long tassets. It was frequently worn without greaves or sabatons.

FLINTLOCK

A firearms mechanism in which the priming powder in a shallow pan is fired by the sparks from the striking of a piece of flint held in a cock against the steel or battery. In the developed flintlock the steel is L-shaped and formed in one piece with the pan-cover (cf. snaphance lock). The mechanism was invented about 1605 by Marin le Bourgeoys at Lisieux, Normandy.

FOOT COMBAT

A duel, either of a serious or a sporting nature, on foot within an enclosure, the *champ clos*. The contestants wore a *Kempfküriss* or a special close-fitting foot-combat armour and practically any type of weapon was used including the sword, dagger, spear and pole-axe.

FREIRENNEN

Duel on horseback in reinforced field armour with light lances and swords; frequently a preliminary to the *Freiturnier*.

FREITURNIER

Group-combat in specially reinforced armour on horseback, using lance and sword. The reinforcing pieces were the pate plate or escufia, bevor, plackart to strengthen the breastplate, and the extra defences for the left shoulder, elbow and hand.

FUSSTURNIER

A German name for the group-combat on foot over a waist-high barrier. The contestants were armed with pike and sword and wore special armour.

FUSSTURNIERHARNISCH

Special armour for the *Fussturnier*; usually a half-armour without lance rest but with a visored helmet.

GLAIVE

A hafted arm with a straight, knife-like blade. In its developed form it was the weapon of guards.

GOLDSCHMELZ

A decorative technique in which the pattern is etched in the steel and the pitted areas filled with amalgam. Under heat the mercury is fumed off to leave the gold adhering to the steel, the bright parts of which are chemically tarnished to a deep blue colour.

GORGET (or collar)

Defence for the neck, throat and upper thorax, generally formed of several lames, each in two parts front and rear, joined by a hinge on one shoulder and fastening with a stud on the other.

GREAVE

A plate defence for the lower leg, extending from below the knee to the ankle, or in some forms to the base of the heel.

GUILD MARK

A mark applied by the guilds to their members' work which had passed a quality inspection. It usually took the form of the city arms and was stamped near the maker's mark.

HALBERD

A hafted weapon with a head combining an axe and a spear, with a fluke at the rear. It was the weapon of infantry and later of bodyguards.

HARNASCH

An Augsburg term for the harness of the heavy infantry and its officers, a half-armour without lance-rest.

HARNESS

A generic term for armour to protect the body and or the limbs.

HELMET

Any protection of plate for the head; the term includes all subsidiary forms.

HILT

The complex of bars and shells around the sword grip to protect the user's hand.

HORSE ARMOUR

Also known as a "bard": in its most complete form it consists of a chanfron to protect the animal's head, crinet for the neck, peytral for the breast, saddle, crupper, and flanchards to protect the flanks. It was usually of steel but moulded leather bards are also known.

JOUST

A combat between two mounted contestants. The joust of peace was fought with rebated arms with the intention of breaking lances or unhorsing. In the jousts of war, real arms were used until one of the combatants was disabled or killed.

KEMPFKÜRISS

An Augsburg term describing foot-combat armour with flared metal bases.

KNEE-COP

A domed plate to protect the knee, often attached to both the greave and the cuisse of a cap-à-pie armour.

KNUCKLE-BOW

That part of a sword guard which curves from the base of the grip to the pommel to protect the knuckles.

KOLBENTURNIER (club tournament)

Group-combat between horsemen armed with wooden clubs; a form of tournament which died out towards the close of the 15th century.

LAMES

Metal plates that overlap to form a flexible defence by the riveting of each to leather straps at the back or by making the rivets of one lame slide in slots on the next.

LANCE REST

A rigid or hinged bracket on the right of the breastplate to support the couched equestrian lance and absorb the shock of impact.

LOCK

See matchlock, miquelet, percussion, wheel-, and flintlock.

LOCKPLATE

A metal plate on the stock of a firearm to unite and carry the elements of the ignition mechanism.

MAIL

The network of interlinked metal rings used to make extremely flexible defensive garments.

MAKER'S MARK

The personal mark of the armourer or weaponsmith stamped with a punch on his finished work. It frequently included his initials.

MATCHLOCK

The earliest efficient firearms ignition system. When the trigger is pressed a burning slowmatch clipped in the cock is lowered into the powder-filled pan. It first appeared in Germany in the first quarter of the 15th century and was still in common use in Europe in the 17th century.

MIQUELET LOCK

A Spanish form of the flintlock in which the sear operates horizontally through the lockplate and the mainspring is mounted externally on the lockplate in front of the cock.

MOUNTS

The metal parts of a firearm used to protect and decorate the wooden stock and to attach the barrel, lock and ramrod to the stock.

MUSKET

The heavy, long-barrelled gun of the musketeer; a military weapon, in its earlier forms it was fired from a forked rest.

PALLASCH

Originally an East European broadsword with a sabre hilt and a straight, single-edged blade; a cavalry weapon early examples of which date from the 17th century.

PARTISAN

A spear whose long, tapering blade has two upturned lugs at its base.

PAS D'ÂNE

A 17-century French term indicating one of the two lobes of a shell-guard. Since about 1850 it has been used to describe the two branches between the quillons and the lower guard.

PAULDRON

A shoulder defence of metal plates which reached its highest development in 15th-century Italian armour.

PAVISE

A shield carried by infantry, it was usually of wood covered with canvas or hide and painted. In its larger forms it had a prop at the back so that it could stand alone as a protection for archers as they shot.

PERCUSSION LOCK

A firearm mechanism in which the charge is ignited by a detonating cap exploded when struck by the cock. The cap is fitted over a pierced nipple which serves as an anvil and through which the flash is carried to the charge.

PICKADILS

Projecting leather or fabric tabs used to decorate the main edges of an armour's padded linings.

PIKE

A thrusting weapon of the infantry, formed by a small leaf-shaped head set usually on a very long haft.

POMMEL

An enlarged terminal at the grip of a sword or dagger serving to counterbalance the weight of the blade and to give a more secure hold. Also refers to the butt-terminal of a pistol. On all three weapons the pommel took many forms.

PRODD (or bullet crossbow)

A light crossbow shooting bullets of metal or clay, used to kill small game and birds.

QUILLON

An element of almost all sword and dagger guards, formed by a straight or recurved bar set at the base of the grip in the plane of the blade.

QUILLON-BLOCK
The metal block on the hilt at the junction of blade and grip from which the quillons spring.

RAPIER
A sword primarily for civilian use, with a long narrow thrusting blade, short grip and a more or less complex guard to protect the hand.

RENNEN
A German form of joust, an equestrian duel in special armour using heavy, sharp lances.

RENNZEUG
Special armour for the *Rennen* with sallet and long tassets but without arm or lower leg defences. The right arm and shoulder were protected by a semicircular vamplate, the left by a large rigid shield.

RIFLE
A hand-held firearm with longitudinal spiral grooves cut in the inside of the barrel to impart a rotary motion to the projectile and so stabilise its flight for increased accuracy.

RONDACHE
See Target.

SABATON
Armour for the foot: a metal shoe formed by a toe-cap and metal lames covering the instep and, on most 15th-century examples, a heel-plate.

SABRE
A sword of East European origin with a broad, curved, single-edged blade and a simple hilt consisting of grip, pommel and knuckle-bow with a short rear quillon.

SALLET
A form of helmet used in sport and war. In its classic German form of c. 1480 it is the most graceful of all head defences, close-fitting at the front and sides and extending backwards in a long tail. Its shape has been compared with that of a sou'wester.

SNAPHANCE LOCK
A form of flintlock with separate steel and pan-cover, the former pivoted on a short rod, the latter opened at the moment of firing by a lever linked to the tumbler.
The mechanism appears to have been developed in Germany in the second quarter of the sixteenth century and local forms were used in Sweden from c. 1556, England from c. 1580, and in Spain and Naples from c. 1600 to the middle of the nineteenth century in the "Miquelet" or "Mediterranean" form.

SPONTOON
A late form of the partisan, the weapon of guards and the badge of rank of some officers of infantry.

STECHZEUG
A special German and Austrian form of armour for the joust in which a heavy helm is bolted to a reinforced breastplate worn with open-fronted pauldrons, tilt targe, left vambrace and gauntlet. Leg harness is worn in the German joust, but not in the Italian version which is fought over a barrier separating the contestants.

TARGET or TARGE
Usually a fairly large circular shield of wood, leather or metal fitted with enarmes (i.e straps) for attachment to the left arm or shoulder. The word, which is used to describe certain other types of shield used in the joust, derives from the Moorish *adarga*. Occasionally the word "rondache" is used for this type of shield.

TASSET

A metal plate or plates hung from the lowest fauld-plate to protect the thigh.

TILT

A form of joust in special equipment with heavy blunt lances. The horses were separated by a wooden barrier, the tilt or *pallia*. The sport was known in Germany as the Pallia – or Italian joust.

TILT HARNESS

Cap-à-pie armour with rigid lance rest, open-fronted pauldrons and the following double-pieces: tilt breastplate with integral fauld and tassets, rigid bevor, steel tilt targe on the left shoulder, pasguard reinforce for the left elbow and a tilt gauntlet for the left hand.

TOURNAMENT

Any one of many forms of mock combat involving groups of horsemen as opposed to jousts between two contestants only. *(See Freiturnier.)*

TRABHARNISCH

A South German term for a half-armour without a lance-rest.

TROUSSE *(or trousse de chasse)*

A set of hunting implements used to gralloch and dismember the kill. It usually consisted of a heavy chopper in a metal-mounted sheath which had a number of small knives and tools in separate pockets on the front.

VAMBRACE

The term used by 19th-century writers to describe the lower arm defence only, but it is obvious from early texts that it meant the entire arm defence below the shoulder.

VAMPLATE

A steel plate, usually funnel-shaped, fitted to the equestrian lance to protect the user's hand.

WENDER

A German term which describes firearms with two or more barrels loaded individually and brought to the firing mechanism in turn by rotating them about their common axis.

WHEEL-LOCK

A firearms mechanism in which the priming is ignited by means of a piece of iron pyrites held against a serrated steel wheel rotated by a strong V-spring when the trigger is pressed. The resulting sparks fire the priming powder. The invention may have been Leonardo da Vinci's, but it saw its greatest use in Germany where it continued to be made until the 18th century.

WINDER

A mechanism for bending a crossbow, either the West European windlass type or the German cranequin.

SOURCES OF PHOTOGRAPHS

Norman Blank: Beverley Hills (Plate 76)
L. H. Hildyard: London (Plate 86)
W. Keith Neal: Warminster (Plate 96)
E. Rouiller: Geneva (Plate 16 a)
Hans Schedelmann: Salzburg (Plates 10, 59)
Lilly Stunzi: Zurich (Plates I, 1, 2, 7, 9, 12, 13, 14, 17, 18, 19, 26, 27, 28, 32, 35, 36, 37, 40, 41, 44, 45, 48, 52, 53, 54, 55, 63, 70 b, 71, 72, 79, 81, 84, 88, 91)

Coburg: Kunstsammlungen der Veste (Plate 4)
Copenhagen: Rosenborg Slot (Plates 73, 95)
Dresden: Historisches Museum (Plates 5, 47, 66, 68)
Florence: Museo Nazionale (Plates 23, 65)
Innsbruck: Tiroler Landesmuseum (Plate 20)
London: Tower Armouries (Plate 6 b)
London: Victoria & Albert Museum (Plate 93 a)

London: Wallace Collection (Plates 70 a, 93 b)
Madrid: Real Armería (Plates 24, 25, 31, 34)
Munich: Bayerisches Nationalmuseum (Plates 67, 83, 87, 94)
Munich: Deutsches Jagdmuseum (Plate 50 a)
New York: Metropolitan Museum of Art (Plates 15, 29, 42, 56, 60, 82, 85, 97)
Stockholm: Kungliga Livrustkammaren (Plates 39, 64, 77, 78)
Turin: Armeria Reale (Plate 62 b)
Vienna: Heeresgeschichtliches Museum (Plate 75)
Vienna: Historisches Museum der Stadt (Plate 89)
Vienna: Waffensammlung des Kunsthistorischen Museums: (Plates 16 b, 33 a, 49, 90 – 3, 6 a, 8, 11, 21, 22, 30, 33 b, 38, 43, 46, 50 b, 51, 57, 58, 61, 62 a, 69, 74, 80, 92 – Elisabeth Schwenk)

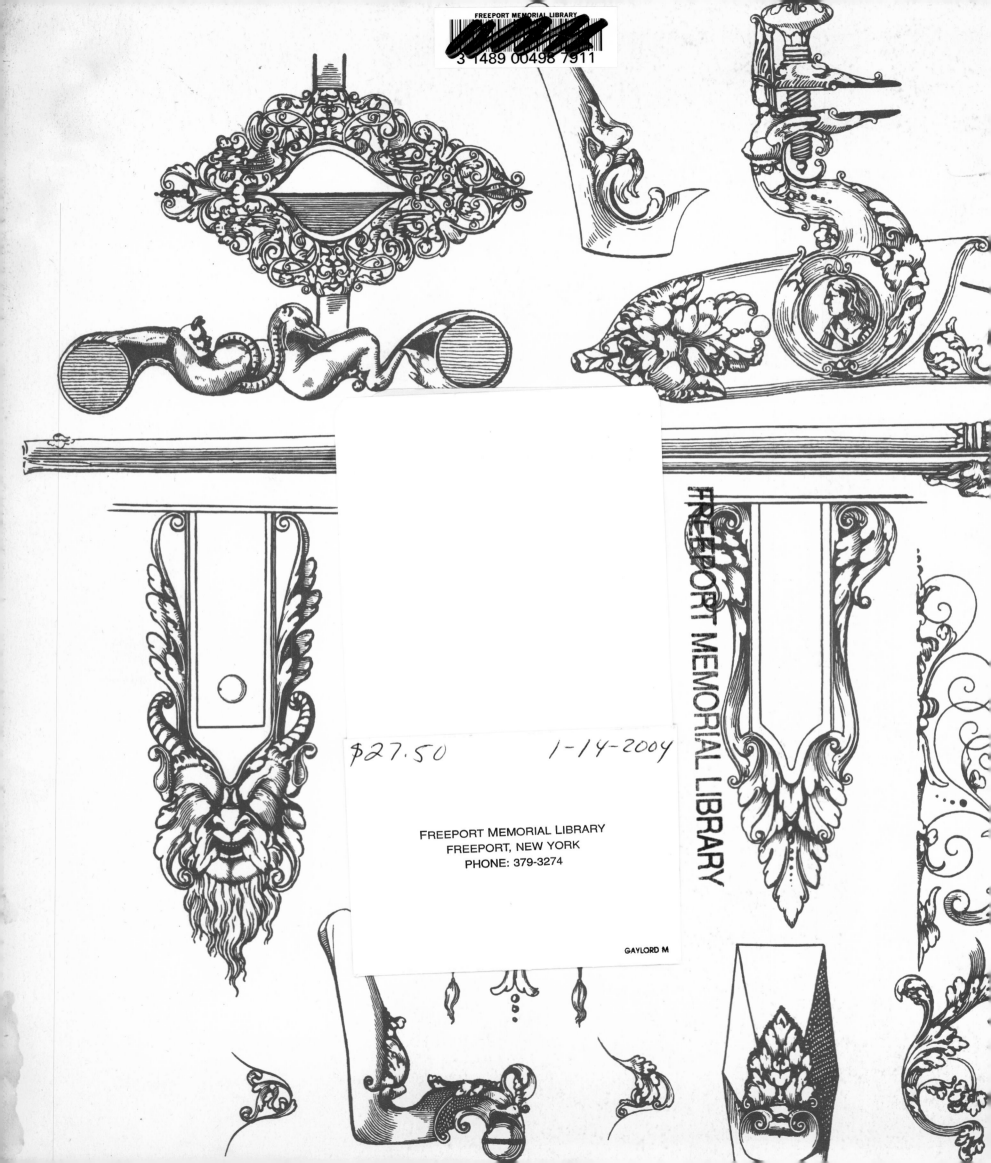